D1247194

Divided Loyalties

Kentucky's Struggle for
Armed Neutrality in the Civil War

James W. Finck

SB

Savas Beatie

California

First edition, first printing

Library of Congress Cataloging-in-Publication Data

Finck, James W.
Divided Loyalties : Kentucky's Struggle for Armed Neutrality in the Civil War / James W. Finck—First edition.
pages cm
Includes bibliographical references and index.
ISBN 978-1-61121-102-3
1. Kentucky—History—Civil War, 1861-1865. 2. Kentucky—Politics and Government–1861-1865. 3. Neutrality, Armed—Kentucky—History—19th Century. 4. Kentucky–Defenses—History—19th Century. 5. Allegiance—-Kentucky—History—19th Century. I. Title.
E509.F56 2012
976.9'03—dc23
2012035936

SB

Savas Beatie LLC
989 Governor Drive, Suite 102
El Dorado Hills, California 95762

www.savasbeatie.com (web)
sales@savasbeatie.com (email)

Savas Beatie titles are available at special discounts for bulk purchases in the United States by corporations, institutions, and other organizations. For more details, please contact Special Sales, P.O. Box 4527, El Dorado Hills, CA 95762, or you may e-mail us at sales@savasbeatie.com, or visit our website at www.savasbeatie.com for additional information.

Printed in the United States of America.

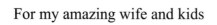

For my amazing wife and kids

Contents

Contents (continued)

List of Photos

List of Photos (continued)

List of Charts

List of Maps

Foreword

The oft-cited aphorism attributed to Abraham Lincoln in 1861 that "I hope to have God on my side, but I must have Kentucky," is almost certainly apocryphal. Certainly, at the least, no authentic contemporary source in his own hand or in one of his speeches has yet been found that contains the famous phrase. Certain it is, however, that Lincoln did write that for the Union to lose Kentucky would be tantamount to losing "the whole game." Moreover, if asked, Jefferson Davis, president of the Confederate States of America, almost certainly would have expressed the same sentiments from his point of view.

A Confederate Kentucky would have given the South the wide Ohio River as its central northern border from the Appalachians to the Mississippi, with only one bridge spanning it at Cincinnati. That would make invasion from the North far more challenging and difficult than simply marching legions across an artificial state line on dry land. A Union Kentucky meant no river to cross, easy access to the Tennessee and Cumberland Rivers as routes of naval advance into the Southern heartland, and every road running south a potential avenue of invasion. Moreover, mountainous eastern Kentucky held the key to access to what was soon to be West Virginia, and even more to Southwest Virginia, that resource rich region so vital to Jefferson Davis, not least because it held the only direct rail connections between Richmond and the western Confederacy.

It requires only a cursory look at Richmond's efforts to take Kentucky away from Lincoln to demonstrate just how important the Bluegrass State was to the South. West of the Appalachians the Confederacy launched only two major campaigns of invasion outside its own borders, and the largest of these was General Braxton Bragg's fall 1862 Perryville Campaign. Even before that, and continually afterward, Confederate authorities set smaller campaigns afoot to take Kentucky's star for its own banners [in fact a star representing Kentucky did appear on Confederate national and battle flags, another indication of Southern aspirations]. The very last Southern offensive of the war, General John Bell Hood's Tennessee Campaign of late 1864, had the Ohio as its ultimate goal.

Far more work has been done on how North and South viewed and vied for the state, than on what Kentuckians themselves felt about their unique—and uniquely hazardous—position between the contending parties. James Finck's *Divided Loyalties: Kentucky's Struggle for Armed Neutrality in the Civil War* is the first discrete work to speak for them, or rather, to look at and interpret how they spoke for themselves. Challenging the long-held post-war assumption that Kentuckians were overwhelmingly pro-Union from the outset, Finck skillfully analyzes their political expression through local, state, and national elections, the actions of their legislature and governor, and the Bluegrass press, to find a body politic far more conflicted, and far more motivated by self-interest and survival than ideology or sectional loyalty. His challenges to old assumptions are going to require historians for some time to come to rethink old truisms. Even those who may reject Finck's conclusions are still going to have to address them head-on.

Finck concentrates his study on the first year of the war, the year in which Kentucky made its choice—or was forced into it, depending on one's point of view. Yet there are other later indicators that he is right in suggesting that all was not as it has seemed for so long. Another old aphorism about the state is historian E. Merton Coulter's statement that Kentucky "waited until after the war was over to secede from the Union." What Coulter meant, of course, was the phenomenon of the state, which during the war rejected the Confederacy, falling politically and socially into the hands of its own former Confederate leaders for half a century after Appomattox. If a man entertained any hope of political success in the state, he almost had to demonstrate wartime service in gray. Paducah-bred Irwin S. Cobb capitalized on this phenomenon after the turn of the century when he wrote his charming Old Judge Priest, whose plot turned repeatedly on the necessity for a Confederate pedigree to get ahead even in small-town Kentucky, and on how some former Unionists retroactively "galvanized" their pasts to suit.

In short, what happened after the war can be read to suggest that sentiment in the state for secession and the Confederacy before the war was far greater than believed. Kentuckians during Reconstruction and after were doing what they felt they had to do to survive in their contemporary world, just as in 1860-1861, as Finck argues, they did what they had to do less from ideology than from an instinct for self-preservation. The lot of the man in the middle in a crisis is rarely a happy one, as almost all of the moderate Kentucky leaders of 1861-1861 discovered to their cost. John C. Breckinridge, Beriah Magoffin, Lazarus Powell, and more, saw their political careers destroyed in their efforts to find a middle way between secession on the one hand, and siding with the North in a war on fellow Southerners on the other. In such a climate, survival is reduced to a very personal and individual level.

Divided Loyalties is about just that, survival. The crisis and the war that followed were everyone's contest, and everyone's tragedy, yet in Kentucky the choices were harder, and the stakes greater, as men and brothers faced the awful prospect of having to choose not against some distant enemy, but against family and friends. No matter what route to survival a Kentuckian chose, it was sure to put him on the road to a collision with the people most dear to him.

William C. Davis

Introduction

hat set Kentucky apart from other states during the Civil War was its interesting relationship with both the North and the South. Although numerous books and articles have been written to explain why states broke their ties with the Union, far fewer have been written to explain why one particular slave state remained loyal. Officially, Kentucky sided with the Union during the Civil War; yet Kentuckians were connected culturally, economically, socially, and through the practice of slavery with the Confederacy. Kentucky sat on the border between the two nations and had loyalties to both.

One reason for the lack of attention to Kentucky's choice of allies derives from past historians, mainly E. Merton Coulter. He argued that Kentucky's decision was easy to make: Kentucky remained in the Union simply because it had much stronger loyalties to the Union than the Confederacy. However, an examination of the evidence yields a different conclusion. Kentucky tried to remain apart from the two warring powers by declaring itself neutral. In the beginning of the secession struggle, Unionists fought for neutrality when they believed their state might follow other slave states into the Confederacy; later, a switch occurred as secessionists picked up the banner of neutrality when they saw their own hopes fading. Ultimately, Kentucky made a decision based upon self-preservation rather than loyalty to either side.

This book is an in-depth study of the twelve months that decided Kentucky's fate, November 1860 to November 1861. By focusing exclusively on one state, one issue, and one year, it uncovers important details that helped lead to Kentucky's decision. The book looks at the roles of the state legislature, the governor, other leading Kentuckians, and average citizens to understand how Kentuckians felt about the prospects of war and secession, and how—they hoped—bloodshed could be avoided.

The various chapters explore several themes, including the political history of Kentucky from the 1840s to 1860. Kentucky, like most of the other border states, was able to maintain its two-party system during these difficult political years. The Whig Party, founded by Kentuckian Henry Clay, never lost its attractiveness in Kentucky even though it was forced to appear under different names, such as the Know-Nothings. This strong two-party system played an important part in keeping Kentucky in the Union.[1]

Yet the emergence of the secession crisis transformed the political landscape of the Commonwealth. Kentuckians divided themselves according to three separate ideological positions: unconditional Unionists, who could not foresee any issue that would justify secession; secessionists, who felt the Union had overstepped its authority and, with the election of Lincoln, saw a necessity to join the Confederacy; and lastly, the largest group in the state, the conditional Unionists. The latter believed the nation could in fact be restored, but did not deem secession to be out of the question if their rights were not protected. These new ideological positions manifested themselves in the realignment of politics into two new parties, the Democratic Unionist Party and the States Rights Party.

Both new parties would come to support Kentucky neutrality. Governor Beriah Magoffin entertained ambassadors from the seceded states, but decided that Kentucky would only consider secession after all possible attempts at reunification and peace had failed. There were three major attempts on the national level to solve the problems: the Corwin Amendment, the Crittenden Compromise, and the Peace Convention. All three had similar elements—the protection of slavery and southern rights—and Kentuckians played a major role in shaping what became of all of them.

However, as compromise efforts began to fail, Kentuckians, knowing their state could become a battleground, began to see the idea of neutrality as their best chance to avoid bloodshed. Adherents of all ideological positions had

---

1   For more on the importance of the two-party system in the border states, see Daniel W. Crofts, *Reluctant Confederates* (Chapel Hill: The University of North Carolina Press, 1989).

different reasons to support neutrality. The legislature had rejected calling for a state convention to decide the issue of secession, but secessionists and Unionists still held relatively equal power, so that decision could be overturned with any unforeseen future event. With such close competition in the state, neutrality seemed the only answer that satisfied, or at least propitiated, everyone.

Much of this book focuses on the difficult endeavor of keeping Kentucky neutral, especially after the fall of Fort Sumter. Men with feelings for each side were leaving the state to fight for their cause, and those who remained behind were pushing the limits of neutrality. One of the biggest obstacles in remaining neutral was the "Lincoln Guns" being delivered in the state by Union supporters. Other causes for concern included the Mayville Convention, at which representatives of the Jackson Purchase section of the state met to decide whether they should sever their ties with Kentucky and join Tennessee. At the same time, the Union created the military department of Kentucky and began actively recruiting troops from the state. The department created military camps just across the Ohio River in Ohio and Indiana to receive and train new recruits. Lincoln also closed down trade into Kentucky of goods that were being sent south to aid the Confederacy.

In the month of July, the situation in the state only worsened. Kentuckians were still trying to remain neutral, but were receiving pressure from within and without the state. The Battle of Manassas and General Fremont's proclamation in Missouri freeing the slaves worried Unionists. However, the August election for the state legislature resulted in a resounding victory for the Democratic Unionists, causing the States Rights Party to push even harder for neutrality and to call a Peace Convention to try to keep their state out of war. With the victory in the August election, the Union took a bold step by setting up Camp Dick Robinson within the state to raise and train Union troops. Finally, in September, the Confederacy—deeming the operation of Camp Dick Robinson a breach of neutrality, and fearing possible invasion by U. S. Grant to capture the high ground over the Mississippi River—invaded the state. When the Confederacy refused to pull out of Kentucky, the legislature voted to embrace the Union, and neutrality was ended.

Another important aspect of this book is its examination of the evidence used by historians such as Coulter and Thomas Speed to prove their thesis of overwhelming Union support. To make their arguments, they used the voting records from important elections held in 1860 and 1861, including the 1860 presidential election. These historians have suggested that Kentucky's loyalty can be proven by counting all the votes for Douglas, Lincoln, and Crittenden as a vote for unconditional unionism and a vote for Breckinridge as a vote for secession. According to this theory, four out of every seven Kentuckians favored unconditional unionism. However, an examination of the campaigns run in Kentucky show that both Breckinridge and Crittenden ran on the similar platform of a government without Lincoln and the protection of slaves within the Union. With seven out of every nine Kentuckians voting for either Breckinridge or Crittenden, Kentuckians were not voting for unconditional unionism, but for a nation that guaranteed Southern rights.

Two important state elections took place in Kentucky in 1861. The first, in May, was the election to the Border State Convention being held in Frankfort. Just as with the presidential election, historians have used the Democratic Unionists' victory as proof of a dominant Unionist sentiment; but once again further examination tells a different story. The Democratic Unionists ran an effective campaign of claiming that a vote for them was a vote for neutrality and peace, while a vote for their opponents meant war. In July, a second vote took place to elect members to a special session of Congress. Again the Democratic Unionists won, and again all the same arguments and disagreement apply.

Lastly, the number of enlistments into the Union army have been used as evidence supporting their thesis of strong unionism. However, if one looks at enlistments before the loss of neutrally, the number of men willing to fight favors the Confederacy. It was only after Kentucky sided with the Union—and was thus subject to the Union draft, as well as having men volunteer out of state loyalty, not national—that more men joined the Union army.

As will be shown, Kentucky's ultimate decision to remain loyal to the Union was not an easy one to make. The state's first preference was not to side with the United States, but instead to avoid any conflict with either side and remain neutral. However, maintaining neutrality would prove to be a difficult task, with men on both sides favoring neutrality for their own agendas. Remaining in the Union was never a foregone conclusion; it was Unionists who first suggested neutrality when they believed Kentucky's membership in the United States was threatened. It was the Democratic Unionists who ran and campaigned on the idea of neutrality. These men would never have done so if they felt Kentucky was firmly in the arms of the Union.

In the end, it was the desire for self-preservation, feelings of state loyalty, geographical location, and the chaos in the state during 1861 (including the breach of neutrality by the Confederacy) that brought reluctant Kentuckians into the Union camp.

Acknowledgments

I have been very fortunate to study under some of the greatest minds in the history world, and in some way they all contributed to helping me get to this point. In each case not only are they gifted writers and historians, but true teachers who cared about my education. They not only supported my learning but pushed me to excel. As an undergraduate at William and Mary, Carol Sheriff helped me see the social side of the Civil War and mentored me as I began my historical journey. As a Master's student, I sat at the feet of both James I. Robinson and William C. Davis, arguably the greatest historical pairing at any university. Professor Davis has been a great help since I left Virginia Tech, both reading my manuscript and connecting me with Savas Beatie Publishers. I also want to thank him for agreeing to write a Foreword for this book, bringing it more credibility than I ever could. As a Ph.D. student at the University of Arkansas, I continued to learn under an excellent historian, Daniel Sutherland. He guided me through the process of writing this manuscript, reading it several times and giving me constant feedback. All four of these historians started out as my professors, but today I consider them good friends.

Another person I need to thank is Dr. Aaron Crawford. He has been a great friend since our days at grad school and has served as my unofficial editor and sounding board during the writing process. Many other people have read my manuscript over the years, including my grandfather, James Ellis, and my parents, Dan and Connie Finck. With each reading I have been able to improve my work. My parents and in-laws also deserve thanks for supporting me in many ways through my schooling.

When it comes to research, the staffs of the special Collections at the University of Kentucky and Western Kentucky University were very helpful, as well as the staff at the Filson Historical Society and the Kentucky Archives. A special thank you to the staff at the Kentucky Historical Society, especially Lynne Hollingsworth, for their assistance with information as well as for granting me a research fellowship. I want to thank Shayna Woidke for her help with the maps and pictures.

I also want to extend a thank you to Savas Beatie's managing director, Theodore P. (Ted) Savas, my editor Rob Ayer, and the entire publishing staff at Savas Beatie for all their help in making this book possible.

I need to thank my kids, Jacob, Savannah, and Jackson; they are my inspiration for everything. Most importantly, I need to thank my wife Melissa. She deserves a Ph.D. as much as I do, having been at my side since my freshman year and supported my every decision. She has read each chapter more than once and has learned more about Kentucky and the Civil War than she ever wanted to. Thank you, and I love you very much.

James W. Finck
Chickasha, Oklahoma

Chapter 1

Kentucky's Political System:

1840 to 1860

In November of 1860, Kentucky, like the rest of the nation, gathered at the polls to elect a new president of the United States. However, this election differed from previous ones in that the very survival of the nation was at stake. Many Southerners saw the possible election of Abraham Lincoln as the ultimate betrayal of their rights and a justification for secession. Unlike the major parties during the antebellum period, the Democrats, Whigs, and Know Nothings, Lincoln and the Republican Party represented only the Northern half of the country. Southerners worried that Lincoln's sectional views and his party's free-soil tendencies could threaten the future of slavery. When Illinois Republicans nominated Lincoln as their candidate for the Senate in 1858, he had accepted their nomination with his now famous "House Divided Speech." In his speech, Lincoln professed his belief that the nation could not survive half slave and half free, leading Southerners to believe that Lincoln intended to attack slavery once he took office. The platform adopted by the Republicans in 1860 even rejected the Dred Scot decision and called for the outlawing of slavery in new territories.[1]

---

1 Avery Craven, *The Coming of the Civil War* (Chicago: The University of Chicago Press, 1957), 391, 417; David Potter, *The Impending Crisis, 1848-1861* (New York: Harper & Row Publishers, 1976), 336-339.

Lincoln, a native-born Kentuckian, was the sixteenth president of the United States. He did not poll well in Kentucky, winning only .9% of the popular vote. Lincoln understood the importance of keeping Kentucky in the Union and walked a fine line between accepting its neutrality and cultivating Kentuckians' loyalty. *Library of Congress*

Kentucky, like every other slave state, had strong concerns about the election of Abraham Lincoln. Although Lincoln was a native son of Kentucky, the majority of the population did not accept his sectionalism and free-soil ideology. Slavery had been an institution in Kentucky since its statehood. In the 1830s, Kentucky had one of the highest ratios of slaves to whites at 24 percent, and the number of slaves within the state grew over the next thirty years. However, the large influx of white immigrants changed the percentage of slaves from nearly one-quarter (24 percent) to about one-fifth (19 percent), with a total slave population of 225,483 by 1860.[2]

Most Kentuckians in 1860 did not own slaves, and a small population within the state believed slavery to be morally wrong. However, for most people, whether one owned slaves was purely a question of expense. A slave in antebellum Kentucky cost an average wage earner about two years' salary. Even with the high expense, 28 percent of Kentucky families did own slaves. This was a very high number compared to the rest of the South, with only Virginia and Georgia having a higher percentage of slave owners. The difference between Kentucky and the cotton states was the number of slaves a family owned. Only five families in Kentucky owned more than 100 slaves; most owned around five or six. The number of slaves in Kentucky was smaller mainly due to the fact that the state's agriculture was not as labor-intensive. The shift in Kentucky's economy away from labor-intensive crops led to the profitable business of selling Kentucky's surplus slaves to the cotton states.[3]

With families owning fewer slaves but more families owning them, slavery tied the state to the rest of the South. The slave trade from Kentucky south only strengthened the bond. With the prominence of slavery and the importance of the slave economy, Kentuckians had no interest in supporting Lincoln or the Republican Party.

While most Kentuckians generally disagreed with Lincoln, they also disagreed with the argument that Lincoln's election was grounds for secession. The *Louisville Daily Journal* declared itself full of sorrow and anxiety over Lincoln's possible election and prayed he would not be successful. However, the paper did not believe in abandoning the Union in its time of crisis, and insisted a legally elected president should be supported. It also maintained that the Congress, being controlled by the South, would be too strong to allow Lincoln to harm slavery in any way. The *Journal* saw no reason to fear a Republican president. Even one of Kentucky's most famous and respected

---

2　For the history of slavery in Kentucky, see Harold Tallant, *Evil Necessity: Slavery and Political Culture in Antebellum Kentucky* (Lexington: University Press of Kentucky, 2003); Lowell H. Harrison, *The Civil War in Kentucky* (Lexington: The University Press of Kentucky, 1975), 1; Lowell H. Harrison and James C. Klotter, *A New History of Kentucky* (Lexington: University Press of Kentucky, 1997), 167-168; William W. Freehling, *The Road to Disunion: Secessionists at Bay*, 2 vols. (Oxford: Oxford University Press, 1990), 2:132, 199.

3　Harrison, *Civil War in Kentucky*, 1; Barbara Fields, *Freedom: A Documentary History of Emancipation 1861-1867*, Series I, 9 vols. (Cambridge: Cambridge University Press, 1985), 1: 493-494; Harrison and Klotter, *A New History of Kentucky*, 167-168.

statesmen, John J. Crittenden, tried to cool passions raised by the chances of Abraham Lincoln's election. Crittenden delivered a speech in August of 1860 in which he questioned what would happen if Lincoln won while the South still controlled the Congress and the courts. Crittenden did not agree with Lincoln's politics, but he knew him and believed him to be a good and decent man—and one smart enough to marry a Kentucky girl. Crittenden's one complaint was not with Lincoln himself but with the Republican Party. Crittenden feared that Lincoln had to follow the ideology of the Republican Party, leading to more sectional agitation for the country; but this factor alone, he said, did not justify secession.[4]

One positive thing that Lincoln did for Kentucky was to unite the state. Unfortunately for Lincoln, however, it was in opposition to him. When it came to the other three candidates for the presidency, things became much more confusing. Two of the candidates, John C. Breckinridge and Stephen Douglas, considered themselves Democrats, while the third, John Bell, belonged to the Constitutional Union Party, an organization running a candidate for the first time. To better understand the confusion regarding these remaining three candidates, it is necessary to provide a brief history of political parties in Kentucky.

Since the 1830s, the Whig Party had controlled the state of Kentucky. Henry Clay, founder of the Whig Party, was arguably the most famous and respected politician in antebellum Kentucky. Clay was part of the generation that transformed Kentucky from a frontier outpost to something at least similar to tidewater Virginia. He pushed the "Bluegrass System" within his state that led to government support of industrialization. On the national level, Clay made his name fighting against President Andrew Jackson while Speaker of the House of Representatives. He outlined the policy known as the American System, which grew out of the Bluegrass System. This policy was meant to make America economically stronger by raising tariffs and building a better infrastructure for trade. He ran for the presidency in 1824, only to lose to John Quincy Adams, who then appointed him secretary of state. Between 1832 and 1844, Clay was considered a possible Whig candidate for each presidential election. He received the nomination both times, but lost on both occasions. It

---

4 *Louisville Daily Journal*, October 8, 1860; John J. Crittenden, *The Union, the Constitution, and the laws: speech of the Hon. John J. Crittenden, at Mozart Hall, on the evening of August 2d, 1860* (Louisville: Bradley & Gilbert, 1860), 6.

Henry Clay served as a congressman and senator from Kentucky, as well as Secretary of State and Speaker of the House. He was one of the most powerful and influential politicians of his era and became known as the "Great Compromiser" because of his efforts to save the nation from civil war. Clay was also one of the founders of the Whig Party during the Second American Party System. *Library of Congress*

was not until the 1850s that the Whigs lost their hold on the state, beginning in 1852 with the death of Clay.[5]

In the late 1840s, problems arose within the Whig Party that continued to plague it. The party ran its last presidential candidate, Winfield Scott, in 1852, only to lose to Franklin Pierce. In Kentucky, the decline began in 1848 when Clay (who had professed retirement) threw his hat into the presidential ring when it looked as if the Whigs could win. Clay's return put Kentucky Whigs in a difficult position; many had given support to Zachary Taylor, but now Clay demanded his state's allegiance, thus creating a split that never healed.[6]

As for the rest of the Southern Whigs, it was the perceived betrayal of Taylor that led to the party fracture. In 1850, Taylor supported the statehood of California, which wanted to enter the Union as a free state. Southern Whigs feared the admission of another free state and criticized Taylor for not protecting their welfare. They also criticized him for not addressing the issues of the fugitive slave law and the proposed ban of slavery in the capital. To solve the problem and patch up the Whig Party, Clay proposed the Omnibus Bill as a compromise. The bill would admit California as a free state, but the rest of the land gained from Mexico would be organized without restrictions on slavery. The slave trade would be outlawed in Washington, D.C., but slavery itself would be allowed to continue. Clay also called for a stronger fugitive slave law. Taylor, however, wanted California admitted immediately and did not support the compromise efforts of Clay, which caused more Southern Whigs to become frustrated with their party. When President Taylor died suddenly, the new president, Millard Fillmore, supported the compromise plan, but by then it was too late. Stephen Douglas led a movement among the Democrats and some

---

5   Stephen Aron, *How the West was Lost* (Baltimore: The Johns Hopkins University Press, 1996), 122-129; Harrison, *The Civil War in Kentucky*, 3-4; Melba Porter Hay, "Henry Clay," in John Kleber, ed., *The Kentucky Encyclopedia* (Lexington: The University of Kentucky Press, 1992), 200-202. For more information on Henry Clay, see Robert Remini, *Henry Clay: Statesman for the Union* (New York: W. W. Norton, 1991). For more information on the Whig Party, see Michael Holt, *The Rise and Fall of the American Whig Party: Jacksonian Politics and the Onset of the Civil War* (New York: Oxford University Press, 1999). For more information on the fascinating history of early Kentucky, see Stephen Aron's *How the West Was Lost*. Aron's monograph traces the growth of Kentucky from the wild lands of Daniel Boone to the land of law under Henry Clay.

6   Craven, *The Coming of the Civil War*, 250-252; Harry August Volz, "Party, State, and Nation: Kentucky and the Coming of the American Civil War" (Ph.D. diss., University of Virginia, 1982), 39-41.

Northern Whigs that took over the efforts to work out a plan; he passed the Compromise of 1850 based on Clay's original Omnibus Bill.[7]

Kentuckians generally saw the Compromise of 1850 as a success. Order was restored and the fugitive slave law passed. Politically, however, the landscape changed. The Democratic Party accepted credit for the Compromise and claimed its new role as upholder of the Clay legacy of compromise. During the debates over the Compromise and the bickering within the Whig Party, many men had jumped ship and joined the Democrats to see the Compromise pass. The old issues that used to divide the parties, such as banks and internal improvements, had lost their importance to the bigger issues of slavery and states rights, and the Democrats claimed they were the party of Southern rights. After all, it was a Whig president who had created the problem.[8]

After 1852, the Whig Party ceased to play a significant role as a national institution. The Northern and Southern wings of the party could not agree on the issue of slavery, and with Scott's failed bid for the presidency and the Democrats capturing states-rights Whigs, the party dissolved. The border states, however, never lost their Whig loyalty and attempted to hold on to the party as long as possible, or resurrect it as part of the American Party. In the mid-1850s elections, the former Whigs, in the American Party, stood their ground as best they could against the Democratic onslaught that captured the cotton states. In most of the border states, the Democrats did gain the advantage, but never by large majorities. In Kentucky, the last election with an official Whig candidate was 1853, a good year for the Democrats, who finally pulled even with Whigs. The difference between Kentucky and most other border states, however, was that Kentucky Democrats would have to wait until 1856 to overtake their opponents. In 1853, ten United States Congressional seats were up for grabs, and the two parties won five each. The Whigs kept their majority in both houses of Congress that year, but they lost the most important federal congressional race. The Ashland district, Clay's old district, was captured by John C. Breckinridge, who tied himself to the legacy of Henry Clay and supported the Compromise of 1850. Even with important wins in 1853, the Democrats would not hold a majority in Kentucky until 1856, and in Kentucky as well as many other border states, the Whigs—under the names of the

---

7   Craven, *The Coming of the Civil War*, 250-252; Volz, "Party, State, and Nation," 56-59.

8   Volz, "Party, State, and Nation," 60-67.

Opposition and Constitutional Unionists—took back those majorities in 1859 and 1860.[9]

The year 1854 brought new challenges to American politics. During that year, two seminal events occurred: the passage of the Kansas-Nebraska Act and the formation of the Republican Party. In order to build a new railroad across the country to California, the territory over which it would run had to be organized. In 1853, Congress created the Nebraska Territory, made up of the land between Indian Territory and the Canadian border. The political problem with the new territory was that it sat north of the Missouri Compromise line. In 1820, Congress had decided that all new states created above the 36' 30" parallel would be free states, while all the new states south of that line would be slave states. Southerners saw the organization of Nebraska and new states that might come from it as a loss of more political power. They had just lost California, and they were determined not to lose Nebraska as well. To solve the new national crisis, Stephen Douglas once again took the mantel of Clay and proposed a compromise. His proposal embraced what had been a key part of the Compromise of 1850, popular sovereignty. Douglas believed that when a territory became a state, the people of the new state should decide whether it would be a slave state or a free state. The second part of his plan divided the land into two territories, Kansas and Nebraska.

Douglas' Kansas-Nebraska bill caused more of an uproar than the original problem. If passed, the bill would overturn the Missouri Compromise, and Northerners, with a growing population of free-soilers and abolitionists, would fight that possibility every step of the way. Northerners saw the split of the territory as a compromise with slavery, which might allow Kansas to become a slave state.

Once again in Kentucky, Democrats supported Douglas and the new bill. They saw popular sovereignty as the best way to keep slavery out of the national discussion by making it a local issue, not a national one. In Kentucky, Democrats also saw the Kansas-Nebraska bill as an opportunity to rid their party of all free-soilers, by making the bill a touchstone for party membership. Democrats wanted to show Kentuckians they supported Southern rights—and

---

9   Daniel W. Crofts, *Reluctant Confederates: Upper South Unionists in the Secession Crisis* (Chapel Hill: The University of North Carolina Press, 1989), 50-54; Thomas Speed, *The Union Cause in Kentucky* (New York: The Knickerbocker Press, 1907), 1; Volz, "Party, State, and Nation," 131-139.

what better way than to push out any member who did not believe the people themselves had the right to slaves in a new state if they chose to have them. In doing this, Democrats could paint the Whigs as the abolitionist party. Democrats claimed that most Northern Whigs and some in the South opposed the Kansas-Nebraska bill; Democrats spun such opposition to be the equivalent of abolitionism. Within Kentucky, the bill divided the already fragile Whig Party even more. The Whig party's gubernatorial candidate, Charles Morehead, supported the bill, with the idea of solving sectional issues in the state. The pro-Nebraska wing of the Whigs also did not want to look soft on Southern rights and slavery, which would lend credibility to the Democratic portrayal of their party as anti-slavery. Crittenden, with his ever-faithful national views, led his wing of the Whigs to oppose the Kansas-Nebraska bill. He correctly foresaw the crumbling of what was left of any type of national Whig alignment. Northern members simply could not accept the dismantling of the Missouri Compromise, and Southern Whigs had little choice but to accept it or risk being called abolitionists. Crittenden's worst fears came true. When Congress finally voted for the bill, Northern Whigs voted against it while Southern Whigs, along with the majority of Kentucky's congressmen, voted in favor of it. Kentucky's Whigs showed the Democrats they were not abolitionists after all—but at a very high price: the Kentucky Whigs sacrificed what remained of the party that had been founded by their beloved Henry Clay.[10]

In the North, many Whigs still rejected the Kansas-Nebraska Bill and did not believe a question as big as slavery should be left to individual states. These Whigs, along with abolitionists and some Democrats who favored federal government involvement, formed anti-Nebraska coalitions to stop its passage. Ultimately, these coalitions would evolve into a new party, the Republicans. The Republicans hoped to capture all the old Whigs.[11]

But in the border states and the cities of the North, the Republicans met a new challenge: nativism. Nativism manifested itself as the American Party, more popularly known as the Know-Nothings. Nativists, who had been around since the turn of the century, saw the growing immigrant population as a threat

10 Harrison, *The Civil War in Kentucky*, 182; Volz, "Party, State, and Nation," 164-171.

11 Harrison and Klotter, *A New History of Kentucky*, 121-124; Volz, "Party, State, and Nation," 172-184.

to their way of life, and they feared the power of the Catholic church, which they saw as anti-democratic.[12]

Entering the 1855 elections, Kentucky Whigs had to admit to themselves that their party was gone. If they hoped to pass any of their agenda, they would need to join a new party. The three parties that ran candidates for Kentucky elections in 1855 were the Democrats, the short-lived Temperance Party, and the Know-Nothings. To former Whigs, the Democratic Party was never an option. The temperance movement had been around for decades but did not run a national political candidate until 1854. The Know-Nothings had worked in secret societies for several years, so their sudden emergence as a party on the national and state scene in 1855 surprised everyone. The Temperance Party ran only a small slate of candidates. In contrast, the Know-Nothings contested all offices, including running Charles Morehead for governor. The importance of Morehead was that he had been a Whig. The Whigs realized they could not run their own candidate without a national party to back them, and believed that by backing Morehead they could at least advance part of their agenda. The principal goal Whigs hoped to accomplish via the Know-Nothing Party was to remove slavery from the national debate by replacing it with nativism.

The Know-Nothing Party emerged victorious in the 1855 elections, capturing the governorship as well as both houses in the state legislature. However, most Whigs did not join the Know-Nothings out of a hatred of immigrants, even though some members did blame immigrants for Clay's loss in 1844. The lack of nativist policies proposed by Kentucky's Know-Nothings after their victory in 1855 is evidence for the lack of strong nativism among the party.[13]

In the approaching presidential election of 1856, Know-Nothings hoped their new-found popularity would manifest itself in a victory for their candidate, Millard Fillmore. The election turned out to be a three-way race, with the Democrats running James Buchanan for president and Kentucky's own John C. Breckinridge for vice president. The new Republican Party ran the great

---

12 Volz, "Party, State, and Nation," 172-184; Frank F. Mathias, "Know-Nothing Party," in Kleber, *The Kentucky Encyclopedia*, 523-524; Harrison and Klotter, *A New History of Kentucky*, 121-124.

13 Mathias, "Know-Nothing Party," in Kleber, *The Kentucky Encyclopedia*, 523-524; Volz, "Party, State, and Nation," 184-228; James Robertson, "Sectionalism in Kentucky from 1855 to 1865," *The Mississippi Valley Review*, 14 (June 1917), 51-53; Harrison and Klotter, *A New History of Kentucky*, 121-124.

explorer, John C. Frémont, for president. In Kentucky, this was the first presidential election without a Whig candidate, and all three national parties hoped to dominate the state in the future. To the displeasure of the Know-Nothings, the old Whig Party platform of banks and internal improvements combined with their nativist platform did not interest voters. Instead, the debate focused on slavery. The Know-Nothings also found they could not agree among themselves. Some ex-Whigs did not support Fillmore because he had abandoned them so soon for the Know-Nothings. Other Know-Nothings worried more about the possible election of a Republican president than a loss by their own party. A victory for the Republicans meant a split in the nation and the possibility of civil war, and Know-Nothings worried that they and the Democrats might so divide their vote as to allow the Republicans to snatch a victory. Many Know-Nothings who thought this way voted Democratic as the lesser of two evils. This allowed a Democrat to win Kentucky's presidential vote for the first time in history.[14]

After the presidential election, the national Know-Nothing Party went the way of the Whigs and drifted into obscurity, but in Kentucky the party did retain some support. Through the state elections of 1857, Know-Nothings remained strong by holding to the old Whig issues of internal improvements and banks. The Know-Nothings relied on the old issues because they were the only things that separated them from the Democrats. Both parties claimed they were the party of Southern rights. They both supported popular sovereignty and the repeal of the Missouri Compromise line, and both claimed the other side would hurt the South. The Know-Nothings tried to expose the Democrats by showing that, while they backed popular sovereignty and slavery in the South, the Northern half of the party wanted to make Kansas free. The Kentucky Know-Nothings planned to wait until Kansas came into the Union as a free state, then portray the Democrats as anti-Southern.[15]

In 1856, Kansas emerged as the national political question. The pro-slavery and anti-slavery crowds in Kansas had both organized their own territorial governments and fought over control of the future state. The pro-slavery government was based at Lecompton, while the anti-slavery government called

---

14 Mathias, "Know-Nothing Party," in Kleber, *The Kentucky Encyclopedia*, 523-524; Volz, "Party, State, and Nation," 245-248, 258-267; Robertson, "Sectionalism in Kentucky," 53-54; Harrison and Klotter, *A New Kentucky History*, 121-124.

15 Volz, "Party, State, and Nation," 267-290.

Topeka home. The Lecompton government called a constitutional convention friendly to slavery, drafted a constitution, and then applied for statehood. Closely on its heels, the Topeka government sent its own constitution to the president.

Buchanan was placed in a difficult situation; he had won the presidency because of Southern Democratic votes, yet he knew the Lecompton constitution had not been endorsed by a majority of Kansans. To the horror of Kentucky Know-Nothings, Buchanan supported Lecompton. Know-Nothings had placed their bets that a Democratic president would reject Lecompton, thereby giving the Know-Nothings the ammunition they needed to prove the Democrats' disregard for Southern rights. Instead, more of the Know-Nothing support slipped away.[16]

The national Democratic Party did not come out unscathed from the Lecompton matter. With the support of Buchanan and Southern control of the U.S. Senate, the Lecompton constitution seemed likely to pass. However, in the House, the Democrats had only a very small majority, and if any Northern Democrats voted against the party, the constitution would be defeated. The debates in Congress were fierce, and when the vote was finally taken, several Northern Democrats broke with the party and voted against Lecompton, splitting the party along sectional lines and defeating the Lecompton constitution. Most prominent amongst the Democrats who voted against Lecompton was Stephen Douglas, who had his sights set on the White House and knew a vote for Lecompton would kill his chances of being nominated by his party.[17]

Going into 1858, both the Kentucky Democrats and Know-Nothings were badly divided, seemingly on the brink of disaster. By that point, the Know-Nothing Party had ceased to exist nationally, but because of the lack of any other viable option, old Whigs in Kentucky tried to maintain it. They realized they needed to overcome a major obstacle: if they wanted to challenge the Democrats, they needed the support of a national party. The only two national parties remaining were the Democrats and the Republicans. The Republicans seemed a good fit for the Know-Nothings if only they could get the Republican leadership to soften its stance on slavery. A large portion of the

---

16 *Ibid.*, 290-296.

17 Robertson, "Sectionalism in Kentucky," 55-57.

Republican Party was made up of old Northern Whigs, and if both sides were willing to compromise, they could create an anti-Democratic coalition. Southern Know-Nothings were willing to sacrifice their stance on nativism, which was never a comfortable position for them, if the Republicans would accept the Dred Scott decision and agree not to push for outlawing slavery in the new territories.[18]

However, many Kentucky Know-Nothings were uneasy about an alliance with the Republicans. Know-Nothing leaders had to convince them that a moderate base existed within the Republican Party. It was the Lincoln-Douglas Debates of 1858 that ultimately made any coalition impossible. In his Freeport Doctrine, Douglas asserted that it was the right of the people of a territory to exclude slavery by passing legislation against the practice, despite the contrary finding of the U.S. Supreme Court in the landmark 1857 Dred Scott case. This stance made Douglas very unpopular with Southern Democrats. Douglas' stance was important for the Know-Nothings because the perception that Douglas and Northern Democrats were opposed to slavery forced the Republicans to take an even stronger stance against the practice, as articulated in such addresses as Lincoln's "House Divided" speech and William Henry Seward's Irrepressible Conflict speech—both of which made any compromise with Southern Know-Nothings impossible. In fact, Kentucky Know-Nothings had to issue public denials of any flirtation with the Republicans.[19]

After the Republican and Know-Nothing fusion fell apart, Kentucky Know-Nothings had to admit their attempts to keep the party alive had failed. Still unwilling to support the Democratic Party, they attempted to create an anti-Democratic coalition of former Whigs, Know-Nothings, and even conservative Democrats. For lack of a better name, they began calling themselves "the Opposition." At a convention to select a candidate for the 1859 Kentucky governor's race they decided upon Joshua Bell as the best man to bring the old Whigs and old Know-Nothings together and beat the Democrats. Also at the same convention, they announced they would support sectional peace and the end of the slavery argument. They blamed the Democrats for creating and fostering sectional strife. Lastly, they called for the

18 Volz, "Party, State, and Nation," 305-307.

19 *Ibid.*, 307-312.

nomination of John J. Crittenden as their presidential candidate in the 1860 election.[20]

During their campaign that year, the Opposition came out for and strongly supported slavery and Southern rights. They attacked the national Democratic government for corruption, especially because of the Lecompton constitution. They claimed the Democrats were responsible for all the sectional difficulties and condemned them for threatening to secede if a Republican won the presidential election the following year. They reminded Kentuckians of the Democrats' opposition to Lecompton and their support of the Freeport Doctrine, and insisted that slavery should be legal in all territories.[21]

When the Democrats met in their convention to choose a candidate for the governorship, they too struggled to hold their party together. Lecompton and Dred Scot divided the national party and even some Democrats in Kentucky. Several men surfaced as candidates, with William Preston taking the lead, but when Preston accepted an appointment as ambassador to Spain the election was left wide open. Linn Boyde made a strong candidate but was seen as having presidential aspirations, something Kentucky Democrats had reserved for someone else. They wanted to show Kentuckians that they too were the party of slavery and Southern rights, so after five ballots they chose a candidate with a strong record on Southern rights, Beriah Magoffin from Harrodsburg.[22]

Bell and Magoffin ran on similar platforms. Both men supported slavery and states rights and both claimed loyalty to the Union. The Democrats denied rumors that they supported secession and said the best way to avoid secession was a Democratic victory. The Democrats tried to compromise within their own party by claiming that Congress had the power to pass laws to protect slavery in the territories but should not use that power.[23]

---

20 Harrison and Klotter, *A New Kentucky History*, 124; Volz, "Party, State, and Nation," 305-317; Albert D. Kirwan, *John J. Crittenden: The Struggle for the Union* (Lexington: University of Kentucky Press, 1997), 341.

21 Harrison and Klotter, *A New Kentucky History*, 124; Volz, "Party, State, and Nation," 317-332.

22 Kirwan, *John J. Crittenden*, 341-342; Volz, "Party, State, and Nation," 316-348; Lowell H. Harrison, "Beriah Magoffin," in Kleber, *The Kentucky Encyclopedia*, 603-604.

23 N. S. Shaler, *Kentucky: A Pioneer Commonwealth* (Boston: Houghton Mifflin Company, 1884), 231-234; William T. McKinney, "The Defeat of the Secessionists in Kentucky," *Journal of Negro History*, 1 (Oct. 1916), 377; Volz, "Party, State, and Nation," 324-348; Kirwan, *John J. Crittenden*, 341; Speed, *The Union Cause in Kentucky*, 1; Robertson, "Sectionalism in Kentucky," 55-77.

When the votes were counted, Magoffin won, 76,187 to 67,283. The Democrats had won the governorship and the majority in the state legislature, but not by as many votes as they wanted. The Opposition had made some solid gains by running a strong Southern rights campaign. The election showed that, while Democrats still controlled the state, Kentuckians did not support secession. Further evidence was that the new legislature elected Breckinridge as U. S. senator, while he was still the vice president. Both Magoffin and Breckinridge exemplified the Kentucky hope of maintaining Southern rights within the Union.[24]

This was the situation Kentuckians faced as they headed into the presidential election of 1860. The Democrats were divided, the Opposition did not have a national party, and the Republicans had no real support in Kentucky. For the Democrats nationally, Douglas had been the frontrunner and was the choice of Northern Democrats, but his recent stance on Lecompton and his own Freeport Doctrine hurt his chances with Southern Democrats. As for Kentucky Democrats, they were willing to forgive Douglas for his Lecompton stance, but he was not willing to renounce what Kentuckians called "squatter rights," or popular sovereignty.

As the national convention in Charleston, South Carolina, approached, Kentucky Democrats divided over who they should support. Half of them wanted to kill any chance that Douglas had to win. They wanted a platform that called for federal protection of slavery in the territories. This group wanted to see a strong Southern rights man and decided to push their own James Guthrie, who had a long history of supporting Southern rights issues. More moderate Kentucky Democrats supported Breckinridge. Southern moderates did not want to antagonize Douglas supporters, and so hoped Breckinridge would be their second choice when they realized Douglas could not win Charleston.[25]

In the Kentucky state Democratic convention, the majority report attempted to compromise in hopes of unifying the party. They agreed to support popular sovereignty rather than federal protection of slavery, but did acknowledge circumstances when the federal government might intervene. The

24 Shaler, *Kentucky: A Pioneer Commonwealth*, 231-234; McKinney, "The Defeat of the Secessionists in Kentucky," 377; Volz, "Party, State, and Nation," 324-348; Kirwan, *John J. Crittenden*, 341; Speed, *The Union Cause in Kentucky*, 1; Robertson, "Sectionalism in Kentucky," 55-77.

25 Harrison, *The Civil War in Kentucky*, 3-4; Volz, "Party, State, and Nation," 339-359.

majority also endorsed James Guthrie, but left open the possibility of change. The minority represented the strong Douglas men who backed popular sovereignty completely and insisted the federal government should never interfere with the territories. They saw this platform as the only possible way to keep the slavery question out of national politics and save the party. They too loosely endorsed Guthrie, but with the intention of switching to Breckinridge as the compromise candidate at the Charleston convention.[26]

In April, the Democrats held their national convention in Charleston to nominate a presidential candidate. Much of the discussion at the convention dealt with secession. Southerners believed that they had put up with attacks on slavery and their way of life long enough and demanded that the party support the South by insisting on federal protection of slavery. Some delegates, such as William Yancey, even called for secession if Southerners did not get a president who supported Southern rights.[27]

Yet each faction within the party arrived at the convention still believing it could achieve victory. The Douglas faction believed it had the national party on its side. Douglas had told Southern Democrats that Northerners would not accept a platform that guaranteed slavery in the territories, and that such a platform could give the Republicans a victory by throwing Northern Democrats over to their side. The radicals wanted Guthrie and came prepared to fight for him. They hoped to bring the entire South with them by showing that Guthrie was the only candidate who would protect the South. The moderate wing of the party hoped that Breckinridge could unite Democrats by maintaining his Southern support while also appealing to a sizable number of Northern delegates. However, when the moderates put Breckinridge's name forward, he refused to run as long as Guthrie remained a candidate. In the end, it did not matter because Douglas had the strength necessary to win. Even with Douglas running on the issue of popular sovereignty, Southerners did not unite against him. However, the seven original states that would make up the

---

26 Harrison, *The Civil War in Kentucky*, 3-4; Volz, "Party, State, and Nation," 362-364.

27 E. Merton Coulter, *The Civil War and Readjustment in Kentucky* (Chapel Hill: University of North Carolina Press, 1926), 20-22; Harrison and Klotter, *A New Kentucky History*, 183-184; Volz, "Party, State, and Nation," 377-379; Michael Fellman, Lesley J. Gordon, and Daniel E. Sutherland, *This Terrible War: The Civil War and its Aftermath* (New York: Longman Press, 2003), 70-71.

Confederacy, plus Arkansas, walked out of the convention rather than support the senator from Illinois.[28]

Kentucky Democrats as well as delegates from the other border states showed they did not support secession by remaining at the convention and attempting to heal the wounds of the party. Kentuckians still believed in the spirit of Clay and wanted to work out a compromise. But the Democrats remaining in Charleston could not form a quorum, so they decided to meet again in six weeks in Baltimore, Maryland. Kentuckians saw the best chance for peace within the party being to push for either Guthrie or Breckinridge, though most now favored Breckinridge. Guthrie would keep the South in the party but would alienate the Northern Democrats; Breckinridge, they hoped, could be supported by everyone. When the Baltimore convention met, the Douglas Democrats who controlled the meeting refused to allow the Southern Democrats who had walked out at Charleston to retake their seats. Following this mistreatment of their fellow Southerners, six more slave state delegations walked out, as well as half of the delegates from Kentucky and Missouri. Historian David Potter saw the Democratic conventions as a microcosm of secession. Except for Arkansas, the states that left at Charleston were the ones that first seceded and created the Confederacy; the ones who joined them in Baltimore left after Fort Sumter, and Kentucky and Missouri split, just as they would in 1861.[29]

The state delegates who abandoned the Charleston and Baltimore conventions decided to meet and create a new party that would stand for Southern rights. They formed the National Democratic Party and endorsed a platform that called for the federal protection of slavery. They wanted to support a candidate who believed in Southern rights but was not so radical that he could not win a national election. They backed Kentucky's favorite son, John C. Breckinridge. With Douglas and Breckinridge both running for president, the last of the old national parties had fallen. Within Kentucky, the Democrats also split, with some of them supporting Douglas and the rest backing Breckinridge. It was an opportunity the Opposition could have only dreamed

---

28 Coulter, *The Civil War and Readjustment in Kentucky*, 20-22; Harrison and Klotter, *A New Kentucky History*, 183-184; Volz, "Party, State, and Nation," 377-379; Fellman, Gordon, and Sutherland, *This Terrible War*, 70-71.

29 Coulter, *The Civil War and Readjustment*, 20-22; Volz, "Party, State, and Nation," 377-379; Potter, *The Impending Crisis*, 413-414.

would happen. With the Democrats split nationally as well as in Kentucky, the Opposition had a chance to win back the state.[30]

The Opposition had held a convention that February at Frankfort in hopes of creating a national party. They called for anyone who wanted peace and compromise; what they got were old Whigs, old Know-Nothings, and some moderate Democrats. Most of their support came from the border states, the same region where the Whig Party had survived in spirit if not in name. They based their platform squarely on the Union. They still believed in the importance of Southern rights and criticized radical leaders on both sides for their stance on slavery. They also believed in supporting the Constitution and called for compromise between North and South. Some men still held out hope for a fusion with the Republicans, if only they would nominate someone without a record against slavery. However, to the disappointment of the Opposition, the Republicans nominated Lincoln, which killed any chance of a last-minute compromise. With hopes of unity over, the Opposition renamed itself the Constitutional Union Party and nominated John Crittenden, the leader of the party, for the presidency. At seventy-four, Crittenden felt too old to run and instead supported the eventual Union candidate, John Bell of Tennessee.[31]

By the summer of 1860, the struggle to nominate the presidential candidates was finished—but the battle for the presidency had just begun.

---

30 Coulter, *The Civil War and Readjustment*, 20-22; Volz, "Party, State, and Nation," 380-384; Potter, *The Impending Crisis*, 413-414; Harrison and Klotter, *A New Kentucky History*, 183-184; Fellman, Gordon, and Sutherland, *This Terrible War*, 71.

31 Robertson, "Sectionalism in Kentucky," 57-58; John V. Mering, "The Slave-State Constitutional Unionists and the Politics of Consensus," *Journal of Southern History*, 43 (Aug. 1977), 401-403; Fellman, Gordon, and Sutherland, *This Terrible War*, 72; Volz, "Party, State, and Nation," 352-353; Otis K. Rice, "Constitutional Union Party," in Kleber, *The Kentucky Encyclopedia*, 224.

C hapter 2

The Presidential Election:
October to November 1860

By the summer of 1860, the presidential candidates were in place. The *Louisville Courier* described the campaign in true Kentucky fashion—by comparing it to a horse race. There were four horses in the race. The first horse, Free Soil, was ridden by his jockey Old Abe, dressed in black and using a piece of rail to whip his horse. Next was the great stallion, States Rights, ridden by John C. Breckinridge, who wore a red cap, blue coat, and white pants. Then, Old Union was ridden by Bell, who wore a liberty cap with a stars-and-stripes coat. Lastly, Little Squatty was jockeyed by Stephen Douglas, who wore a green cap, a striped gray coat, and black pants. Squatty hoped to ride on the heels of States Rights, but broke his girth and fell behind. As for the pedigree of the horses, Free Soil, trained by a black man, was sired by abolition and born from Old Spoil, who was fathered by False Philanthropy and born from Imported Africa. States Rights was sired by Constitution and born from Fair Play. Constitution was sired by Revolution and born from the Spirit of '76, who was out of Magna Carta. Old Union was fathered by Compromise and also born from Old Spoils. Compromise was sired by Shrieking Kansas and born from Brown Raid. Lastly, Squatty was sired by Abolition and born from Young America. Abolition and his brother Old Spoils were both sired by Free States.[1]

---

1 *Louisville Courier*, October 19, 1860.

The *Louisville Courier* represented the views of the Breckinridge Democrats, so it did have its own slant, but it effectively summed up the candidates from a Kentucky perspective. For those who do not speak the language of horse racing, the *Courier* said that Lincoln represented the party that Southerners dubbed the Black Republicans. It was a party created by abolitionists that hoped to end slavery. The *Courier* saw the Constitutional Union Party in a positive light, conceived as it was from compromise, but the party had a dark side with its connection to Old Spoil. In other words, both the Republicans and Constitutional Unionists had the same source, the old Whig Party, and so they had more in common than people might know. The father of Old Spoil was False Philanthropy, which was a reference to slave colonization. The Whigs and, more importantly, Henry Clay had supported emancipation of slaves and recolonization to Africa. The *Courier* wanted to stress that John Bell and the Constitutional Unionists sought compromise but came from the same background as the Black Republicans, and so might compromise on slavery. Throughout the campaign, the *Courier* reserved its harshest criticism for the Douglas Democrats; it did not see Lincoln as a threat to win Kentucky. Douglas' horse, Squatty, was named after squatter rights, a negative term for popular sovereignty. The important Louisville paper saw the Northern Democrats as being as much influenced by abolitionists as the Republicans. Squatter rights conflicted with Dred Scot and had the potential to kill slavery. Finally came John C. Breckinridge and States Rights. The Southern Democrats believed in following the Constitution and the Supreme Court's decision in Dred Scot. They saw the other three parties as endangering the laws that the founding fathers had created to protect slavery forever. Where the *Courier* fell short was in showing that most of the nation, including many Kentuckians, believed—for good reason—that the Breckinridge Democrats were the party of secession.[2]

As campaigning began, only three of the four parties had a chance in Kentucky: the two Democratic parties and the Constitutional Unionists. All three knew that if the Republicans won the election overall, secession was possible. The three parties blamed each other for helping give the Republicans a chance to win, believing that their own party would win if it were a two-candidate race. They wanted to use the election to send a message to the rest of the nation that they supported the Union, but they supported it in

2 *Ibid.*

different ways. The Constitutional Unionists and the Douglas Democrats each believed that only they could maintain the Union. If Lincoln won, the South would secede, and if Kentucky voted for John C. Breckinridge, the lower South would gain more confidence, believing there existed a united slave front. If Kentucky voted for either Bell or Douglas, not only would one of those men achieve victory, but they would steal some of the thunder from the lower South. The Breckinridge Democrats saw things differently. Unless the South stood together to elect Breckinridge, the nation would divide. Breckinridge had to win so that the North would respect the South's political power and the South would not have to secede.[3]

Four days before the election, the *Louisville Courier* reported that Douglas Democrats were being asked to vote for John Bell in the upcoming election. The Douglas camp saw its chances for victory in Kentucky as minimal, but was not about to give up. If nothing else, Northern Democrats hoped to have the election thrown into the House, where a compromise candidate could win. Because of this dynamic, these two parties in Kentucky refrained from attacking each other. They both reserved their opposition for the perceived extremists, the Southern Democrats and Republicans. In two Northern states, the two parties were able to unite and run on a fusion ticket, but in Kentucky and the South the Constitutional Unionists could not afford to mesh with the Douglas Democrats for fear of losing their identity as a pro-Southern party. Bell already had to defend himself against Southern Democratic attacks of being an abolitionist. The Louisville paper had reported on a speech given by Pennsylvania Republican Thaddeus Stevens in which the influential Northerner claimed Bell would be a perfect candidate for a cabinet position in a Republican White House because he agreed with many Republican policies. Though Stevens must have meant well, the Kentucky Constitutional Unionists could not have been happy about his endorsement. Bell needed to prove to Kentucky that he stood for Southern rights. Joining with Douglas might pick up a few Democratic votes, but it could cost him the race by pushing away more support than he attracted.[4]

---

3   Harry Volz, "Party, State, and Nation," 388-390.

4   *Ibid.*, 388-395; Albert D. Kirwan, *John J. Crittenden: The Struggle for the Union* (Lexington: University Press of Kentucky, 1962), 357-360; *Louisville Courier*, October 23 and November 2, 1860.

Illinois Senator Stephen Douglas was the Democratic candidate in the 1860 presidential race. Famous for his 1858 debates with Lincoln, Douglas was also responsible for the division in the Democratic Party when Southern Democrats refused to accept his nomination and instead chose John C. Breckinridge. Douglas did not make a good showing in Kentucky, coming in third with 17% of the popular vote, ahead of only Lincoln. *Library of Congress*

As for Douglas, he tried to run in the South and did some campaigning. Within Kentucky, he still retained some support (he would receive 17 percent of the popular vote on election day). The main Douglas platform in Kentucky was still popular sovereignty. He believed people within a territory had the right to allow or outlaw slavery as they saw fit. His supporters also promoted the idea that Breckinridge supported secession. The *Louisville Daily Journal* reported a speech given by Douglas in which he challenged Breckinridge's right to be called a Democrat. Douglas pointed out that the Democratic convention had voted for him, whereas the only way Breckinridge had received a nomination was by Southern members throwing away their loyalty to the party. As far as Douglas was concerned, the men who had left the Charleston and Baltimore conventions to nominate Breckinridge were traitors because he was the one man who would accept the votes of traitors. Breckinridge was a hypocrite, exclaimed Douglas, because he had been elected as a senator from Kentucky to support not just Southern rights but also the Union. Douglas openly questioned why Breckinridge did not resign his senate seat, since he could not possibly believe in the Union while also representing the party of secession. Lastly, Douglas accused Breckinridge of splitting the Democratic vote, giving Lincoln a good chance of winning the election. If Southern Democrats voted for Douglas, he could win the election, but votes for Breckinridge practically ensured victory for Lincoln.[5]

As mentioned, the principal paper of the Breckinridge Democrats—the *Louisville Courier*—used Douglas as its punching bag. Its goal was to show that Breckinridge was the only true Democrat running and that Douglas had betrayed the Democratic Party to the Black Republicans when he abandoned states rights for squatter rights. Squatter rights played right into the hands of the Republican Party by allowing it to break with Dred Scott and outlaw slavery in the new territories. According to the paper, the convention that nominated Douglas was not a Democratic convention because all true Democrats had walked out. Their criticism of Douglas was that his candidacy might allow Lincoln to win. Maintaining the concept that Douglas did not belong to a national party, the *Courier* insisted that he lacked the strength to win in the North, and that he might pull votes away from Breckinridge in the South. It believed that if the election was between Lincoln and Breckinridge, the latter

---

5   William C. Davis, *Breckinridge: Statesman, Soldier, Symbol* (Baton Rouge: Louisiana State University Press, 1974), 242; *Louisville Journal*, October 1, 1860.

could easily win; but with the Democratic votes split and the Constitutional Unionists likely to siphon crucial votes, Lincoln had a good chance to win. To make matters worse, if Lincoln did win and the South seceded, the *Courier* feared that Lincoln would whip the South back into the Union.[6]

In Kentucky, the election came down to a race between Breckinridge and Bell. Kentuckians would have struggled to find any major differences between the two men's campaigns in the state. However, according to some prominent Kentucky historians, the first evidence of Kentucky's unionism surfaced when the state voted for Bell. Yet, as evidenced by their campaigns, that is not a logical conclusion. A vote for Breckinridge could be as much a vote for the Union as could a vote for Bell, and a vote for Bell could mean secession as much as could a vote for Breckinridge. Both parties claimed to be the party of Southern rights and slavery, and both rejected secession. In fact, each accused the other of favoring secession. Breckinridge backers pointed to a speech given by Bell in 1850 called the "Give Me Disunion" speech, in which Bell advocated constitutional protection for slavery and said he did not want to live in a nation kept together by force. The Bell backers admitted that Breckinridge had never called for secession, but they attacked him because leading members of his party did talk of leaving the Union. In Kentucky, Breckinridge had said that a vote for him was a vote for the Union, but too many people were reading the rantings of other Breckinridge Democrats, including Robert Rhett in the *Charleston Mercury*, who openly demanded secession if Breckinridge lost.[7]

Historian John Mering has shown the relationship between the Constitutional Unionists and the Southern Democrats by looking at voting patterns in Congress from December 1859 to June 1860. He found that the thirty-three Southern Congressmen—members of both parties—voted the same way on every occasion except for two. The two exceptions were over partisan, not ideological, issues. The first instance was the vote to select the Speaker of the House, and the second was a vote on whether to investigate corruption in the Buchanan administration. According to Mering, both parties held the same pro-South, pro-slavery ideology, with the Constitutional Unionists being as strong a Southern party as the Southern Democrats. He pointed out that in the upper South most secessionists supported Breckinridge, but so did many anti-secessionists. Modern historians have always portrayed

6   *Ibid.*, October 15, 18, 20, 22, and November 2, 1860.

7   Coulter, *The Civil War and Readjustment in Kentucky*, 22; Davis, *Breckinridge*, 242.

John Bell from Tennessee was the candidate of the Constitutional Union Party in the 1860 presidential election won by Abraham Lincoln. The Constitutional Union Party formed as a compromise party as a way to keep the peace. It chose Bell because he was seen as acceptable to both Northerners and Southerners. His only success was in the border states, including Kentucky, which he won with 45% of the popular vote. *Library of Congress*

Breckinridge as the pro-secession candidate because of his supporters and because of the dramatic fashion in which he later quit the Senate to join the Confederacy. However, what is not so often mentioned is that Bell also joined the Confederacy, and did so before Breckinridge.[8]

John Bell had been a leader of the newly-developed Whig Party in the 1830s and had served several terms in the U.S. House of Representatives and the Senate. He came from one of the wealthiest families in the South and owned a large slave force. He received acclaim from the North when he opposed the Kansas-Nebraska Act and the Lecompton Constitution. Members of the old Whig Party hoped to run a candidate who would draw support from both North and South, and they saw Bell and John Crittenden as their best chances. When Crittenden refused to run because of his age, the new Constitutional Union Party decided on Bell. The *Louisville Daily Journal* supported Bell's candidacy because it believed neither half of the splintered Democratic Party could win, and unless the people voted for Bell, Lincoln would win and the Union would be dissolved. Bell's most important supporter in Kentucky was Crittenden, who hit the campaign trail to convince Kentuckians that their best and only option was Bell. He argued that slavery in the territories should not be the important issue; popular sovereignty did not matter because geographically there was nowhere left to take slaves. The important issue was who could keep the peace, and the answer was Bell. He was the one candidate acceptable to all. The Republicans were backed by abolitionists. The two wings of the Democratic Party were fighting each other. Douglas could not be accepted by the South, and, although Breckinridge was not a secessionist, his party was labeled as such.[9]

The *Louisville Courier* disagreed with Bell's and Crittenden's assessment of the situation. It saw the national election as a duel between Breckinridge and Lincoln, with a vote for Bell helping the latter. It did not dislike Bell; it believed he was an able man, but he could not be trusted as a true friend of the South. His party allegiance may have changed several times, but his Whig ideology had not, and, as a Whig, he had been connected with the same people who made up the

---

8   John V. Mering, "The Slave-State Constitutional Unionists and the Politics of Consensus," *Journal of Southern History*, 43 (August 1977), 399-409.

9   Crofts, *Reluctant Confederates*, 19; *Louisville Journal*, October 3, 1860; Mary Scrugham, *The Peaceable Americans of 1860-1861* (New York: Columbia University Press, 1921), 36-40; Volz, "Party, State, and Nation," 392-395; Kirwan, *John J. Crittenden*, 360-363.

Republican Party. His voting record proved it. Even though Bell voted against the Kansas-Nebraska Act—the *Courier* reported that he had voted to repeal the Missouri Compromise line—in every other way he had voted the same as the men who now made up the Republican Party. He had even started to lean toward squatter rights. The paper feared that if Bell received enough votes he could throw the election into the Congress, where Lincoln had the best chance to win. In the end, said the Louisville paper, if Kentucky voted for Bell it would show that the South was not unified, which could give the North the courage it needed to repress the Southern people.[10]

The Democrats seemed to have the advantage in Kentucky going into the final days of the presidential race. Their candidate, John Breckinridge, was not only from Kentucky, but had served Kentucky for years as a states-rights Democrat. He came from a well-respected family and, most importantly, had just won a victory over the Opposition candidate for the United States Senate. Before Breckinridge entered politics, he graduated from Centre College in Kentucky, attended the College of New Jersey (known today as Princeton University), and studied law at Transylvania University in Kentucky. He practiced law in Kentucky until the Mexican War, in which he served as a major of volunteers. Upon returning from the war, he won a position in the state legislature in 1849 and two years later ran for Congress from the Ashland district, the old district of Henry Clay. The Ashland district was strongly Whig, but Breckinridge used his family name, his military rank, and his excellent speaking and political skills to win the seat. While in Congress, he became known as a defender of states rights and argued that the Constitution did not give the president or Congress the power to interfere with slavery in any way. In 1856, the Democrats chose him as Buchanan's running mate to help secure the Southern vote.[11]

In Kentucky, Breckinridge had one major hurdle in 1860: he had to prove that he was not a secessionist. His support of slavery and Southern rights could not be denied by the other candidates, so they challenged his devotion to the Union. The *Louisville Journal* regarded Breckinridge with affection for his service

---

10 *Louisville Journal*, October 18, 19, 20, 1860.

11 Davis, *Breckinridge*, 1-57; Lowell H. Harrison and James C. Klotter, *A New History of Kentucky* (Lexington: University Press of Kentucky, 1997), 182-184; Volz, "Party, State and Nation," 86-87; James C. Klotter, "John Cabell Breckinridge," in John Kleber, ed., *The Kentucky Encyclopedia*, 117-118.

to Kentucky, but claimed he had surrounded himself with secessionists, so it could no longer support him. The paper also looked unfavorably on his record as a compromiser. As for Breckinridge himself, he believed his nomination for the presidency came about because the Democrats wanted to prove their loyalty to the nation, not push for secession.[12]

Breckinridge gave only one major campaign address in Kentucky. On September 5, 1860, he told a crowd of over ten thousand gathered at Clay's home in Lexington that his party's platform did not endorse secession. At no time, Breckinridge continued, had he ever said he wanted to see his beloved country destroyed, and he challenged anyone to point to a time when he had attacked the Union. He said his platform was to stand behind the Supreme Court and the Dred Scot decision. He denounced both Douglas and Lincoln: Douglas for refusing to accept the decision of the courts; and Lincoln for being the real disunionist, meaning that Lincoln's policies, as outlined in his "House Divided" speech, had started the secession talk. Even so, Breckinridge could not escape the cloud of secession. Too many Kentuckians saw the Southern Democrats as conspiring to break up the nation by having Lincoln win and giving them a reason to secede.[13]

November 6, 1860, was election day. Kentuckians knew they faced a dilemma. As one man put it, he opposed both secession and abolitionists. "The thought of civil war is to me most horrible," he explained, "but we can't live as we are for the abolitionists are unbearable when they come among us as they do." With the two strongest candidates both claiming they met Kentucky's needs, Kentuckians had a difficult choice to make. Many decided not to make the choice at all. Kentuckians turned out to vote at only 67.1 percent, high by modern standards but one of Kentucky's lowest to that point; the presidential election voter turnout in 1856 had been 70.8 percent. In fact, it was the first time since 1824 that Kentucky's turnout was lower than the national average.[14]

---

12 Coulter, *Civil War and Readjustment*, 22; Davis, *Breckinridge*, 228-230; *Louisville Journal*, October 1, 1860.

13 Coulter, *Civil War and Readjustment*, 22; Wilson Porter Shortridge, "Kentucky Neutrality in 1861," *Mississippi Valley Historical Review*, 9 (March 1923), 284; *Louisville Courier*, November 6, 1860; Harrison and Klotter, *A New History of Kentucky*, 182-184.

14 Unknown to Tom, October 23, 1860, in Thomas Walker Bullitt Collection, Filson Club; Jasper Shannon and Ruth McQuown, *Presidential Politics in Kentucky, 1824-1948* (Lexington: Bureau of Government Research, College of Arts and Science, University of Kentucky, 1950), 32.

After the votes were counted, Bell had won the day in Kentucky with 45.2 percent of the votes. After Bell came the two Democratic candidates, Breckinridge with 36.4 percent and Douglas with a surprisingly low 17.5 percent. Lincoln came in last with only 0.9 percent of the vote. One interesting statistic is that the two Democrats together received more votes than Bell. Democratic predictions were correct: by dividing, they had allowed the state to select Bell. If the party's members had remained united, they might have carried the state.[15]

On the national level, the worst fear of Southerners came true. With a split in the Democratic Party, Abraham Lincoln was elected with 39.8 percent of the popular vote and 180 electoral college votes. Besides New Jersey, in which he split the vote with Douglas, Lincoln captured every Northern state and California and Oregon. Breckinridge followed Lincoln with seventy-two electoral college votes, but he captured only 18.1 percent of the popular vote. Breckinridge won all of the deep South as well as Maryland, North Carolina, Arkansas, and Delaware. John Bell followed with thirty-nine electoral college votes and 12.6 percent of the popular vote. Bell won the border states of Kentucky, Tennessee, and Virginia. Douglas came in last with only twelve electoral college votes, even though he took 29.5 percent of the popular vote. Douglas won only the state of Missouri and half of New Jersey.

Lincoln's election gave Southern firebrands the ammunition they needed to push for secession. William Bodley, a Louisville lawyer active in public affairs, expected the cotton states to rush foolishly out of the Union at the first moment. South Carolinians had wanted disunion since 1833, he said, and had tried to coerce the rest of the South into supporting them; but with the election of Lincoln, South Carolina could finally convince the rest of the cotton states that slavery was doomed within the Union. As for Kentucky, Bodley said the state's sympathies were with the South but against secession, and he spoke prophetically when he guessed that if war came it would be ten times worse for the border South.[16]

There are two contradictory ways of viewing the 1860 presidential election in Kentucky, both of which dispute the traditional theory of the state's

---

15 "Secretary of State of Kentucky Election Results," 1855-1872, manuscript volume, Kentucky State Archives.

16 William Bodley to A. Beerswell, November 26, 1860, in Temple Bodley Papers, Filson Club; Bodley to Unknown, November 22, 1860, in Temple Bodley Papers, Filson Club.

overwhelming Union support. Two historians who helped create the traditional view are Thomas Speed and E. Merton Coulter. Speed, a Union veteran of the Civil War, originated the theory in 1907 when he published *The Union Cause in Kentucky*. Coulter wrote his classic account of the border state, *The Civil War and Readjustment in Kentucky*, in 1926. Both men believed that the 1860 election was the first sign that Kentuckians would never accept secession. Speed saw votes for Bell, Douglas, and Lincoln as votes for the Union, while a vote for Breckinridge was a vote for secession. His interpretation was that, with 93,026 votes for the "Union" candidates and only 52,836 for Breckinridge, four of every seven Kentuckians rejected secession.[17]

However, even if the November election was a referendum on secession, it can be looked at in an entirely different way. By combining the Constitutional Unionists with Douglas and Lincoln, Speed effactually turned them into unconditional Unionists, which they were not. As seen earlier, Bell ran on a platform that was strongly pro-Southern rights. Constitutional Unionists believed in the Union, but only a Union that guaranteed slavery. When looking at the election numbers, 75 percent of the counties having over a 40 percent slave population voted for Bell. Counties that had a slave population in the 30 to 39 percent range voted for Bell by 93 percent. Lastly, counties having less than ten percent slaves voted for Bell only 38 percent of the time. In other words, Kentuckians most intent on protecting slavery voted for Bell, while those who dealt the least with slaves did not. A vote for Bell did not mean unconditional support for the Union; it meant compromise. A vote for Bell meant living in a nation without Black Republicans running the country, and with a government pledged to protect Southern institutions.[18]

Support for this conclusion may be found in the elections in Virginia and Tennessee. Both states selected Bell, who ran there on the same platform of fighting for Southern rights within the Union as he did in Kentucky. If Speed's theory was correct, and a vote for Bell meant a vote for the Union, then why did Virginia and Tennessee both secede after electing Bell? To go one step further, if Bell was an unconditional Unionist, why did he later join the Confederacy?[19]

---

17 Speed, *The Union Cause in Kentucky*, 18.

18 Mering, "The Slave State Constitutional Crisis," 404-406.

19 The issue of support for state over the federal government for men like Bell will be discussed in a later chapter. *Louisville Courier*, January 22, 1861; Mering, "The Slave State

Further evidence against Speed's interpretation may be found in the national vote. The highest percentage of votes that Bell received in a non-slave state was 13.2 percent in Massachusetts, followed by 4.4 percent in Vermont. In eight of the fourteen free states, Bell polled lower than two percent, and in five states he polled less than one percent. If people in the North wanted peace and the Union, then why not vote for Bell? The answer is that most saw Bell as a Southern-rights candidate, not a conditional Unionist. Thus, based on Northern perceptions, Speed's argument could be reversed, with the votes of the "secessionists" Breckinridge and Bell combined. This shows that the people of Kentucky strongly opposed Lincoln and supported Southern rights, by 119,194 votes to 27,002, or seven out of nine Kentuckians.[20]

1860 Presidential Votes for Bell by State

State	Bell %	State	Bell %
Arkansas	30.9%	Mississippi	36.2%
Alabama	37%	Missouri	35.3%
California	7.6%	New Hampshire	0.6%
Connecticut	2%	New Jersey	Fusion
Delaware	24.1%	New York	Fusion
Florida	36.1%	North Carolina	46.7%
Georgia	40.3%	Ohio	2.8%
Illinois	1.4%	Oregon	1.5%
Indiana	1.9%	Pennsylvania	2.7%
Iowa	1.4%	Rhode Island	Fusion

Constitutional Crisis," 401-499; Volz, "Party, State, and Nation," 369-399; Shortridge, "Kentucky Neutrality," 744-750.

20 Mering, "The Slave State Constitutional Crisis," 401-409; Shannon and McQuown, *Presidential Politics in Kentucky*, 32-36; Volz, "Party, State, and Nation," 396-399; Shortridge, "Kentucky Neutrality," 744-750.

State	Bell %	State	Bell %
Kentucky	45.2%	South Carolina	0%
Louisiana	40%	Tennessee	47.7%
Maine	2%	Texas	24.5%
Maryland	45.1%	Vermont	4.4%
Massachusetts	13.2%	Virginia	44.6%
Michigan	0.3%	Wisconsin	0.1%
Minnesota	0.1%		

The second possible explanation for the Kentucky vote, which contradicts the first but still argues against Speed, is that people continued to vote along old party lines. Research by historians such as Daniel Crofts shows that people in much of the upper South in the 1860 election voted for the same parties they had always supported. In other words, they were not voting for the Union or secession but for Democrats and Whigs, regardless of the party platforms. For example, in Arkansas the Whiggish, slave-holding region of the southeast voted for Bell, while the strong Democratic area of the northwest voted for Breckinridge. However, when Arkansas voted for secession, it was the southeast that supported secession while the northwest fought against it.[21] Seemingly, then, Arkansans voted in November according to party allegiances.

A similar pattern existed in Kentucky, but since Kentucky never voted for secession it is impossible to make a direct comparison. There were 100 counties in Kentucky whose votes were recorded for the presidential elections of 1852, 1856, and 1860. Seventy-nine of the counties voted the same way in 1852 and 1856, with Whigs being replaced by Know-Nothings in the latter elections. In those 79 counties, 87 percent continued to vote the same way in the 1860 election, the Whig and Know-Nothing vote being replaced by the

---

21 Crofts, *Reluctant Confederates*, 55-64; Robert Childers, "The Secession Crisis and Civil War in Arkansas Through the Eyes of Judge David Walker, Conditional Southern Unionist from Fayetteville" (M. A. Thesis, University of Arkansas, 2001), 17; James Woods, *Rebellion and Realignment: Arkansas's Road to Secession* (Fayetteville: University of Arkansas Press, 1987), 107-114, 151-164.

Constitutional Unionists. But when examined closer, 61 percent of the counties that continued to vote the same voted for John C. Breckinridge, while only 29 percent voted for Bell. Of the nine counties that voted for the same party in 1852 and 1856 but changed parties in 1860, eight switched from the Whig/American Party to the Democrats, while only one switched in the other direction.[22]

County	1852	1856	1860
Adair	Dem	Dem	Dem
Allen	Dem	Dem	Dem
Anderson	Dem	Dem	Dem
Ballard	Dem	Dem	Dem
Barren	Whig	Amer	Union
Bath	Dem	Dem	Dem
Boone	Whig	Amer	Dem
Bourbon	Whig	Amer	Union
Boyle	Whig	Amer	Union
Bracken	Whig	Whig	Dem
Breathitt	Dem	Dem	Dem
Breckinridge	Whig	Amer	Union
Bullitt	Dem	Dem	Dem
Butler	Whig	Amer	Union
Caldwell	Dem	Dem	Dem
Calloway	Dem	Dem	Dem

22 Shannon, *Presidential Politics in Kentucky,* 26-36.

County	1852	1856	1860
Campbell	Dem	Dem	Dem
Carroll	Dem	Dem	Dem
Carter	Dem	Dem	Dem
Casey	Whig	Amer	Union
Christian	Whig	Dem	Union
Clarke	Whig	Amer	Union
Clay	Whig	Amer	Dem
Clinton	Dem	Dem	Dem
Crittenden	Dem	Dem	Union
Cumberland	Whig	Amer	Union
Daviess	Whig	Dem	Dem
Edmonson	Dem	Dem	Dem
Estill	Whig	Dem	Dem
Fayette	Whig	Amer	Dem
Fleming	Dem	Amer	Dem
Floyd	Dem	Dem	Dem
Franklin	Whig	Amer	Dem
Fulton	Dem	Dem	Dem
Gallatin	Dem	Amer	Dem
Garrard	Whig	Amer	Union
Grant	Dem	Dem	Dem
Graves	Dem	Dem	Dem

County	1852	1856	1860
Grayson	Whig	Dem	Dem
Green	Dem	Dem	Dem
Greenup	Dem	Dem	Union
Hancock	Whig	Dem	Dem
Hardin	Whig	Amer	Dem
Harlan	Whig	Amer	Union
Harrison	Dem	Dem	Dem
Hart	Dem	Dem	Dem
Henderson	Dem	Amer	Union
Henry	Dem	Dem	Dem
Hopkins	Dem	Dem	Dem
Hickman	Dem	Dem	Dem
Jefferson	Dem	Amer	Union
Jessamine	Whig	Amer	Union
Johnson	Dem	Dem	Dem
Kenton	Dem	Dem	Dem
Knox	Whig	Amer	Union
Laurel	Whig	Amer	Union
Lawrence	Whig	Amer	Dem
Letcher	Dem	Dem	Dem
Lewis	Dem	Dem	Dem
Lincoln	Whig	Amer	Union

County	1852	1856	1860
Livingston	Whig	Amer	Union
Logan	Whig	Amer	Union
Madison	Whig	Amer	Union
Marion	Whig	Dem	Dem
Marshall	Dem	Dem	Dem
Mason	Whig	Amer	Union
McCracken	Dem	Amer	Union
Meade	Whig	Amer	Union
Mercer	Dem	Dem	Dem
Montgomery	Whig	Amer	Union
Monroe	Whig	Dem	Union
Morgan	Dem	Dem	Dem
Muhlenburg	Whig	Dem	Union
Nelson	Whig	Amer	Union
Nickolas	Dem	Dem	Dem
Ohio	Whig	Dem	Dem
Oldham	Dem	Dem	Dem
Owens	Dem	Dem	Dem
Owsley	Dem	Dem	Dem
Pendleton	Dem	Amer	Dem
Perry	Whig	Dem	Dem
Powell	Dem	Dem	Dem

County	1852	1856	1860
Pulaski	Dem	Dem	Union
Pike	Whig	Dem	Dem
Rockcastle	Whig	Amer	Union
Russell	Whig	Amer	Union
Scott	Dem	Dem	Dem
Shelby	Whig	Amer	Union
Simpson	Whig	Dem	Dem
Spencer	Dem	Dem	Dem
Taylor	Dem	Dem	Dem
Todd	Whig	Amer	Union
Trigg	Dem	Dem	Dem
Trimble	Dem	Dem	Dem
Union	Dem	Dem	Dem
Warren	Whig	Amer	Union
Washington	Dem	Dem	Dem
Wayne	Whig	Dem	Dem
Whitley	Whig	Amer	Dem
Woodford	Dem	Amer	Union

Seventy-two percent of Kentucky counties voted the same party in 1852, 1856, and 1860 with the Whigs being replaced in 1856 by the American Party and in 1860 by the Constitutional Union Party.

After the election, the vast majority of Kentuckians continued to reject separation as the cure for their troubles. They did not believe Lincoln's election required rash actions. One Kentuckian wrote as much in his journal the day after the election. "Lincoln," he offered, "gave no encouragement to the disunionists." The state's two largest papers, published out of Louisville, expressed loyalty to the Union, although neither news organ embraced unconditional Unionism. Instead, both papers insisted that Southern rights be protected under Republican rule. They even discussed joining in a common cause to help Kentucky in this time of crisis, though they did so for different reasons.[23]

Even though John Bell supporters stood for Southern rights, the fear of secession growing stronger each after the election convinced them to make a call through the *Louisville Journal* for a Union meeting as a way of demonstrating to the rest of the nation their loyalty to the United States. Bell's supporters hoped to follow ex-governor Charles Wickliffe's advice, "[to] proclaim to the Country that Kentucky will stand by the Union or perish with it." In particular, they wanted to send a message to the deep South that Kentucky would not join in any secessionist movement. They hoped this would slow secession talk in the South. Most believed that if other border states followed Kentucky's lead, Southern fireaters would realize they were a minority and back off from secession. Kentuckians realized that their actions over the next couple of weeks

1860 Presidential Election by County

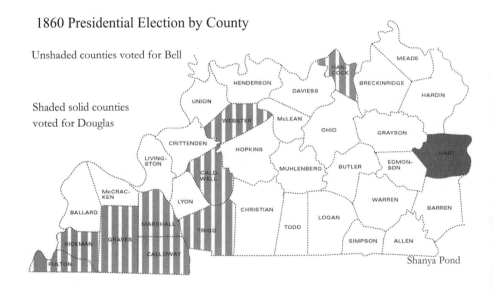

23 John F. Jefferson Diary, November 7, 1860, in John F. Jefferson Papers, Filson Club; *Louisville Journal*, November 10, 1860; *Louisville Courier*, November 13, 1860.

could decide the fate of the nation, and saw a meeting to endorse the Union as a positive first step.[24]

Kentucky Democrats were hurt by their loss in the election, but their spirits were not crushed; they had lost before and had always bounced back. For the moment, they needed to refocus and fight for what was important. They agreed with Bell's party that it was necessary to oppose secession, but they opposed any public meeting or organized opposition to secession. They thought that would send the wrong message to the wrong people. The *Louisville Courier* claimed that no Kentuckians had called for secession, so it was not necessary to speak against it. They feared putting Kentucky in a false position of supporting the Union unconditionally. Instead, Kentucky needed to show that, while it would not submit to Republican bullying, it did not see secession as a useful weapon.

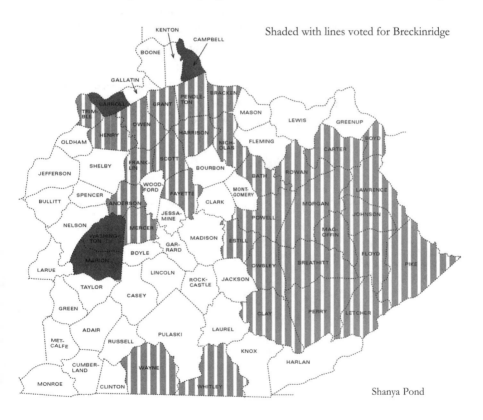

Shaded with lines voted for Breckinridge

Shanya Pond

24 Charles Wickliffe to Lewis Harvie, November 13, 1860, in Wickliffe/Preston Papers, University of Kentucky; *Louisville Journal*, November 10, 1860; Volz, "Party, State, and Nation," 403-404.

The best way to stop secession, in the opinion of the Democrats, was to show the deep South how committed they were to fighting for the cause of the South within the Union. By showing they were clearly not unconditional Unionists yet willing to fight for their rights alongside the South, they hoped the deep South would not feel the need to secede.[25]

The state's two major newspapers commented on this division over tactics, but they took unexpected positions. The *Louisville Journal*, the more pro-Union paper, feared the resolutions by Bell supporters were too strong. They wanted Kentuckians to endorse the Union but also emphasize that their sympathies were with the South. They wanted it known that if the South came under attack and called for help, Kentucky would answer the call. The *Journal* reminded readers that if the South seceded, the days of prosperity in Louisville (to be discussed in the next chapter) were over. Interestingly, the more pro-secession paper agreed with the Union meeting's resolutions. The *Courier* believed Kentucky should support the Union as long as Southern rights were guaranteed.[26]

Even with the election of Lincoln, most Kentuckians were not confused or torn. They were for all intents and purposes Southern—but they still saw their greatest chance of peace and prosperity within the Union.

25 *Louisville Courier*, November 13 and 14, 1860; Volz, "Party, State, and Nation," 402-405.

26 *Louisville Journal*, November 24, and 27, 1860.

C hapter 3

Secession, Slavery, and Economic Prosperity:
November 1860 to February 1861

O n December 17, 1860, the *Charleston Mercury* published "A Southern Manifesto," calling for the slave states to secede from the Union. The manifesto declared that all attempts to remain in the Union, meaning Congressional legislation and Constitutional amendments, had failed and that, for its own protection, the South needed to form a separate confederacy. Three days later the state of South Carolina officially declared itself independent from the United States. Over the next few weeks, Mississippi, Florida, Alabama, Georgia, Louisiana, and Texas all joined South Carolina in passing secession ordinances. On February 4, 1861, representatives of these seven states met in Montgomery, Alabama, to create the Confederate States of America.[1]

Political leaders had convinced sufficient numbers of Southerners in those states that Lincoln's election marked an end to slavery and their way of life. Southern leaders claimed that Lincoln and the Republicans wanted to position

---

1   Charles B. Dew, *Apostles of Disunion: Southern Secession Commissioners and the Causes of the Civil War* (Charlottesville: University of Virginia Press, 2001), 24; Michael Fellman, Lesley J. Gordon, and Daniel E. Sutherland, *This Terrible War: The Civil War and its Aftermath* (New York: Longman Press, 2003), 76-77.

blacks over whites and make slaves of free men. Worst of all, blacks would be turned loose on white women to destroy their innocence.[2]

To promote their cause of racial fear and secession, the five Southern states of Mississippi, Alabama, South Carolina, Georgia, and Louisiana sent official delegates to slave states that had not seceded to persuade them to join their cause. On December 26, 1860, Stephen Hale, a commissioner from the state of Alabama, arrived in Frankfort, Kentucky, to talk to Governor Beriah Magoffin. Hale told Magoffin that Alabama wanted to consult with other slave states and discuss "common grievances and the measures necessary to be adopted to protect the interests, honor, and safety of their citizens." Hale insisted that the South had the right to break from the Union under the contract theory of government. Individual states, he explained, had no obligation to recognize a national government that ignored its contract with the states to protect their rights. When the Constitution was created, Hale argued, slavery existed in all thirteen states, and even though the North no longer practiced slavery, the government's responsibility to protect slavery had not changed. What had changed was how the North now attacked the institution of slavery in every way possible, in literature, schools, press, and pulpit. Northern states ignored fugitive slave laws and actively tried to help slaves escape. And then, Abraham Lincoln was elected solely by the Northern votes. The incoming president represented all the wrongs committed against the South over the past several years.[3]

Hale claimed that if Southerners remained in a Union under Lincoln's direction, they would submit themselves to complete ruin. "The slave-holder and non-slave-holder must ultimately share the same fate," Hale insisted forcefully, "all be degraded to a position of equality with free negroes, stand side by side with them at the polls, and fraternize in all the social relations of life, or else there will be an eternal war of races, desolating the land with blood, and utterly wasting and destroying all the resources of the country." The South would not and could not wait to see what Lincoln might do to the slave-holding states. Indeed, the slave states must strike first, and Kentucky must join them Hale told Magoffin. Disunion was inevitable, and if the South united now it

---

2 Fellman, Gordon, and Sutherland, *This Terrible War*, 76-77; Unknown to Unknown, November 22, 1860, in Temple Bodley Papers, Filson Club.

3 B. Magoffin to S. F. Hale, December 28, 1860, *OR* Ser. 4, vol. 1, 4-13.

could prepare to resist the North if the national government tried to hold the Union together by force.[4]

Governor Magoffin responded to Hale by outlining the policy Kentucky would eventually take toward secession for the remainder of the crisis. His policy also mirrored the attitude of most Kentuckians. As a supporter of states rights, Magoffin agreed with Hale about the wrongs committed against the South. Indeed, Magoffin believed his state had even greater reason to fear Northern fanatics than Alabama because of Kentucky's closer proximity to the North. He saw slavery under attack by journalists, religious leaders, and the new government. However, unlike Alabama, Magoffin said, Kentucky would do all in its power to save the Union. He assured Hale that if that proved impossible, Kentucky would be prepared to join a Southern confederacy; but Magoffin still saw a chance for compromise. If the South stood together, the North would have to compromise, and Magoffin believed that if Northerners were given the chance and time, they would support a guarantee of slavery. The Northern people did not want disunion or war. If the North supported compromise, it could both maintain the Union and avoid war.[5]

Magoffin's policy, therefore, was undergirded by five clear premises. First, Kentucky's loyalties were with the South and slavery. Second, geography put Kentucky in a dangerous location. Third, Kentucky wanted to stay in the Union if at all possible. Fourth, Kentucky's leaders believed compromise was the answer. Lastly, only after every attempt had failed to preserve its people's rights within the Union would Kentucky consider secession. It was only on this last point that Magoffin misjudged Kentucky—and, as it turned out, himself as well.[6]

Beriah Magoffin was born in Harrodsburg, Kentucky, in 1815 and, like his political ally John C. Breckinridge, attended Centre College and law school at Transylvania University. He moved to Mississippi to begin his law practice but returned to Kentucky in 1839. In 1850, he was elected to the state senate as a Democrat. He ran for lieutenant governor in 1855 but lost to the Know-Nothings. In 1859, he won the governorship, making him responsible

---

4   S. F. Hale to B. Magoffin, December 20, 1860, in *The War of the Rebellion: A Compilation of the Records of the Union and Confederate Armies*, 128 vols. (Washington, D.C., 1880-1901), Series 4, vol. 4, 4-11 (hereafter *OR*); Dew, *Apostles of Disunion*, 18, 51-58.

5   B. Magoffin to S.F. Hale, December 28, 1860, in *OR*, Ser. 4, vol. 1, 4-13.

6   *Ibid.*

Beriah Magoffin was the Democratic governor of Kentucky from 1859-1862. His task was to guide Kentucky through the most difficult period in the state's history. Magoffin rejected sending troops to either side and strongly supported Kentucky's right to remain neutral. Unionists viewed him as a Southern sympathizer, and once they took control of the legislature overrode all his vetoes. He agreed to step down as governor, provided a conservative man would take his place. *Library of Congress*

for guiding the state through the roughest waters in its history. Magoffin was a strong states-rights Democrat who would ultimately call for the secession of Kentucky. However, before advocating secession, he worked toward a compromise to save the Union and, equally importantly, to keep Kentucky out of the war.[7]

The first issue Magoffin confronted was slavery. Most people of Kentucky, like the rest of the South, saw slavery as vital to its way of life. American historians have shown that the South's justification of slavery evolved over time: slavery in colonial times was defended differently than it was in the antebellum period. The common way to describe this evolution is to say that slavery went from being an evil necessity to being a positive good. During the colonial and revolutionary periods, many Americans, including leading founding fathers, saw slavery as evil. Even famous slaveholders, such as Thomas Jefferson, feared that God would punish them for practicing slavery. Men who saw slavery in this light knew the institution was wrong but did not see an easy way to abolish it. Slavery was vital to the Southern economy, and the alternative to slavery was a large free black population. Just because slavery was evil did not mean people believed in racial equality, and the thought of a large free black population was intolerable.[8]

However, by the 1840s, abolitionism had changed Southern views. Abolitionists such as William Lloyd Garrison believed slavery was morally wrong, and insisted on the immediate emancipation of all slaves. When the country agreed slavery was evil, the two sides could work together; but when Northerners began to attack Southerners as sinners and demanded rights for blacks, Southerners changed their thinking. Instead of defending slavery as a necessity, they began to celebrate it as a positive good. Slaveholders looked to religion and social conditions to show not only that slavery fit within Christianity, but that it created an ideal labor situation. Slaveholders claimed

7   Lowell H. Harrison and James C. Klotter, *A New History of Kentucky* (Lexington: University Press of Kentucky, 1997), 194; Lowell H. Harrison, "Beriah Magoffin," in John Kleber, ed., *The Kentucky Encyclopedia*, 603-604.

8   Fellman, Gordon, and Sutherland, *This Terrible War*, 28-34. For more on the defense of slavery, see Winthrop Jordan, *White over Black: American Attitudes Towards the Negro, 1550-1812* (Chapel Hill: North Carolina University Press, 1968); Larry Edward Tise, *Proslavery: A History of the Defense of Slavery in America, 1701-1840* (Athens: University of Georgia, 1990); Eric L. McKitrick, ed., *Slavery Defended: The View of the Old South* (Englewood Cliffs: Prentice Hall, 1963); Drew Gilpin Faust, *A Sacred Circle: The Dilemma of the Intellectual in the Old South, 1840-1860* (Philadelphia: University of Pennsylvania Press, 1986).

that slaves, because of their low intellect, thrived under the institution. They even claimed that slaves fared better than workers in the North because slaves did not fear unemployment, hunger, lack of shelter, or old age.[9]

In his book *Evil Necessity*, Harold Tallant made a connection between different regional views of slavery within the South and the timing of secession. The Deep South, which supported the idea of slavery as a positive good, was more willing to fight to protect the institution and much readier to secede when it could not achieve that goal. The states of the Upper South that seceded months after the Deep South did not have the same concerns. Other sources show the same evidence. In examining the secession debates in Virginia and Kentucky, slavery was definitely a primary concern, but it was less important than the threat of Northern coercion—of the North, that is, using military force to keep the South in the Union. In the Virginia secession convention, most delegates were willing to gamble that the Union would not outlaw slavery, but they would not tolerate Northern efforts to coerce Southern states back into the Union.[10]

Tallant believed that most Kentuckians stood apart from the majority of the South because even into the late 1850s they still saw slavery as a necessary evil. Still, that did not lessen their determination to keep slavery in Kentucky. It took the Thirteenth Amendment, in 1865, to force Kentuckians to give up their slaves. Tallant believed that Kentuckians did not embrace slavery as a positive good because much of the state's economy was not as dependent as the deep South on slavery. Kentucky's cereal grain crops were much less labor intensive than the lower South's cotton crop, rendering slavery less important. As previously mentioned, Kentucky had only a 19 percent slave population. Only 28 percent of the population owned slaves, and while many of those people may have been willing to accept the positive good theory, the majority of Kentucky's population never did. So, if Kentuckians saw slavery as evil and did not require

9 Fellman, Gordon, and Sutherland, *This Terrible War*, 28-34.

10 Harold Tallant, *Evil Necessity: Slavery and Political Culture in Antebellum Kentucky* (Lexington: University Press of Kentucky, 2003), 3-9; Harrison and Klotter, *A New History of Kentucky*, 167-168; George H. Reese, *Proceedings of the Virginia State Convention* (Richmond: Virginia State Library, 1965); *Journal of the Called Session of the Kentucky General Assembly of the House* (Frankfort, Kentucky: Yeoman Office, 1861), hereafter cited as *House Journal*. For more information and detail on the Virginia secession, see James Finck, "Honor and Duty: John Janney and the Virginia Secession Convention" (M.A. Thesis, Virginia Tech, 2002), and William C. Davis and James I. Robertson, *Virginia At War, 1861* (Lexington: The University Press of Kentucky, 2005).

the practice, why did they so ardently support slavery, even to the point of advocating secession? The answer was racial control.[11]

There had always been Kentuckians who opposed slavery. They were tolerated by the general population because their arguments against slavery were similar to the ones used to support slavery as a necessary evil. Kentucky anti-slavery sentiments in the early days had been expressed in the form of colonization. Colonization was the practice of shipping freed blacks to Africa. Many people could accept the concept of colonization because it theoretically solved all problems. Those who were pro-slavery liked colonization because it rid the state of free blacks, whose visible independence set a bad example for slaves. People who opposed slavery but were not especially fond of the black race saw colonization as a way of getting rid of slavery while not increasing the free black population. Kentucky's most influential citizen supported colonization: Henry Clay served as the president of the American Colonization Society from 1836 to 1852. Still, actual colonization efforts in Kentucky and elsewhere ultimately failed—they proved too expensive and too difficult to organize.[12]

The state's laws and political debates also illustrate Kentucky's attitude toward slavery. In 1833, the state legislature passed a law banning the importation of slaves into the state. Legislators hoped the law, in conjunction with colonization, would lead to a gradual emancipation of slaves. In the 1840s, the legislature debated outlawing slavery altogether, but proponents could not overcome public fears of free blacks, so the pro-slave forces won the debates convincingly. In 1849, Kentuckians wanted to make a new state constitution. Slavery was only one issue among several that inspired debate, but when it came to voting for delegates, slavery dominated the discussion. Traditional party lines broke down for a while as men campaigned for or against slavery. The anti-slavery candidates ran on platforms of gradual emancipation, claiming that slavery hurt the state's social and economic systems by obstructing the growth of industry and white immigration. The pro-slavery people declared there simply was no acceptable alternative to slavery. Not only did whites not want to

11 Tallant, *Evil Necessity*, 1-9; Harrison and Klotter, *A New Kentucky History*, 167-168; Barbara Fields, *Freedom: A Documentary History of Emancipation 1861-1867*, Series I, 9 vols. (Cambridge: Cambridge University Press, 1985), I: 493-494.

12 Tallant, *Evil Necessity*, 27; Volz, "Party, State, and Nation," 72-73.

live with free blacks, the pro-slavery people maintained, but slavery elevated the status of poor whites.[13]

What hurt the anti-slavery candidates the most was that at the same time they were campaigning there were rumors of violence by slaves. The pro-slavery forces used violence to undermine the anti-slavery position. With an open ballot system in place during the election, most men would not risk voting anti-slavery for fear of being perceived as endangering the white race. In the end, the anti-slavery party won only nine percent of the vote. Consequently, the new constitution required that freed blacks leave the state. With their loss in the election, anti-slavery forces resorted to more radical and violent measures.[14]

In the 1850s, violence both by and against abolitionists grew in Kentucky. What separated Kentuckians from the inhabitants of most slave states was having abolitionists living amongst them. Most slave states dealt with growing attacks against slavery from without, but the reason for Kentucky's volatile situation was the attacks from within. Kentucky's two greatest anti-slavery voices: abolitionist John Fee and emancipationist Cassius Clay. Both despised slavery, but took different approaches to fighting it. Clay was born into a slave-holding family in 1810. He began his schooling at Transylvania University, but left to finish at Yale. While there he heard abolitionist William Lloyd Garrison speak, an experience that changed his life. Upon his return to Kentucky, Clay allied politically with his cousin, Henry Clay, and won a seat in the state legislature. He lost his seat in the next term because of his growing anti-slavery views. In 1845 he began publishing an anti-slavery newspaper called the *Lexington True American*, but a mob closed him down and forced him to move to Cincinnati. After serving in the army during the Mexican War, he returned to Kentucky to continue his work in abolition. That is where he met John Fee.[15]

---

13 Volz, "Party, State, and Nation," 73-74; Tallant, *Evil Necessity*, 93, 112, 135-137, 143-162; Fields, *Freedom*, 494; 1850 Kentucky State Constitution, Article X, Kentucky Historical Society.

14 Volz, "Party, State, and Nation," 73-74; Tallant, *Evil Necessity*, 135-136, 143-163; Fields, *Freedom*, 494.

15 Harrison and Klotter, *A New History of Kentucky*, 177-178; William W. Freehling, *The Road to Disunion: Secessionists at Bay*, 2 vols. (Oxford: Oxford University Press, 1990), I: 462-472; Stanley Harrold, "Violence and Nonviolence in Kentucky Abolitionism," *Journal of Southern History*, 57 (Feb., 1991), 16-19; H. Edward Richardson, "Cassius Marcellus Clay," in Kleber, *The Kentucky Encyclopedia*, 199-200. There were varying degrees of ideological thought in the anti-slavery movement, and, while Fee and Clay worked together, they did not have the same ideological position.

Like Clay, Fee was born to a slave-holding family. Six years younger than Clay, he attended Augusta College in Kentucky before leaving for Lane Theological Seminary in Cincinnati. It was at Cincinnati that he developed his religious anti-slavery views, and over the next few years he helped to establish anti-slavery churches in Kentucky. It was during this time that Fee met Cassius Clay, and the two worked together for emancipation. Clay even gave Fee land in Madison County on which to build a new church and eventually a school, which he named Berea in 1859. Both the church and the school supported black equality. The two men also helped to organize the state's first branch of the Republican Party.[16]

In 1856, however, they had a falling out. Fee saw the Republican Party as soft on slavery. He advocated immediate abolition, and so did not agree with Clay's advocacy of gradual emancipation with colonialization. The two men had made a good fit in the beginning because Clay kept Fee from physical harm. Clay was well known for his ability to protect himself, including challenging enemies to duels, and was justifiably famous for his skill with a Bowie knife. Clay did not believe that violence in protection of personal honor or liberties to be wrong. Fee, however, did not condone violence for any cause, not even self-protection. Still, it was only after the John Brown raid in 1859 that Kentuckians decided they could no longer tolerate John Fee. The citizens of Madison County forced him to flee the state. Fee's eviction was not as remarkable as the fact that he had preached his gospel of abolitionism within the state for over fifteen years. Fee's experience suggests that slavery in the 1850s was not Kentucky's top concern, at least not until Kentuckians saw emancipation of slaves as a real threat with the election of Lincoln.[17]

In 1862, a frustrated Kentucky soldier fighting for the Union wrote a letter home after the Emancipation Proclamation was announced. In it, the soldier described how he did not enlist and was not happy to be fighting for a doctrine that, if announced a year earlier, would have sent Kentucky into the arms of the Southern Confederacy. The soldier summed up the attitude of most

16 Tallant, *Evil Necessity*, 168, 195; Harrison and Klotter, *A New History of Kentucky*, 178; Harrold, "Violence and Nonviolence in Kentucky," 18-26; Richardson, "Cassius Marcellus Clay," 199-200; Richard Sears, "John Gregg Fee," in Kleber, *The Kentucky Encyclopedia*, 312-313.

17 Tallant, *Evil Necessity*, 168; Harrison and Klotter, *A New History of Kentucky*, 178; Harrold, "Violence and Nonviolence in Kentucky," 18-26; Richardson, "Cassius Marcellus Clay," 199-200; Richard Sears, "John Gregg Fee," in Kleber, *The Kentucky Encyclopedia*, 312-313.

Kentuckians: they may have seen slavery as a necessary evil, but they stressed the necessary part.[18]

Lincoln's election, fears of abolition, and the subsequent debate over emancipation brought on a crisis in Kentucky. Kentuckians most feared that losing slavery would lead to a loss of social and racial control. One man reported that a black playmate of his son had said that when the blacks were freed, they would kill any whites who did not run away. Another man heard that slaves had been telling their masters that they would not work for them much longer because Lincoln would set them free. The *Louisville Journal* reported on December 4, 1860, that a white man and fifteen slaves were hanged for plotting a slave insurrection. As seen in Magoffin's letter to Hale, cited earlier, the continued existence of slavery was never the central question when it came to secession. Even the legislature passed a unanimous resolution declaring no truth in rumors that Kentucky was considering freeing slaves. So the question was not whether Kentucky believed in slavery, but which side offered the most protection to slavery.[19]

The question of how best to protect slavery had no obvious answer. As a friend of Brutus Clay, Cassius Clay's brother, asked, "What was a border state to do?" The issue was not whether to secede and keep slavery or to stay in the Union and lose it. In fact, both secessionists and Unionists claimed that only their side would protect slavery. John White Stevenson, Kentucky congressman, gave a speech on January 30, 1861, calling for secession and accusing Lincoln and the Republican Party of breaking both the spirit and the letter of the Constitution. By threatening to exclude slavery from the territories, they ignored basic rights to property, not to mention the Dred Scott ruling. The *Louisville Journal* reported on November 21, 1860, that some Northern states had passed a new series of personal liberty laws that very week—laws that trumped the federal fugitive slave law. If Lincoln did not intend to free the slaves, why did he allow the personal liberty laws to stand? Lastly, secessionists said that remaining in the Union would hurt Kentuckians because they would lose their market in the South to sell slaves, which was of great economic importance to the State. If the Confederacy did not open the foreign slave trade, Kentucky, being foreign, could not sell slaves there. If the Union ever tried to

18 Harrison and Klotter, *A New History of Kentucky*, 179.

19 Unknown to Tom, January 18, 1861, in Thomas Walker Bullitt Collection, Filson Club; *Louisville Journal*, December 4, 1860; *House Journal*, December 20, 1860, 503.

free the slaves, Kentucky would be stuck with a large free black population—the exact thing Kentuckians feared.[20]

As for the Unionists, they continued to downplay the dangers to slavery within the country as a whole. Crittenden, who led the Unionists in Kentucky, offered a good example of their post-election perspective. He owned nine slaves and feared losing them, but his political position was that the Dred Scott decision protected slavery. Robert Breckinridge agreed with Crittenden when he argued, "Our duties can never be made subordinate to our passions without involving our ruin, and . . . our rights can never be set above our interest without destroying both."

In other words, if Kentuckians allowed their passions to force them into secession, they would end up losing slavery. Unionists also stressed that remaining in the Union theoretically allowed them to invoke the Fugitive Slave Law. Under current circumstances, if slaves ran away there was at least some chance of having them returned to their owners. If Kentucky joined a Southern confederacy, they would lose that tool, a significant concern for a border state. The *Louisville Journal* pointed out that all the runaways had been returned in Illinois and Indiana, showing that the law worked. But if Kentucky seceded, what chance did the state's slaveholders have that any slaves would be returned?[21]

Kentuckians reminded their friends farther south that Kentucky slave-owners were the people most likely to have fugitive slaves in the North. According to the *Louisville Journal* noted that Madison County, Kentucky, and Queen Anne County, Missouri, lost more slaves every year than any entire cotton state had ever lost. A similar point was made at the Virginia secession convention. Delegate Waitman Willey accused secessionists of basing their reasons for disunion on the idea that the Northern press and pulpit attacked the Southern way of life and encouraged slaves to run away. Willey openly inquired how secession could stop either thing from continuing to happen. The North would still criticize the South, he argued, and still encourage slaves to run away.

---

20 C. Field to B. Clay, January 1, 1861, in Clay Family Papers, University of Kentucky; John White Stevenson, Speech of Hon. J. W. Stevenson, of Kentucky, on the state of the Union (Washington: L Towers, 1861); James Speech, February 18, 1861, in Governor Beriah Magoffin Records, Kentucky State Archives; *Louisville Journal*, November 21, 1860.

21 Fields, *Freedom*, 494; Kirwan, *John J. Crittenden*, 344-345, 428; Coulter, *The Civil War and Readjustment in Kentucky*, 7-8; *Louisville Journal*, January 11 and 29, 1861.

The only difference, he continued, would be that a separate confederacy would have no legal way to fight back.[22]

Looking ahead to the second wave of secession, the one that jolted the upper South, only four of eight Union slave states seceded after March 1860. A quick look at a map reveals an important geographical consideration in that delayed secession movement. In each case, the states that seceded—Virginia, North Carolina, Tennessee, and Arkansas—had a slave state directly north of it. When they seceded, the four remaining states were either still debating which direction to go or had been occupied by Union troops. Either way, the seceding states had buffering slave states between themselves and the free states. Missouri, Kentucky, Maryland, and Delaware all bordered Northern states, which meant that if they seceded they would share a border with a different country—one that would offer freedom to runaway slaves.

Further complicating Kentucky's consideration of secession, the slave economy was already taking a major hit. William Johnston, lawyer and son of Albert Sidney Johnston, complained on December 2, 1860, that he had not been able to sell his slave Hamitt in the current uncertain political climate. In fact, he observed that slave traders in his part of the state had not been able to sell any slaves for several months. At the last auction, twenty-one blacks had been put on sale but not one received a bid. Another Union man reported that he could only sell his slaves at barely a quarter of their value, and that property value in general was falling. With the possibility of war on the horizon, crop prices were falling so fast that it was not worth planting.[23]

The secession of the lower South caused a depression in Kentucky that continued into the spring of 1861. A Kentucky women wrote in her journal one February night, "I have heard talk of the scarcity of money but I have never witnessed anything like the present time, the best men cannot pay the ordinary family expenses. The merchants unable to collect or unable to lay in the usual supply of food. Add to all this great scarcity of food for stock here, and starvation for the people in some places." One Kentucky merchant tried to buy as much cotton as possible because he did not see the problem getting any

---

22 *Louisville Journal*, November 28, 1860; George H. Reese, ed., *Proceedings of the Virginia State Convention of 1861* (Richmond: Virginia State Library, 1965), I: 352-361.

23 William Johnston to George W. Johnson, December 2, 1860, in George W. Johnson Papers, Kentucky Historical Society; Charles E. Yonkers, "The Civil War Transformation of George W. Smith: How a Western Kentucky Farmer Evolved from a Unionist Whig to a Pro-Southern Democrat," *The Register of the Kentucky Historical Society*, 103 (Autumn, 2005), 670.

better, especially if other states left the Union. The economic situation was bleak, with thousands of workers being laid off in the cities. For Kentuckians, secession was about more than states rights and slavery; they also had to decide which side offered Kentucky the best chance of economic prosperity.[24]

Kentucky, a predominantly agricultural society and economy, ranked eighth in the country in 1860 for the highest number of farms. In the early days of Kentucky, farmers relied on the river trade to sell their products, the majority of goods being sent down the Mississippi River. The most important city for Kentucky merchants was New Orleans. Kentucky's trade in the early antebellum period further solidified that city's place in the Southern economy. However, with the growth of Northern manufacturing and the development of railroads and steamboats, Kentuckians were in the fortunate position of being able to open markets in the North as well. The South used its land to grow commercial crops, while the North invested in manufacturing. Kentucky produced crops and livestock needed by the people of both North and South. The principal crop for Kentuckians was tobacco; they produced twenty-five percent of the nation's output. Second to tobacco was hemp, but livestock and grains were also in demand. Kentucky ranked fourth nationally in the production of rye, ninth in oats, and tenth in wheat. In terms of livestock, Kentucky ranked seventh in horses, second in mules, fourth in swine, eighth in sheep, and tenth in cattle. In most cases, Kentucky only trailed behind other border states that supplied the same products.[25]

As for manufacturing, Kentucky ranked twelfth nationally, but among slave states trailed only Virginia and North Carolina. The principal manufacturing export for Kentuckians was bourbon, which they started distilling commercially in 1789. They also had a rich supply of iron ore and developed a fair number of iron works companies. After 1851, they even began to make steel. Kentucky also offered other manufactured goods, including textiles and paper.

24 Wallace Journal, February 12, 1861, in Wallace-Sterling Family Diaries, Kentucky Historical Society; George Black to C. Field, January 3, 1861, in Clay Family Papers, University of Kentucky; Mary to sister, November 22, 1860, in Hunt-Morgan Family Papers, University of Kentucky.

25 Harrison and Klotter, *A New History of Kentucky*, 142-143; Kenneth H. Williams and James Russell Harris, "Kentucky in 1860: A Statistical Overview," in *The Register of the Kentucky Historical Society*, 103 (Autumn 2005), 753-757.

The state's exports were important to both North and South, but which customer would prove the most vital to Kentucky? Unfortunately, the commonwealth stood to lose economically whichever way it went, leading some manufacturers ultimately to endorse neutrality.[26]

Unionists claimed that Kentucky's geographical location made it impossible not to side with the North economically. The state had a 700-mile border with three Northern states, each with a population larger than Kentucky's and desiring Kentucky goods. Crittenden said that even a moment's reflection would show the ruinous consequences of disunion to Kentucky's economy. Tariffs became an important issue for many Kentuckians. Kentucky had long been one of the few slave states to benefit from high national tariffs, but another consideration now confronted people. If Kentucky went with the Confederacy, and assuming the Confederate States achieved independence, Northern tariffs would make the cost of trading with the North too high; whereas, if Kentucky remained in the Union, it could ship goods and produce south without paying a tariff. Also, if Kentucky remained in the Union, seceded states would still trade with them out of necessity. The lower South grew mostly cotton, which could not be eaten. The region still needed to trade for foodstuffs and livestock. Kentuckians also had to consider which section had the stronger economy. During the secession crisis, Kentucky and most of the South saw economic declines. The *Louisville Journal* reported, for example, that the values of South Carolina stocks were down to zero while New York stocks were at a premium and getting stronger. The North had a stable government and proven market. One Kentuckian believed a Southern confederacy would be a drag on the economy of the state. South Carolina's hasty act, he said in January, had reduced the prices of everything in the South and would ultimately ruin many a good Kentuckian.[27]

Unionists identified taxation as another economic reason to remain loyal. The deep South did not support tariffs, so in order to make up the lost income a confederacy would be forced to rely on direct taxation. A new nation, after all, would have to build an army, navy, post office, and all manner of governmental

26 Harrison and Klotter, *A New History of Kentucky*, 139-140; Williams and Harris, "Kentucky in 1860," 755.

27 Coulter, *The Civil War and Readjustment*, 12; Wilson Porter Shortridge, "Kentucky Neutrality in 1861," *Mississippi Valley Historical Review*, 9 (March 1923), 288; Kirwan, *John J. Crittenden*, 429; *Louisville Journal*, January 7, 1861; Curd to Mr. Cornell, January 26, 1861, in John Curd Miscellaneous Collection, Filson Club.

support. Direct taxes might prove beneficial to the cotton states, but they could damage Kentucky's growing manufacturing enterprise and affect farmers. In the Union, farmers paid twenty cents on every hundred dollars in taxes, but if they joined a Southern confederacy the *Louisville Journal* predicted they would be forced to pay closer to two dollars on every hundred dollars.[28]

Secessionists saw things quite differently. They blamed the current depression on the fact that Kentucky had not seceded and aligned with its principal customers. Speaking strictly economically, the South had a great deal of appeal to Kentucky. Most of the state's trading partners came from the South. The South grew mainly cotton and had little industry, both factors that could benefit Kentucky for trade purposes. As mentioned earlier, Kentucky was a major food supplier, and if the Midwestern states were eliminated as competition, Kentucky's agriculture output could become even more profitable. Kentucky's manufacturing output was small in comparison to the North, but if the state joined the South, it would be among the leaders in Southern industry. Kentucky could even take over the North's textile business by keeping the cotton in the Confederacy and not sending it North. The North could survive without Kentucky's crops, but the Southern states absolutely needed them. In the North, Kentucky would rank twelfth industrially, but in the South, with its food sources and manufacturing, it would be one of the richest states.[29]

After Kentuckians considered slavery and the economy, they had to consider their dangerous geographical position, being in such close proximity to a potential enemy. The same map that showed why Kentucky's debate over secession was affected by runaway slaves and the economy also showed how being on the wrong side in a war would have dire consequences. If Kentucky joined the seceded states and the U. S. government decided to force them back into the Union, Kentucky would be the first state to feel the effects of war. South Carolinians, observed the *Louisville Journal*, were willing to risk war because their distance from the Ohio River made them relatively safe. Even looking at the secession debates in Virginia, there is no comparison to the importance Kentuckians placed on their proximity to the North. Virginians also

28 *Louisville Journal*, January 14 and 30, 1861.

29 Coulter, *Civil War and Readjustment*, 9-10; *Louisville Courier*, January 17, 1861; Kirwan, *John J. Crittenden*, 429; James Headly to Father, no date, in Thomas Henry Hines papers, University of Kentucky.

feared invasion, but they did not mention it in debate half as often as did Kentuckians. Geographically speaking, the issue that was raised the most during Kentucky's secession debate was the 700 miles along the winding Ohio River. In other words, just above Kentucky were the states of Ohio, Illinois, and Indiana, with a combined population of more than five million people; (Kentucky had fewer than one million). The seven major railroads leading from those three Northern states into Kentucky offered convenient logistical routes for invasion.

Kentuckians never admitted to being scared. In fact, just the opposite; they continued to point out that, if called upon, brave Kentuckians would defend the state. A better way to describe the feeling in Kentucky is to say people acted cautiously. They knew that if there was a war, their land would be the battleground—it would be their homes destroyed and their crops burned. William Bodley, a Louisville lawyer, insisted that while Kentucky's sympathies were with the South, few people endorsed secession. If war came, he said, the border states would suffer ten times more than the deep South, and so the border states would not support secession or war.[30]

No matter which direction Kentucky turned, it could not avoid serious consequences. The best possible outcome would be not to choose sides at all, and for that reason Kentuckians pushed for a compromise and peace. When that effort failed, the only way to save Kentucky would be to remain neutral. With neutrality, Kentuckians hoped they could keep their slaves, trade with both sections of the country, and avoid war, all at the same time.

---

30 Kirwan, *John J. Crittenden*, 429; *Louisville Journal*, November 28, 1860, January 15 and February 12, 1861; William Bodley to A. Beerswell, November 26, 1860, in Temple Bodley Papers, Filson Club.

C hapter 4

Choosing Sides:
January to February 1861

E ver since the presidential election in November, Kentuckians had seen themselves as the best chance of peace for the nation. If they could act as moderators, through compromise, they could restore the South to its rightful place in the Union. However, by mid-January, some in Kentucky had lost their optimism about the possibility of maintaining peace. Tom Bullitt, a lawyer, received a letter claiming that if the people of the United States looked to Kentucky to save the Union, the Union was doomed. Kentucky, he said, was too bitterly fragmented.[1]

Kentuckians did, however, agree on some issues. First and foremost, they wanted peace. Second, most people agreed that they wanted to remain in the Union; it was the way to accomplish these goals that led to Kentucky's division. With the crisis facing the nation, the traditional political parties in Kentucky began to collapse as people gathered with like-minded individuals to push their own agendas. The old parties were the foundation for the new parties, though not all voters remained loyal to their old allegiances. Some men who had voted for John Bell saw Lincoln's election as a reason to secede. But most Constitutional Unionists and Whigs joined with Douglas Democrats to form

---

1 Unknown to Tom Bullitt, January 18, 1861, in Thomas Walker Bullitt Collection, Filson Club.

the Democratic Union Party, while most of the new States Rights Party had been Breckinridge Democrats. In the months to come, neither party would take extreme positions, hoping to recruit as many followers as possible.[2]

There were three contending ideological positions when it came to secession in post-1860 Kentucky. First were the unconditional Unionists. They could not foresee any circumstance that would justify Kentucky leaving the Union and pledged their allegiance to the nation without qualification. Most unconditional Unionists lived in the northern part of the state, bordering Ohio, Indiana, and Illinois. Cassius Clay represented this ideology. He loved the Union because of its stability and liberty and saw no reason to secede. Clay even supported war if it was required to save the Union and end slavery; the nation may as well settle these issues now, he said, or it would surely face them again in the future.[3]

Next there were the secessionists. They believed that even compromise efforts were not enough to make up for the grievances against Kentucky and the South. One Kentucky doctor pointed out that with the secession of South Carolina the exodus had already begun. Secessionists believed their loyalties, and the best possible chance for prosperity, now lay with a Southern Confederacy. Most Kentucky secessionists lived along the Tennessee border or in the Jackson Purchase.[4]

Third were the conditional Unionists, who made up the majority of Kentuckians. Conditional Unionists did not reject the possibility of secession, but they considered it a drastic step. They placed their hopes on the compromise efforts in Washington. The two new political parties to emerge after the election, the Democratic Union Party and the States Rights Party, officially embraced this third position, even though some of their members believed in the other positions. Both parties wanted Kentucky to remain in the Union, but they disagreed over the extent of the state's ultimate loyalties. The biggest difference between them was that it would take a drastic action, such as declaring war against the Confederacy, for the Democratic Unionists to accept

2   Volz, "Party, State, and Nation: Kentucky and the Coming of the American Civil War," 413-415; *Louisville Journal*, February 8, 1861.

3   Kirwan, *John J. Crittenden*, 428-429; Clay to Rollins, January 8, 1861, in Cassius Marcellus Clay Papers, Filson Club; Mary Allen Bernard, "Joseph Holt, Judge Advocate General, 1862-1875" (Ph.D. diss., University of Chicago, 1927), 53.

4   Kirwan, *John J. Crittenden*, 428-429; Bernard, "Joseph Holt, 53; W. Sutton to Unknown, December 26, 1860, in Orlando Brown Papers, Filson Club.

secession, while the States Rights Party was prepared to secede for only minor infractions.[5]

As for the secessionists, their argument was clearly stated in a long letter written by James Headley, a lawyer, to his father in January 1861. Headley had lived in Kansas for some time. He had known many abolitionists there, and the experience convinced him that secession was the only recourse for Kentucky. He made a comparison to business. He asked his father what he would do if his business partner accused him of a great crime while the partner stole from him at the same time. Would his father not be justified in ending the business relationship? That was how the North had treated the South. It told the world that Southerners were committing a sin by having slaves, yet northerners benefited from the profits that the South made from slave labor. Headley believed that the right of secession had become a moot point. The only decision left for Kentucky was which side to join. Kentuckians could join the North, which hated them, or with their friends, family, and like-minded people of the South.[6]

Headley went on to explain to his father why compromise would not work. The North was not interested in compromise; northerners would only work with the South if Southerners were willing to change completely. Northerners had broken compromises in the past and would continue to do so, especially now that they held the power of the presidency. The *Kentucky Statesman* concurred; it wrote that with some Southern states abandoning the Union, with more surely to follow, the Republicans would be left in full control of the Federal government. Once the Republicans were in charge, they would try to subjugate Kentucky and the rest of the South.[7]

Analyzing the problem further, Headley also noted that the most frequently mentioned compromise proposal, the Crittenden Amendment, had several drawbacks. Crittenden had proposed that: the Missouri Compromise line be reestablished; Congress could pass no laws against slavery; slavery could not be abolished in Washington, D.C.; Congress could not interfere with the interstate slave trade; a stronger fugitive slave law be enacted; and finally, no future

---

5   Kirwan, *John J. Crittenden*, 428-429; Bernard, "Joseph Holt, 53.

6   James Headley to Father, January 17, 1861, in Thomas Henry Hines Papers, University of Kentucky.

7   James Headley to Father, January 17, 1861, in Thomas Henry Hines Papers, University of Kentucky; *Kentucky Statesman*, January 4, 1861.

congress could null and void the compromise. One problem was that Crittenden was not Henry Clay. He simply did not have Clay's influence with the American people that had enabled him to make compromises. The time constraints on passing the amendment were impossible; it would take a couple of years to have any amendment to the Constitution passed, and what were people to do in the meantime—just wait? The only solution for Southern security was for the South to leave. Crittenden should be honored for his efforts, but ultimately, Headley said, "Mr. Crittenden after the whole matter is settled will be standing at the door of the Capitol with his proposition in his hand asking everybody that comes to look at it." The South could not be asked to compromise any longer; it had given everything and received nothing. The rest of Headley's arguments for secession were similar to ones mentioned previously: preserving slavery and the economy.[8]

The idea that compromise was doomed was a popular theme among secessionists. The *Louisville Courier* reported on a speech given by William Henry Seward, who was offered a position in Lincoln's cabinet. In the speech, Seward claimed the government had the authority, if necessary, to suppress the South by force. The paper went on to claim that the "submissionists," a derogatory term for Unionists, were telling the people of Kentucky that the Republicans wanted peace. However, it editorialized, Seward's speech made it was clear that Republicans supported neither peace nor compromise. The *Kentucky Statesman* agreed with the *Louisville Courier*, arguing that all the so-called "compromising" was moving in the wrong direction because the Republicans were showing no spirit of compromise at all. Kentucky Congressman William Simms blamed the failure to compromise squarely on the Republicans. Civil war was rapidly approaching, he exclaimed, yet the Republicans did nothing to stop it and closed their ears to any proposal for peace. According to Simms, the Republicans gave their allegiance to the Chicago Platform, not too the United States Constitution. The party claimed it was trying to save the Constitution, but by supporting its own platform, which outlawed slavery from the territories and rejected Dred Scott, it was actually destroying it.[9]

---

8   James Headley to Father, January 17, 1861, in Thomas Henry Hines Papers, University of Kentucky.

9   *Louisville Courier*, January 15, 1861; *Kentucky Statesman*, January 4, 1861; William Simms, *State of the Union: Speech of Hon. Wm. E. Simms, of Kentucky, delivered in the House of Representatives, February 9, 1861* (Washington: H. Polkinhorn's Steam Job Press, 1861), 3.

Robert Breckinridge, a Presbyterian minister who was uncle to John C. Breckinridge and a leading Unionist statesman, received several letters from secessionists trying to understand his stance on the Union. In one such letter, Breckinridge was told that no compromise effort would be successful, and Kentucky deserved its share of the blame for this failure. The state had wavered so long on deciding which side to support that both sections were convinced that Kentucky would eventually side with them. This gave the North confidence to impose its will on the South and reject any compromise. According to the letter, the only blameless Kentuckians were those who voted for Breckinridge's nephew, John Breckinridge, and he wondered why Robert Breckinridge did not do the same. In another letter, a man calling himself "One of the People" professed love for Breckinridge's sermons but questioned why he wished to remain in a nation the South had been fighting politically for over thirty years. He pleaded with Breckinridge to stop advocating the Union. The minister's influence was strong, and he might sway Kentuckians in what "One of the People" feared was the wrong way.[10]

During the remainder of January and February, secessionists attacked all Unionists as submissionists who were willing to accept any action by the future Lincoln government. They tried to call a state convention in order to take Kentucky out of the Union. A separate convention was required, independent of the state legislature, to change the state constitution and pass an ordinance of secession. When the convention was blocked, by sending the issue to the Committee on Federal Relations, the secessionist legislators played a waiting game until national compromise efforts had played themselves out and Lincoln was inaugurated. They also organized, or at least were accused of organizing, new branches of a secret society known as the Knights of the Golden Circle, whose mission was to bring about secession of all the slave states. Secessionists denied knowledge of the Knights, but the Unionists were convinced of their existence. Tom Bullitt received a letter accusing the submissionists of being too willing to accept anything the national government did. The author of the letter claimed that the North first needed to see the "beam" in their own eyes, take care of their own people, and allow the South to secede. In the end, he predicted, the North would pay for not allowing the South and Kentucky to

10 G. Anderson to Robert Breckinridge, December 27, 1860, and "One of the People to R. Breckinridge," January 29, 1861, in Breckinridge Family Papers, Library of Congress.

leave the Union peacefully and denying them their rights as Christians who were free to choose.[11]

John Curd summed up the unconditional Unionists' position. Curd could not imagine Kentucky ever wanting to secede; he believed that all of Kentucky's problems could be better settled within the Union and that secession would cause financial ruin for the people. The one issue on which Curd allowed his unconditional Unionism to slip was coercion. He hoped that the North would not threaten the South in ways that would force Kentucky to secede. However, even if the North tried to coerce the South, Curd would rather try to form a middle confederacy than join what he called the reckless South. The *Journal* agreed with Curd's assessment of the devastation that would follow if Kentucky seceded. The paper argued that secession would lead to ruin, as already seen by the crash of credit in the South. With secession, the rich would become poor while the laborers starved. Yes, Kentucky would be united with the great slave states in the South, but a much more powerful nation still sat on its Northern border, and in a time of war that nation could easily take away Kentucky's slaves.[12]

Unconditional Unionists based their position only partly on love for the Union; it was based, too, on their disdain for the seceded states, especially South Carolina. The *Louisville Journal* wrote that the time to work with the seceded states was over. Kentuckians should not worry themselves with these turncoats, for the seceded states had not worried about Kentucky: they seceded without asking the state's opinion or caring about its problems. They formed a government with laws that Kentucky would have to accept without having any input. The Louisville paper also claimed that South Carolina had not seceded over issues that concerned Kentucky—such as personal liberty laws which allowed states to ignore the Fugitive Slave Law—but did so in order to reopen the African slave trade, which would hurt the economy of the border states. South Carolina only used the personal liberty laws in an effort to convince the border states to join it. All the Palmetto State politicians really wanted was to use those states to create a buffer zone between themselves and the North,

---

11 Wilson Porter Shortridge, "Kentucky Neutrality in 1861," *Mississippi Valley Historical Review*, 9 (March 1923), 285-287; *Journal of the Called Session of the Kentucky General Assembly of the House* (Frankfort: Kentucky Yeoman Office, 1861), 255; Unknown to Tom, January 18, 1861, in Thomas Walker Bullitt Collection, Filson Club.

12 Curd to Mr. Cornell, January 26, 1861, in John Curd Miscellaneous Collection, Filson Club; *Louisville Journal*, January 12, 1861.

Warner Underwood was both a state and federal legislator. He represented the anti-Lincoln, pro-Union stance and was a powerful voice in the state. He was the father of diarist Johanna Louisa Underwood Nazro. *Library of Congress*

argued the paper, and if it came to it, the borders states would be nothing more than a bloody battleground. Anna Dicken wrote to her sweetheart Henry Rust, a legislator in Frankfort, that she was angry at the course taken by South Carolina and wished a few Carolinians would be hanged as traitors. Now, it seemed to her, their action would lead to the death of hundreds of good men.[13]

13 *Louisville Journal*, January 7 and 8, 1861; Anna to Henry, February 11, 1861, in Dicken-Troutman-Balke Papers, University of Kentucky.

Another unconditional Unionist, and possibly the best diarist in their ranks, was a young woman named Johanna Louisa Underwood Nazro, or Josie for short. The Underwoods were a prominent family in Bowling Green. Josie's father, Warner Underwood, was a United States congressman and her uncle Joseph Underwood had been both a congressman and a senator. The Underwoods were strong Southerners but also strong Unionists. They hated to hear people speak joyfully about the separation of the nation or to say they would die to protect Southern rights. Josie did not understand why such men could not fight for their rights within the Union. Nonetheless, she recognized a difficult challenge for unconditional Unionists: how could they support the Union without supporting Lincoln? She wrote how difficult it was to speak out for the Union because, like most Southerners, she opposed Lincoln. George Washington, she claimed, could never have dreamed that such a low-born clodhopper would ever be elected to the presidency. Yet she did not see his election as grounds for secession. Her uncle and father had done all in their power to prevent Lincoln's election, but her family still loved the nation, no matter who was president.[14]

Josie's family was not the only one that struggled with the difficulty of supporting a Republican president. John Jefferson, a medical doctor, did not think his new president worth the difficulties he caused Unionists. When the newly-elected Lincoln stopped at Pittsburgh to make an address in mid-February while en route to Washington for his inauguration, Jefferson declared, "Old Abe would act more wisely if he would keep his mouth shut." Lincoln entered the slave state of Maryland under police protection, and when threats were made against his life in Baltimore, he passed quietly through the city rather than stop and make a public address. Jefferson responded to the news by commenting, "The old coward sneaked through . . . what a humiliating spectacle . . . afraid Lincoln is not the man in the times." When Lincoln finally arrived in Washington in March 1861, Jefferson wrote, "He appeared among the folks at D.C. to see the people and to let them see him. I suppose in the sight he has the best of the bargain."

The *Covington Journal* chimed in with a few remarks about the president-elect. The paper described Lincoln's speech at Cincinnati a blunder, and told its readers that the paper supported the Union—but not Lincoln. The *Journal*

14 Johanna Louisa Nazro Diary, December 10, 1860, to January 8, 1861, in Underwood Collection, Western Kentucky University.

Although he is usually associated with Mississippi, the state where he owned a plantation and won a U.S. Senate seat, Jefferson Davis was in fact a native-born Kentuckian. He was also the first and only president of the Confederate States of America. His administration prudently recruited Kentucky for the Southern Confederacy. Although he did not give the order, Davis was ultimately responsible for the breach of its neutrality. *Library of Congress*

hoped that Lincoln would not speak again until he took office, which would be on March 4, 1861. The *Kentucky Statesman* and the *Covington Journal* both agreed with the assessment; they claimed that Kentuckians were loyal to the Union, but would not submit to Lincoln or the Chicago Platform.[15]

In her diary, Josie continued to explain her stance as an unconditional Unionist. The big question for all of Bowling Green was the status of the Union. Her father believed it was up to Kentucky and the border states to preserve the nation. The first step in keeping Kentucky loyal was to block a state convention on secession, and Josie rejoiced when many of the oldest and most prominent men of the state came out of retirement to fight for the Union. They, more than many people, realized that if Kentucky seceded the state would become "the dark and bloody ground." These older and wiser men also knew that secession would also end slavery by allowing Kentucky slaves to escape into the Union. Yet the Unionism of Josie's family did not make its members anti-Southern. She described her mother as a true Southerner who hated everything about the North, especially abolitionists, but someone who equally hated the thought of abandoning the old flag. Her father was also described as someone who hated the North and loved the South, but saw the doctrine of secession as ultimately destructive. His Southern congressman friends kept trying to persuade him to change his position, but he could not justify the disintegration of the Union.[16]

Josie described how the conflict was dividing the town of Bowling Green. She believed her town would stand firm for the Union, but it had many rowdies who made a lot of noise over secession. She believed the supporters of a Southern confederacy had an advantage, too, in that they could cheer for their emerging leader, Jefferson Davis, whereas Unionists despised Lincoln and had no one to celebrate. Old friends in the town had started to fight, and even she had quarreled with her dearest friend over the question of allegiances. She found she was losing many old friends who held political ideas different from her own. Josie represented many Kentuckians in the early months of 1861: the people were choosing sides and preparing for conflict.[17]

---

15 John Jefferson Diary, February 16, 25, and 26, in John F. Jefferson Papers, Filson Club; *Louisville Journal*, February 15, 1861; *Kentucky Statesman*, January 15, 1861; *Covington Journal*, January 5, 1861.

16 Nazro, Diary, February 5, 1861.

17 *Ibid.*, February 5 and 10, 1861.

Ultimately, though, it would be the conditional Unionists who decided the fate of the state. These people wanted to remain loyal to the Union; but, as the *Louisville Courier* reported, if the Republicans continued to block compromise efforts, Kentucky might be forced to secede. Similarly, if the North attacked the seceded states, Kentuckians would be forced to help their Southern brethren. Anna Dicken wrote that she had little sympathy for South Carolina, but if Kentucky was endangered in any way, she wanted Rust to be a patriot and stand up for their rights. The Northern states needed to know that Kentuckians had spunk. Many Kentuckians repeated these same themes again and again in early 1861. A man called Uncle Billy insisted that Kentuckians would stick to the Union if they did not have to compromise their rights. He disagreed with South Carolina but wished Kentuckians would stand up for their rights the way South Carolinians had done. The *Louisville Courier*, a pro-Southern paper, claimed Kentucky should remain loyal—but not passive. If war began, the state would be the battleground. Kentuckians must do everything to avoid that end. Conditional Unionists agreed. Their worst fear was that one of the two sides would act in haste and light the spark that would start a war. They pleaded with the North not to coerce the South. James Bacon hoped the seceded states would have the wisdom to avoid violence, but he no longer expected wisdom from the South.[18]

Many people preferred to wait and see how Lincoln would act toward slaves. He had promised not to free any slaves in areas where the practice already existed, and they wanted to find out in practice whether Lincoln would be true to his word. Lincoln, others noted, only controlled the executive branch, with the judicial and legislative branches controlled by Democrats. Even those Kentuckians who would become famous Confederate soldiers, such as John Hunt Morgan, argued early on that Lincoln should be given a chance to keep his promises and so fought against secession.[19]

With such subtle yet crucial differences dividing Kentuckians, the post-election political maneuvering took some interesting twists and turns. The Douglas Democrats started things by calling a meeting for all who supported

---

18 *Louisville Courier*, December 11, 1860; Anna to Henry, January 9, 1861, in Dicken-Troutman-Balke Papers, University of Kentucky; Uncle Billy Meeting, Filson Club; *Louisville Courier*, January 5, 1861; James Bacon to Brother, February 3, 1861, in Fall Family Papers, Kentucky Historical Society.

19 William Freehling, *The South vs. The South* (Oxford: Oxford University Press, 2001), 37-38.

the Union. Seeking support from the conditional Unionists, they said they expected to keep Kentucky in the Union if the North promised not to interfere with slavery. It so happened that the Constitutional Unionists also wanted a statewide meeting; and, not to be left out, the Breckinridge Democrats were calling for a united Southern convention, intended to support a constitutional amendment that protected slavery. The *Louisville Journal* disagreed with all of these suggestions, urging instead a regional convention of Missouri, Kentucky, Tennessee, Virginia, Maryland, Delaware, New Jersey, Pennsylvania, Ohio, Indiana, and Illinois.[20]

The state's two Unionist-inclined parties ignored the *Louisville Journal*'s plea and set a date for their own combined meeting on January 8. When the day arrived and the two groups met, they worked out a merger in hopes that, by joining forces, they could guarantee their success; they thus began the Democratic Unionists. They needed to support each other, too, because the Breckinridge Democrats, meanwhile, had joined with like-minded men to form the States Rights Party. The States Rights Party had great strength in Kentucky, especially from its leadership, which started with the governor of the state, Magoffin.[21]

The new Democratic Unionists ran the gamut of attitudes, from unconditional Unionists such as Joshua Bell, who did not believe there was any reason to leave the Union, to James Jackson, who said that sectional peace was impossible but did not want to leave the Union. Still, the founding delegates agreed that if the North granted a few concessions, including protection of slavery in the territories, all might yet be well. If Kentucky were to secede now, it would lose all rights to help influence the unorganized Federal territories and would leave abolitionists in complete control of the North. They also believed that if the eight slave states of the upper South remained in the Union, the non-slave states could not justify a war to abolish slavery.[22]

To these ends, the delegates came up with four resolutions. First, they called for a border state convention, so that those states could act in concert.

20 *Louisville Journal*, December 4, 1861; John Jefferson, Diary, January 8, 1861; Speed, *The Union Cause in Kentucky*, 4, 57; Volz, "Party, State and Nation," 415-416.

21 John Jefferson Diary, January 8, 1861; Speed, *The Union Cause in Kentucky*, 4, 57; Volz, "Party, State and Nation," 415-416.

22 *Louisville Journal*, January 9, 1861; *Louisville Courier*, January 11, 1861; Volz, "Party, State, and Nation," 415-416, 421-425; Harrison and Klotter, A New History of Kentucky, 187.

Second, they called for the passage of the Crittenden Amendment. Third, they condemned any coercion of the South; they insisted that a Union held together by force was not worth the name. Last, they rejected a state convention to decide the issue of secession in Kentucky. The resolutions passed unanimously but for one vote, showing that unconditional Unionism was dead amongst the Democratic Unionists.[23]

The last resolution became the most important issue in Kentucky, and it completely divided the state. Democratic Unionists opposed a convention because they feared that delegates might get caught up in the excitement of the moment and hastily decide to secede. Instead, they hoped to delay any such decision until late March, well after Lincoln had been inaugurated, to allow passions to cool. But the Democratic Unionists knew that secessionist forces, led by the governor, would do all in their power to call a convention. Democratic Unionists also feared the secret societies and Southern rights clubs being organized in the state to push for secession. The States Rights Party was already collecting signatures to petition the legislature for a convention, and the *Louisville Journal* guessed correctly that they wanted the voting for delegates to be in early March, when the weather would likely yield a low voter turnout.[24]

The States Rights Party, for the very reasons the Democratic Unionists feared, hoped to see a convention called at the earliest possible moment. The logic of their plan is confirmed by historian Daniel Crofts, who identified the first two stages toward secession in the border states. The first was a strong push for secession in the South that crested in the middle of January. Kentucky secessionists were riding the high wave of Southern secession and hoped to act before the second stage, which, according to Crofts, was a Unionist backlash. The States Rights Party's push for a convention was supported by sitting U. S. Senator John C. Breckinridge. By mid-January, when it seemed that any hope of compromise had failed, Breckinridge informed Governor Magoffin that he supported a state convention. He claimed the time had passed for a Southern convention, or even a border state convention, because Congress had no

---

23 *Louisville Journal*, January 10, 1861; *Louisville Courier*, January 11, 1861; Volz, "Party, State, and Nation," 415-416, 421-425; Harrison and Klotter, *A New History of Kentucky*, 187.

24 *Louisville Courier*, January 22, 29-30, 1861; *Louisville Journal*, January 14, February 9, and March 21, 1861; Harrison and Klotter, *A New History of Kentucky*, 187; Coulter, *The Civil War and Readjustment in Kentucky*, 37.

intention of passing the Crittenden Amendment.[25] Consequently, Magoffin called for a special session of the legislature to meet in January to authorize a secession convention. The *Kentucky Statesman* and the *Covington Journal* both joined the call for a convention. Both agreed that the current legislature had no authority to sever ties with the Union and needed to call the convention to know the will of the people. Kentucky must call a convention, the *Statesman* stressed. All the other Southern states were holding conventions, and without one, how could the rest of the nation know where we stand?[26]

When the legislature met on January 17, the politicians were strongly divided, with neither side having a clear advantage. Most men were expected to vote along old party lines, but a change of party for just a few legislators could swing the state in unpredictable ways. All in attendance knew they had been called to sanction a state convention, but it would take some time just to debate the idea. J. T. Boyle, a lawyer, accused Magoffin of inciting revolution in the state and declared that calling a special convention was against the state constitution. In fact, Kentucky's constitution foresaw the problem of an emotional decision being made by an excited minority and put time restrictions of over a year between the time a convention was called and when it met.[27]

Be that as it may, and apparently ignoring this constitutional restriction, the special session started with an address from the governor, who informed the legislature that a revolution had already begun and that Kentucky must decide how to respond. He called for nonpartisan support for a convention for the good of the state. He also blamed Lincoln and the anti-slavery faction in the North for creating a sectional crisis. He blamed the Republicans for blocking all compromise efforts in Congress. Magoffin would not let Kentucky submit to such inequality or dishonor. All the South required to remain loyal, Magoffin said, was for the national government to recognize the legality of slavery and protect property in the territories. Kentucky had done much for the Union, he insisted, and still supported it, but the state had no future in a nation governed by fanatics and devoid of compromise. All other border states were putting the

---

25   Daniel W. Crofts, *Reluctant Confederates* (Chapel Hill: The University of North Carolina Press, 1989), xvi-xviii; *Louisville Journal*, January 15 and 28, 1861; Davis, *Breckinridge*, 254-255.

26   *Ibid.*, 254-255; *Kentucky Statesman*, January 1 and 15, 1861; *Covington Journal*, January 5, 1861.

27   Volz, "Party, State, and Nation,"430-431; *Louisville Courier*, January 22, 1861; House Journal, 4-6; *Senate Journal*, 4-5.

question of secession to the people, and he expected Kentucky to do the same.[28]

The *Louisville Courier* reported that the legislature was divided into four groups, which roughly reflected divisions in the general population. The first two groups composed the minority and represented the extremes of secession and unconditional Unionism. The third group wanted to delay calling a convention until all hopes of a compromise in Washington had collapsed. The fourth group opposed secession but saw coercion as the greater of the two evils. These legislators hoped a convention would show the Northern states that they meant to resist hostile action. They hoped the mere summoning of a convention would deter the North from such a course.[29]

Legislators then devoted themselves to a full week of staking out their positions, with nothing done about the proposed convention. George Hodge, speaking beyond the assembly, appealed to the Confederacy to rejoin the Union on the basis of a shared past. At the same time, he warned the North against coercion. Ben Cissell argued that Kentucky should urge compromise one last time before seceding. Finally, John Prall, who saw the Union as the best way to preserve Southern rights, insisted on holding to the Union until the bitter end. Only if the Crittenden Compromise was rejected, he said, should Kentucky consider war a probability. On January 19, much time was given over to discussing whether or not the United States flag should be flown over the capitol during the proceedings. The legislators decided to fly it by 66 votes to 23. The *Louisville Courier* disparaged the flag debate as an attempt by "submissionists" to avoid a vote on the convention.[30]

On January 21, questions about a possible convention finally arose, only to be tabled and sent to the Committee on Federal Relations. The vote was 54 to 35 against debate. The "no" votes came mostly from the Jackson Purchase, the mountains, and northern Kentucky. Only slightly more than half the delegates who voted "no" came from counties that had voted for Breckinridge in the presidential election, showing that not everyone followed party lines. The same day, W. C. Richardson resolved that if the two parties could not agree, honor alone demanded that Kentucky join with the seceded states. His resolution was

28 Volz,"Party, State, and Nation,"430-431; *House Journal*, 4-6; *Senate Journal*, 4-5.

29 *Louisville Courier*, January 17, 1861.

30 *Senate Journal*, 47-49; *House Journal*, 44-45, 53-56; *Louisville Courier*, January 19, 1861.

also sent to the Committee on Federal Relations, by a vote of 68 to 23. Once again the largest portion of the "no" votes came from the Jackson Purchase, with a scattering from the mountains and the Bluegrass region. Only 62 percent of the counties followed November's election results. The most notable change from "no" to "yes" votes from their vote earlier in the day was the loss of northern Kentucky. The rejection of any debate on the central issue led the *Louisville Courier* to complain about the hypocrisy of the legislature. The delegates accused the North of wrongdoing for not allowing the people to vote on the Crittenden Compromise, but they were doing the same thing in Kentucky by not endorsing a convention to give the people an opportunity to vote on the issues.[31]

It became clear by the voting that the legislature was split over holding a convention, but the voting also showed that legislators were united in their attachment to the South. G. W. Ewing offered a resolution after hearing that some Northern states planned to send money and men to put down the rebellion in the South. He wanted to inform the Northern states that if such action took place, Kentucky would help defend the South. When the vote took place in the House, the resolution passed 87 to six. All the "no" votes came from the Bluegrass region, with the one notable exception of Christian County that bordered Tennessee. Then, by a vote of 82 to eight, the House passed an ordinance calling for a national convention to consider the Crittenden Compromise. The same ordinance passed in the Senate 37 to zero. Finally, the House voted 75 to 13 to allow citizens to use the House chambers to discuss current issues—that is, as long as no emancipationists or abolitionists were involved.[32]

The *Louisville Courier* claimed the reason the submissionists voted for these resolutions was out of fear of having to explain themselves to their constituents. This gave the editors of the *Courier* hope that if the current legislature did not call a convention, a new legislature, to be elected in the coming August, would do it. The opinion espoused by the paper would ultimately be proven wrong, but the early voting did show that legislators who were anti-convention were not necessarily anti-South.[33]

---

31 *House Journal*, 64-66; *Louisville Courier*, January 21, 1861.

32 *House Journal*, 68-73, 83-87; *Senate Journal*, 77.

33 *Louisville Courier*, January 22, 1861.

On January 29, the legislature finally made some progress when the Committee on Federal Relations issued its majority and minority reports. The majority report recommended that Kentucky remain impartial and act as a mediator. It asked for the North to compromise and for the South to remain patient. It strongly denounced coercion and supported the passage of the Crittenden Compromise. It did not call for a state convention, but instead recommended that the state wait on further developments.[34]

The minority report disagreed with the majority and accused it of trying to stall a convention until the submissionists took power. The minority believed that Kentuckians could not remain impartial any longer; if they tried, they risked seeing the end of slavery. It did not understand why the state should continue asking the North to compromise when every compromise had been rejected. The minority recommended that if none of the current compromise proposals were approved by May 1, the state should call a convention and allow the people to decide.[35]

In the end, even this meager progress was slowed further when delegates voted in the negative to bring either the majority or minority reports to a vote. It seemed to many Kentuckians, as voiced by the *Louisville Courier*, that the legislators were more concerned with voting their party lines than with fixing the problems of the state.[36]

Next, the legislature tackled the issue of Union property in the South. The great fear was that the seizure of government property, such as forts and arsenals, might lead to bloodshed and spark a civil war. John Harrison wanted Lincoln to remove Federal troops from forts in the South as the best way to keep the peace. His argument was that if bloodshed was avoided, then a peaceful return of the South could be negotiated. It was clear from the eventual passage of Harrison's resolution by a vote of 77 to 17 that Kentuckians wanted to avoid war. What they were still divided over was which side to endorse. The counties that voted "no" were spread around most of the state, and all but one had voted for Bell in November. John A. Finn of Franklin County wanted to add an amendment to the Harrison resolution that made clear that the state disapproved of any attempt by the seceded states to confiscate Union property.

34 *House Journal*, 153-156, 175.

35 *House Journal*, 153-156, 175.

36 *House Journal*, 153-156, 175; *Louisville Courier*, February 1, 1861.

Finn's amendment was challenged by an amendment from Nathan Gaither, which proposed that Union property might be taken if necessary for defense of the South. Gaither's amendment passed by the narrow margin of 51 to 44. Kentuckians agreed they wanted peace, but continued to divide over their support of North or South.[37]

Finally, in early February, the real voting began. Back in January, David Ganaway had offered a resolution stating that when Kentucky's efforts to protect the Union were exhausted, the state should join the seceded states. The resolution had been tabled at the time, but was brought to the floor on February 5. John K. Goodloe of Versailles Country offered an amendment to the original resolution that embraced the majority report. Goodloe urged the seceded states to return to the Union and the national government to avoid coercion. Also, he argued, a national convention should be called to amend the Constitution to guarantee slavery. The resolution won out by the narrow vote of 49 to 47. The two areas with the greatest concentration of "yes" votes were the Bluegrass region and the southern mountain area. The greatest concentration of "no" votes came from the Jackson Purchase, the northern mountain region, and northern Kentucky. There was no clear-cut vote along party lines. Only 57 percent of the "no" votes came from counties that had voted for John C. Breckinridge, but fully 80 percent of "yes" votes came from counties that had voted for John Bell or Stephen Douglas. Officially, nothing had yet been said about a convention or secession, but it was the closest a vote had come to endorsing one side or the other. With two votes separating the legislators, it was also clear that the decision whether to call a convention might come down to a very slim margin.[38]

When the showdown finally came, the House and the Senate together killed the chance of a convention. In the House, W. W. Cleary called for the people to vote on February 22 to decide whether they wanted a convention, and, if so, who should represent them. The legislators defeated the measure 60 to 36. The second vote occurred when it was moved that all legislators resign their seats when the session adjourned so that new elections could be held immediately. The new elections would serve as a referendum on secession, with the voters making their will known through the selection of representatives. The resolution failed in the House 43 to 42. There was no clear-cut pattern as to

37 *House Journal*, 195-196, 214-219.

38 *House Journal*, 229-240; *Louisville Courier*, February 6, 1861.

regions either voting "yes" or "no" on the measure. The most interesting aspect in the votes was the number of counties that did not vote. Twenty different counties did not cast a vote for the resolution; most of the non-votes came from the Jackson Purchase and western Kentucky. If the non-votes had voted the way the rest of the Jackson Purchase and western Kentucky voted, the "yes" votes would have carried the day—basically, for secession.[39]

In the Senate, a resolution was offered to allow the people to vote for a convention. An amendment was added to delay such a vote until national compromise efforts had failed. Both the resolution and the amendment were tabled on a vote of 18 to 14, which practically killed any chance for a convention.[40]

The legislature adjourned on February 11 without calling for a convention. It would not reconvene until March 20, thus allowing Congress time to pass some compromise measure. Neither side claimed victory when the legislative session ended, and both sides knew the fight was far from over. Unionists hoped that, with time, Lincoln could show the South it had nothing to fear, while states righters believed that all compromise efforts fall apart. Many people, pessimistic about the chances for compromise, thought delay favored the cause of the states righters.[41]

The *Kentucky Statesman* was displeased with the legislature. Its members, explained the editors, had worked for 25 days and yet accomplished nothing. The paper blamed the anti-convention forces who were not strong enough to block the convention and for stalling it. The *Statesman* was further upset that the legislature had adjourned without providing for any defense of the Commonwealth, again blaming a few legislators who were accidentally in power and did not represent the state. If war comes, the *Statesman* wrote, we must unite with those in the South with whom we have a common bond; and the only question left for the legislature is, when the revolution comes, will it be brought about in orderly fashion, by them, or be spontaneous?[42]

---

39 *House Journal*, 286-287, 230-234.

40 *Senate Journal*, 185-187.

41 *Senate Journal*, 175-176, 223-224; Volz, "Party, State, and Nation," 433; W. C. Daniell to G. W. Crawford, February 25, 1861, in *The War of the Rebellion: A Compilation of the Official Records of the Union and Confederate Armies*, 128 vols. (Washington, D.C., 1880-1901), ser. 4, vol. 1, 112; Harrison and Klotter, *A New Kentucky History*, 187.

42 *Kentucky Statesman*, February 12, 1861.

Kentucky stood out among most of the other seven border slave states in its legislative failure to call a convention. The only other legislature not to allow a convention was Delaware, a state that had practically given up slavery anyway. Kentucky's lethargy provides a clue to the state's ultimate decision to remain aloof from both sides. Other states took more positive action, in both directions. In Virginia the legislature voted for a convention 141 to 0; in Arkansas 53 to 11; in Missouri 105 to 18.

And when the people of those states voted to ratify the conventions and elect delegates, the fears of Unionists were calmed. Virginians, Missourians, Marylanders, and Arkansans agreed to hold conventions, but they overwhelmingly voted for Unionist delegates. Virginia, for example, voted four to one for Unionists over secessionists. In Tennessee and North Carolina, the people even rejected a convention. That Kentucky was the only significant border slave state in which the legislature frustrated any chance of a convention certainly makes it intriguing.

But the more important part of Kentucky's story is how its decision affected the larger issue of secession. Virginia, Tennessee, North Carolina, and Arkansas proved their Unionism with the convention votes—but three months later, all four states joined the Confederacy. Missouri and Maryland voted for Unionists in their conventions, but failed to take any action before the U.S. Army moved in and occupied them. Kentucky would be unique among the states in that its people opted to remain neutral.[43]

---

43 Daniel Crofts' *Reluctant Confederates* discusses the secession issues of most of the upper South. His primary focus is on Virginia, North Carolina, and Tennessee, but he refers to the other states as well.

C hapter 5

Compromise:
January to April 1861

O n January 30, 1861, J. W. Stevenson gave a speech that recalled past political conflicts the nation had faced and how each one had been peacefully handled with a compromise. On each occasion, the president had either backed down from his position or supported the compromise effort—at least until now. This was the first time in the history of the United States, Stevenson maintained, that the president was not willing to compromise, and in this instance his obstinacy was leading the nation to war. Stevenson had hoped a united South would battle the president-elect to protect constitutional rights, but with the loss of the deep South, the only chance for peace was compromise. The problem for those who wanted to work toward peace was that any compromise had to be endorsed by the Republicans.[1]

It was clear from Governor Magoffin's response to the commissioner from Alabama, Stephen Hale, that Kentucky's priority was to serve as mediator and bridge the gap between the two sections. Magoffin had already given evidence of his stance. On December 9, 1860, he sent a letter to the governors of all the Southern states laying out a six-point plan to stop the movement toward

---

1   J. W. Stevenson, *Speech of Hon. J. W. Stevenson, of Kentucky, on the state of the Union* (Washington: L. Towers, 1861).

secession. If the North would agree to these terms, secession could not be justified.

Magoffin made the following proposals: amend the Constitution to enforce the Fugitive Slave Law; compensate the owners of unreturned fugitive slaves; require that states turn over to federal authority any person indicted for assisting fugitive slaves; create a dividing line between slave territories and free territories along the 37th parallel; amend the Constitution to guarantee the use of the Mississippi River to all states; and amend the Constitution to allow the South to protect itself against anti-slavery legislation.

Magoffin believed he spoke for all Kentuckians; but not everyone in the state wanted compromise. On both extremes there were people who fought against a peace plan. Southern rights radicals opposed compromise because they were already intent on joining with the seceded states. Some extreme pro-Union men did not see any reason to compromise; Abraham Lincoln and the North had given the South no reason to secede. However, most Kentuckians did believe in doing everything they could to save the nation.[2]

As discussed earlier, Kentuckians clearly benefited from a united nation. Disunion would hurt slavery and the economy, and war would severely damage their state. With so much at stake, most Kentuckians embraced any effort that could lead to peace. Starting in December 1860, three different national efforts to bring about a compromise were proposed: the Corwin Amendment, the Crittenden Compromise, and the Peace Convention. In all three cases, Kentuckians played some part in making the plans.

On December 3, 1860, the United States Congress assembled with the hope of finding a resolution that could heal the nation. President Buchanan began the session with an address that asked Congress to consider a bill with three components: the right of the South to own slave property; the protection of that right in all common territories; and the right of masters to have runaway slaves returned. Buchanan hoped his bill would stop the strong movement toward secession by showing the South it had nothing to fear. Unionist members of Congress, believing that the lower South would secede, saw the loyalty of the border states as the best protection for the nation. By protecting

---

2 Harrison and Klotter, *A New History of Kentucky*, 186; R. Bruce Gelston to Mr. Duncan, January 20, 1861, in Duncan Family Papers, University of Kentucky; Harry August Volz, "Party, State, and Nation: Kentucky and the Coming of the American Civil War" (Ph.D. diss., University of Virginia, 1982), 411-412; Mary Scrugham, *The Peaceable Americans of 1860-1861* (New York: Columbia University Press, 1921), 108-112.

slavery, they believed they could secure the border states. With those states loyal to the Union and only seven or so states breaking away, any attempt to create a new government would create one too weak to succeed.[3]

On December 4, a congressman from Virginia, Alexander Boteler, acting on the advice of Buchanan, proposed that Congress create a committee of 33 members, one from every state, to find a way to preserve the Union. Only a small minority of 38 Congressmen voted against the committee, and 37 of them were Republicans. Thomas Corwin of Ohio was appointed chairman. Both sides accepted Corwin. Even though he was a strong Unionist, he was not an abolitionist, and he had a reputation for fairness. The makeup of the committee was lopsided: it contained 16 Republicans, which left only 17 positions for Northern and Southern Democrats and Constitutional Unionists. Francis Marion Bristow, of Elkton, a strong Unionist and member of the Constitutional Union Party, was chosen to represent Kentucky.[4]

On December 6, the Senate followed suit when Kentuckian Lazarus Powell proposed a similar committee of senators to work out a peace plan. There was more opposition to such a committee in the Senate, so the so-called Committee of Thirteen was not established until December 20. The Senate committee was composed of five Republicans, three Northern Democrats, and five Southern Democrats and Constitutional Unionists. Chief amongst them was John J. Crittenden, Kentucky's senior statesman and a man who would propose his own compromise effort when the Committee of Thirteen met.

The House and Senate committees debated different compromises, including the one from Crittenden, but they reached no conclusions. The Republicans were stalling in both houses, awaiting instructions from Lincoln.[5]

While the Congress and its committees debated, the compromise effort most directly influenced by a Kentuckian was presented by Crittenden; it became known as the Crittenden Compromise. Crittenden had accepted the mantle of Henry Clay, and with such a responsibility he took it upon himself to propose a plan to maintain the peace. Crittenden had been pro-Union since his earliest days as a politician. He was born in 1786 in Woodford County,

3   R. Alton Lee, "The Corwin Amendment in the Secession Crisis," in *Ohio History*, 70 (January 1961), 3-7.

4   Lee, "The Corwin Amendment," 8; Harrison and Klotter, *A New History of Kentucky*, 185.

5   Lee, "The Corwin Amendment," 8-17; Harrison and Klotter, *A New History of Kentucky*, 185; Kirwan, *John J. Crittenden*, 378-382.

Arguably the most respected and important Whig politician in the state after Henry Clay, John C. Crittenden served as state legislator, United States Senator, Kentucky's secretary of state, United States Attorney General, and governor of Kentucky. He is most famous for his efforts to craft a compromise to reestablish the Union. He introduced the Crittenden Compromise to Congress and chaired the Border State Convention in an effort to maintain peace. Both measures failed, but his legacy remained intact. *Library of Congress*

Kentucky, and educated in Virginia at Washington College (later Washington and Lee) and the College of William and Mary, where he finished with his degree. Upon graduation he studied law and opened his own practice in Russellville, Kentucky. His first stint as a public servant began in 1811 in the state House of Representatives, where he served six terms. In 1817, he was elected to the U. S. Senate and served two years before retiring to resume his law practice. Between 1819 and 1835, he went back and forth between politics and the law and earned a name for himself in both venues for his speaking abilities. In 1835, he was elected again to the U. S. Senate, but after winning reelection he resigned his post in 1841 to become Attorney General in the cabinet of William Henry Harrison. He resigned from that position when Harrison died a month into office and the less whiggish John Tyler took over the presidency. From 1842 to 1848, Crittenden was back in the Senate until resigning again to run for the governorship of Kentucky. He was victorious, but resigned after two years to become Attorney General to President Millard Fillmore. Finally, in 1854, Crittenden returned to the Senate, where he served as a Whig, Know Nothing, and Constitutional Unionist before his death in 1863. However, nothing he did during his career would be remembered nearly as much as his effort to save the Union in 1860.[6]

Crittenden knew that every previous compromise effort to protect slavery had come through legislative acts. The problem with such acts was that they were subject to change in subsequent legislatures. To quiet the fears of the South, Crittenden wanted to amend the Constitution in such a way as to protect slavery permanently. The South would then have no reason to secede. On December 18, Crittenden proposed a six-part plan to save the nation. First, he wanted to restore the Missouri Compromise line and extend it across all the western territories. Territories north of the line would be free while the ones south of it could be slave. When the territories south of the line applied for statehood, the people of each new state could decide to be slave or free. Second, he wanted to prohibit Congress from abolishing slavery on any government property in the South. Third, he would prohibit the abolition of slavery in Washington, D.C., as long as either Virginia or Maryland had slaves. Fourth, he would forbid Congress to interfere with the interstate slave trade. Fifth, he wanted the owners of unreturned fugitive slaves compensated for their loss.

6 Harrison and Mathias, "John Jordan Crittenden," in John Kleber, ed., *The Kentucky Encyclopedia*, 240-241.

Lastly, but most importantly, he would guarantee that no future amendment could repeal the three-fifths clause of the Constitution or the Fugitive Slave Law, or allow Congress to interfere with slavery in any way.[7]

Two days before the Crittenden Compromise was introduced, South Carolina passed its ordinance of secession. The rest of the deep South called state conventions but seemed willing to delay action on secession until Congress had time to debate compromise efforts. For Crittenden, the pressure was on to heal the political wounds caused by the election. On December 22, the Committee of Thirteen finally met, with Crittenden as the chairman, to deliberate on his compromise. Some of the most important men of the time sat on the committee, including Robert Toombs of Georgia, Jefferson Davis of Mississippi, Stephen Douglas of Illinois, William Seward of New York, and, from the all-important border states, Robert Hunter of Virginia and Crittenden. The committee members seemed sincere in their desire for compromise, but their work would be undone by a man not even present: Lincoln.[8]

Lincoln wanted to work toward a lasting peace, but he made it very clear that he would accept no compromise that extended slavery. He would even agree to an amendment that protected slavery in the South or toughened the Fugitive Slave Law; but Lincoln would not budge on expansion. When William Kellogg, a member of the Committee of Thirty-three, wrote to Lincoln to ask his advice on compromise, Lincoln answered, "Entertain no proposition for a compromise in regard to the extension of slavery. The instant you do, they have us under again; all our labor is lost, and sooner or later must be done over." To make sure his wishes were known, Lincoln maintained a constant communication with Seward and Corwin while they sat in their committees.[9]

In February, Lincoln, fearing the reaction from the border states, wrote part of a speech that he intended to give in Kentucky to explain his position on compromise. Lincoln exclaimed,

> During the winter just closed, I have been greatly urged, by many—patriotic men, to lend the influence of my position to some compromise, by which I was, to some

---

7   Kirwan, *John J. Crittenden*, 374-375; Harrison and Klotter, *A New History of Kentucky*, 185.

8   Kirwan, *John J. Crittenden*, 378-382; Lee, "The Corwin Amendment," 10-12; David Herbert Donald, *Lincoln* (New York: Simon & Schuster, 1995), 268-270.

9   Roy Basler, ed., The *Collected Works of Abraham Lincoln*, 9 vols. (New Brunswick: Rutgers University Press, 1953), 4:150.

extent, to shift the ground upon which I had been elected. This I steadily refused. I so refused, not from any party wantonness, nor from any indifference to the troubles of the country. I thought such refusal was demanded by the view that if, when a Chief Magistrate is constitutionally elected, he cannot be inaugurated till he betrays those who elected him, by breaking his pledges, and surrendering to those who tried and failed to defeat him at the polls, this government and all popular government is already at an end.[10]

The recreation of the Missouri Compromise line in the territories and popular sovereignty for new states was the first order of business for the Committee of Thirteen on December 22. When a majority of the members rejected it, Robert Toombs responded decisively by demanding that it was now time for the rest of the South to join South Carolina. Two days later, William Seward proposed his own compromise to the Committee of Thirteen—a compromise heavily influenced by Lincoln. Seward's plan had three parts. First, Congress would be prohibited from passing any amendment that would outlaw slavery where it existed. Second, a new fugitive slave law would allow runaways a trial by a jury. Third, all states should revise their citizenship laws to conform to federal laws. This last clause was meant to repeal personal liberty laws. Seward's proposal was the only one endorsed by the committee, but it did not receive enough support to have a chance of approval by the full Senate. Therefore, the committee reported on December 31 that it could not agree on a plan.[11]

Chances for a compromise and peace were dwindling when the House Committee of Thirty-three met. Charles Francis Adams took up the torch for the Republican Party by introducing the first part of Seward's bill to this committee on December 28. Adams was a strong anti-slavery congressman, but he knew the only chance for satisfying the South was to pass a constitutional amendment that would prohibit Congress from interfering with slavery. Adams' bill guaranteed slavery as long as at least one state in the Union supported the practice, virtually guaranteeing it would last forever. The debate within the committee lasted for several weeks, but when it finally voted, the

---

10 Basler, *The Collected Works of Abraham Lincoln*, 4:148.

11 Lee, "The Corwin Amendment," 10-17; Kirwan, *John J. Crittenden*, 378-390; Harrison and Klotter, *A New History of Kentucky*, 185.

proposal passed with only three negative votes. The committee reported on the so-called Corwin Amendment on January 21, 1861.[12]

However, two minority reports also came out of the committee that did not support the amendment. A Southern minority report claimed the amendment did not do nearly enough. This report endorsed the Crittenden Compromise, with the added measure that slavery be protected everywhere it currently existed. A Northern minority report rejected the amendment on the grounds that it would never be ratified by the states. But by the time the full House was prepared to debate the Corwin Amendment, on January 21, time was running short, and the Committee of Thirty-three was already discussing an alternative plan.[13]

Crittenden addressed the Senate on January 3, 1861. He believed his compromise was the only plan that could keep the South in the Union. He would not accept its rejection by the Committee of Thirteen and suggested that the question be referred directly to the people. Crittenden did not stand alone in his request. Several congressmen, especially from Kentucky and the other border states, as well as President Buchanan backed the Kentucky senator. Even Stephen Douglas, who saw this as a very unconventional approach, agreed with Crittenden. There was not sufficient time to debate his ideas in Congress; South Carolina had already seceded and other states were planning to follow. Some Kentuckians cheered the idea. They believed that if the people had the right to decide, they would support compromise and peace. One of Crittenden's admirers, who saw him as one of the few unselfish members of Congress, predicted of the compromise, "If submitted to the people [it] will be passed by a large vote."[14]

Republicans in the Senate were in a difficult position. If they voted against sending the compromise to the people, they risked looking anti-democratic; but if they allowed the people to vote and the vote went against them, their position on the non-expansion of slavery was ruined. In the end, the Republicans came out against sending the compromise to the people, and on January 16,

---

12 Lee, "The Corwin Amendment," 17-22.

13 *Ibid.*, 17-22.

14 Kirwan, *John J. Crittenden*, 392-400; James Becon to Brother, February 3, 1861, in Fall Family Papers, Kentucky Historical Society; No author, "Crittenden Compromise," in Kleber, *The Kentucky Encyclopedia*, 241.

Crittenden's proposal was barely defeated, 25 to 23. The Republicans had struck down the best chance to unify the nation.[15]

Kentuckians did not easily accept the rejection of the Crittenden Compromise. The rejection strengthened the secessionists by showing that they had been right all along about Republican intentions to end slavery. One Kentuckian predicted that rejection of the compromise would drive many conservative men toward the South. The *Louiseville Courier* claimed that the time for peace had ended and that Kentucky must now act to protect its way of life. The only solution the paper could see was for Magoffin to call a state convention for the state to secede from the Union. Even the state legislature supported the compromise effort. Both Douglas Democrats and Constitutional Unionists passed resolutions accepting the Crittenden plan, and on January 17, the legislature passed a resolution calling for its passage by Congress.[16]

The last of the three plans for peace began taking shape on January 19, when the Virginia legislature called for a Peace Convention to convene in Washington. It should assemble on February 4 and be attended by representatives from all states. Virginia believed something must be done quickly before the division of the states became permanent. When they issued their call for the convention, Virginians also asked that both the North and the South abstain from any further political or military actions until the convention had ample time to meet and try to resolve the issues.[17]

With only sixteen days in which to call delegates and send them to Washington, the fact that 132 delegates made the trip shows how seriously the state legislatures took the issue of compromise. Unfortunately, thirteen states did not send delegates. None of the seven deep South states sent delegates, as they were by now preparing to create their own nation. California and Oregon were too far away to respond in time. Arkansas' governor supported secession and took advantage of the state's legislature not being in session to ignore the

15 Kirwan, *John J. Crittenden*, 392-400; No author, "Crittenden Compromise," in Kleber, *The Kentucky Encyclopedia*, 241.

16 Scrapbook no. 3, pp. 66-77, in Josiah Stoddard Johnston Papers, Filson Club; *Louisville Courier*, January 15, 1861; Curd to Mr. Cornell, January 26, 1861, in John Curd Miscellaneous Collection, Filson Club; John Jefferson Diary, January 9, 1861, in John F. Jefferson Papers, Filson Club.

17 Howard C. Westwood, "The Real Lost Cause: The Peace Convention of 1861," in *Military Affairs*, vol. 27 (Autumn 1963), 121-122.

meeting. Minnesota, Wisconsin, and Michigan, whose legislatures could not decide whether they should attend, ended up sending no one.[18]

Nonetheless, the delegates who did assemble made a formidable group. Most of them were elder statesman who had been out of office but returned from retirement to support the Union. The convention consisted of 19 former governors, 29 former members of Congress, and two future Lincoln cabinet members, Salmon Chase and Caleb Smith. The most distinguished member was ex-President John Tyler of Virginia. The rest of the delegates consisted of lawyers and businessmen, with the most successful businessman being Kentucky's own James Guthrie, president of the Louisville and Nashville Railroad and a former senator and secretary of the treasury. Kentucky sent a generally strong contingent, including William Butler, a former congressman and major general in the Mexican War; Charles Morehead, a former governor; Joshua Bell, a former congressman and Kentucky secretary of state; Charles Wickliffe, a former governor and U.S. postmaster general; and lastly, to add the Clay legacy of compromise efforts, James Clay, Henry's son. The members of the Peace Convention were instructed by Congress to unite the nation and were given the Crittenden Compromise as their guide.[19]

The first order of business was to elect a president of the convention; the honor went to the most distinguished member, John Tyler. Next, the delegates created a committee to formulate a resolution. The man chosen to lead the committee was Kentucky's own James Guthrie. As with the other compromise efforts, the border states—those with the most to lose if secession succeeded—controlled the meetings. The entire convention was held in secret, so no official record was kept, but historians have a sense of what transpired from participants' personal notes. The committee reported its efforts on February 15 and suggested a plan that mirrored the Crittenden Compromise. For the next two weeks, the convention as a whole debated the proposal and made minor changes before settling on a three-point plan.[20]

First, like Crittenden, the convention wanted to extend the Missouri Compromise line into the territories and allow any new states to decide whether they would permit slavery. Again, this went against everything the Republican

---

18 *Ibid.*, 122; Kirwan, *John, J. Crittenden*, 406-407; Harrison and Klotter, *A New History of Kentucky*, 185.

19 Westwood, "The Real Lost Cause," 121-123; Davis, *Breckinridge*, 259.

20 Westwood, "The Real Lost Cause," 123-125; Davis, *Breckinridge*, 259.

Party hoped for, but the delegates argued that the only territories affected would be the Indian Territory and the New Mexico Territory. They claimed that, while slavery currently existed in both territories, neither one would likely vote for slavery when applying for statehood. Second, no new land—in reference to the foreign filibustering schemes of the 1850s—could be acquired by the United States without the majority consent of both North and South. Third, if a fugitive slave was rescued by abolitionists, the federal government would have to compensate the slave's owner. The new twist, making the proposal different from other similar ones, was that if the slave owner accepted the money, he would have no future claim on the slave. This was meant to satisfy both parties: the South would get money and the North a possible means for gradual emancipation.[21]

The voting records of the upper South at the convention hold some interest. North Carolina delegates voted against all three parts of the plan, while the Virginians voted against the Missouri Compromise line and the new fugitive slave law. Kentucky, Maryland, Delaware, Tennessee, and Missouri voted in favor of all three measures. As seen in the preceding chapter, the upper tier of border states, with more to lose by seceding, fought harder for peace than the lower tier. One reason that has always been attributed for Arkansas' failure to send delegates was its pro-South governor. However, Kentucky's Magoffin, like Arkansas' governor, eventually called for secession; yet he fully supported the peace measure. Further evidence of the division may be seen in Virginia, which had called a state convention in mid-February to debate secession. When Tyler finished his duties at the Peace Convention, he returned to Virginia to take a seat in the convention. While there, Tyler came out against the Washington plan. He argued that it could not help Virginia in any way, and he eventually convinced the state convention not to endorse the Peace Convention plan. By that point, Virginia had decided that the best course for the border South was to call a border state convention so that all eight states might act in unison. Kentucky endorsed this idea, but the state also supported any promising chance for peace, including the Peace Convention plan.[22]

Even with some states in disagreement, by the end of February, the Peace Convention was prepared to submit its proposal to Congress. Many Northern

---

21 Westwood, "The Real Lost Cause," 123-125; Davis, *Breckinridge*, 259.

22 Westwood, "The Real Lost Cause," 127-128; *Proceedings of the Virginia State Convention*, 4 vols. (Richmond: Virginia State Library, 1965), I: 636-679.

delegates worried that the timing was wrong. Lincoln would take over the government in a matter of days, and Congress would not act before then. They proposed a recess of the convention until after Lincoln's inaugural on March 4. The convention could then reconvene and present its conclusions to Congress. The editors of the *Louiseville Courier* agreed with this assessment, but Kentuckian Guthrie led a fight to submit the proposal right away. He and his followers wanted to submit the plan so they could say, in case things went badly after the Republican takeover, that their plan had been made in a climate of good will. The border states won this battle, with some help from a few Northern congressmen, and the Peace Convention's proposal was delivered to Congress on February 27.[23]

Meanwhile, the House of Representatives had been debating the Corwin Amendment for several weeks, and pro-compromise men, with a new Congress due to be seated on March 4, were beginning to panic. As always, Kentucky and the border South supported the compromise effort while anti-slavery forces in the North fought against it. Northern abolitionists hoped to stall the amendment so there would be no time to send it to the Senate for a vote. On February 26, Corwin changed the wording of his amendment to resolve some of the concerns of Northern congressmen. The original wording had denied the right of Congress to pass any law affecting slavery. Corwin adjusted it to say that Congress could not outlaw slavery. The next day, Corwin successfully brought the amendment to a vote; but, with all the Republicans voting in the negative, it failed. However, the day after, February 28, a Republican congressman came to Corwin's aid. David Kilgore of Indiana asked that the vote of the previous day be reconsidered and reminded Republican congressmen that their policy toward slavery was non-interference. If they rejected an amendment that protected slavery where it existed, they would send the wrong message to the border states. The House agreed to reconsider the amendment, and on the second vote it was approved and sent to the Senate.[24]

On March 1, the Senate considered both the Corwin Amendment and the Peace Convention amendment. The Corwin Amendment was taken first, but in order for a resolution to be voted on, it had to be read twice, normally on two different days. However, Stephen Douglas hoped to vote on the Corwin Amendment quickly, so that the Peace Convention proposal might be voted on

---

23 Westwood, "The Real Lost Cause," 126-128; *Louisville Courier*, March 1, 1861.

24 Lee, "The Corwin Amendment," 19-23.

the floor. He pushed successfully to have both readings done on the same day. On March 2, Senator Charles Sumner of Massachusetts, best known for the bloody attack he received on the floor of the Senate after he gave an inflammatory speech about "Bleeding Kansas," blocked any chance for debate or a vote on the amendment by claiming that he had opposed conducting the second reading the day before, but his objection had not been heard. Three other Republican senators supported Sumner's claim, but enough senators backed Douglas to open debate. Republicans continued to try to block the passage of the amendment. They wanted to change its wording and force its return to the House for approval, which would have effectively killed the amendment when Congress adjourned. Once again, it was a Republican who came to the aid of the resolution. Senator Edward Dickinson Baker of Oregon gave the same argument as his counterpart in the House: if Republicans killed the amendment, they would only validate Southern claims that the Republican Party meant to destroy slavery. He told his colleagues that if they wanted to kill the vote, they should simply vote against it, but not send it back to the House.[25]

March 3 fell on a Sunday. Congress normally did not hold sessions on Sundays, but because of the crisis atmosphere it met that evening. Crittenden gave a final speech in an attempt to sway the Senate. He said that all he wanted to do was save the Union. He believed his compromise was the best way to accomplish that mission, but under current time restrictions adoption seemed impossible. The Corwin Amendment may not be perfect, he said, but it was the best chance the nation had to retain the border states. He pleaded with the Senate to pass it. The Senate debated all night and into the next morning. Finally, just hours before Lincoln was to be inaugurated, it approved the measure.[26]

The Corwin Amendment was poised to become the Thirteenth Amendment to the Constitution, but first it had to be ratified by three-fourths of the states. The *Louiseville Courier* did not believe this was possible—especially under the current circumstances. The Confederate government had already been formed, but because the U. S. government still regarded the seven Confederate states as part of the Union, their absent votes must count against

25 Kirwan, *John J. Crittenden*, 412-415; Lee, "The Corwin Amendment," 23-24; Westwood, "The Real Lost Cause," 126.

26 Kirwan, *John J. Crittenden*, 412-413; Lee, "The Corwin Amendment," 23-24; Westwood, "The Real Lost Cause," 126.

the amendment. With some Northern states certain to vote no, the amendment would surely fail. The only possible chance for the amendment to pass was if Lincoln recognized the Confederate States as an independent nation so those states would not be counted, which the *Louiseville Courier* did not see as possible. The *Covington Journal* agreed with the *Courier's* assessment, but for a different reason. The *Louisville Journal* claimed that it might take years for the states to ratify anything, citing other amendments that had taken four years, which would be too long to keep the peace.[27]

The Kentucky legislature met to consider the Corwin Amendment in late March. In its final form, the measure read: "No amendment shall be made to the Constitution which will authorize or give Congress the power to abolish or interfere, within any state, with the domestic institutions thereof, including that of persons held to labor or services by laws of said state." Representative John Goodloe, in the state legislature, felt the proposed amendment fell short of guaranteeing all rights the slave states desired, but it did remove the danger of having slavery outlawed. Goodloe believed that passage of the amendment would demonstrate the North's desire for reconciliation with the South. He proposed that the legislature ratify the amendment. But first it had to pass through the Committee on Federal Relations. On March 27, the committee issued majority and minority reports. Representative John Finn, representing the majority, recommended that Kentucky ratify the amendment. He also recommended that Kentucky elect delegates to attend a conference of border states and continue to work toward peace and passage of the Crittenden Compromise. Representative George Hodge represented the minority, and his recommendation differed little from that of the majority. He agreed to the ratification of the amendment, but emphasized that it should not be considered a final settlement. Hodge, too, supported sending delegates to a border convention, but also wanted the state legislature to petition Lincoln to withdraw all troops from the Southern states. Following only one day of debate, the House passed the amendment 95 to one on March 29.[28]

It seemed as if Kentucky would be one of the first states to prove it wanted compromise, but with the trouble that would come in April, the amendment died after it was sent to the Senate. Indeed, before any state could ratify the

---

27 Kirwan, *John J. Crittenden*, 412-413; Lee, "The Corwin Amendment," 23-24; Westwood, "The Real Lost Cause," 126; *Louisville Courier*, March 1, 1861; *Covington Journal*, February 2, 1861.

28 *House Journal*, 331-423.

amendment, war broke out at Fort Sumter, South Carolina. After that, only a few states ever bothered to ratify the amendment. The first was Ohio, which voted in May 1861, but others did not vote until much later. Maryland, for example, ratified the amendment in January 1862. Ironically, the eventual Thirteenth Amendment would not protect slavery but abolish it.[29]

Kentuckians mourned the loss of the compromise. Congressman J.W. Stevenson had hoped the Crittenden Compromise would keep at least five states in the Union, but he feared the Republicans would never endorse it; he was right. U. S. Congressman William Simms had agreed with Stevenson. Simms believed the Crittenden Compromise was a good deal for both sides and questioned why the Republicans would not support it. He argued that there were "1,600,000 miles [sic] of territory" above the compromise line and only 275,000 miles of territory south of it. Although Simms and everyone else seemed to be ignoring the fact that the Supreme Court's decision in Dred Scott challenged the legitimacy of such an artificial line, he emphasized that Republicans would be getting the better deal.[30]

Kentucky would not stop working for compromise and peace. Unlike the people of the states north and south of them, Kentuckians could not afford to give up. The *Louisville Journal* had predicted that secession would come only if passions overrode common sense, but the *Louisville Journal* had warned correctly that not enough time had elapsed between the election and the rush to secede for cooler heads to prevail. Kentuckians had taken that advice to heart. Instead of diving in on one side or the other, they had urged caution and worked for compromise. Even in the wake of Fort Sumter, they embraced the call for a border convention as yet another chance for peace. Even more importantly, they began to think, should all else fail, about the possibility of maintaining neutrality in the upcoming struggle.[31]

29 Lee, "The Corwin Amendment," 24-25.

30 J.W. Stevenson, Speech of Hon. J. W. Stevenson, of Kentucky, on the state of the Union.

31 *Louisville Journal*, February 1, 1861.

C hapter 6

Neutrality:
March to May 1861

s it began to look to many Kentuckians as if Congressional compromise might fail, the idea of neutrality became increasingly attractive. For people who still held out hope that war could be avoided, a neutral Kentucky now looked like the best potential mediator between the two sides. At the same time, if war came nonetheless and Kentucky found itself standing between two great armies, neutrality might avoid potential disaster. With the Democratic Union Party blocking a state convention yet leaving the States Rights Party still very potent, both sides saw neutrality as the best way of reaching their political ends.[1]

The idea of neutrality was not something new, and had been discussed even before the legislature defeated hopes of holding a state convention. George Smith, who opposed secession, declared as early as late December 1860 that Kentucky could remain both neutral and part of the Union. Josie Underwood thought in early February of 1861 that neutrality was the only safe course for the state. Pondering the issue further, Underwood believed that most Kentuckians understood the inherent advantages of remaining neutrality, but would not

---

1   Speed, *The Union Cause in Kentucky*, 40-41; Tom to Mary, March 13, 1861, in Gunn Family Papers, University of Kentucky; N. S. Shaler, *Kentucky: A Pioneer Commonwealth* (Boston: Houghton Mifflin Company, 1884), 240-241.

endorse it unless their side lost the debate over secession or war threatened to destroy the state.[2]

Those favoring the Union saw Governor Beriah Magoffin as their greatest threat to neutrality. The *Louisville Journal* reported on petitions sent to Magoffin by secessionists that pleaded with him to call a convention during the period when the legislature was adjourned and could not oppose him. The argument of the secessionists was the same as before: that the Fifty-ninth Congress did not represent their views on secession, and so the state needed to hold a convention. The Unionists feared that if Magoffin, who openly supported a convention, received enough signatures, he would be justified in calling one. If he did so, demanded the *Louisville Journal*, Magoffin should be impeached. Once the Louisville paper took the lead, other Unionist papers threatened to denounce the governor if he acted without the legislature.[3]

The Unionist answer to secessionists was to show an equal amount of strength. The *Louisville Journal* listed the secessionists' strategy as fourfold: to hold a disunion meeting at Frankfort during the next legislative session, so as to intimidate the legislators; to collect enough signatures to show the legislature that Kentucky demanded a convention; to create Southern rights clubs around the state; and to exaggerate secessionist strength and thereby force a convention. The *Louisville Journal* called for Union men to retaliate in kind, especially by holding a Union meeting in Frankfort at the same time as the Southern rights meeting.[4]

The *Journal* was correct in saying that Southern rights clubs had sprung up around the state, and its call for Unionists to organize was heard. John Jefferson reported with sadness that a group in Louisville, made up of "several good citizens," had organized and called for secession; but on the night of their meeting the gathering was broken up by Unionists waving a large American flag.[5]

2   Charles E. Yonkers, "The Civil War Transformation of George W. Smith: How a Western Kentucky Farmer Evolved from a Unionist Whig to a Pro-Southern Democrat," in *The Register of the Kentucky Historical Society*, 103 (Autumn 2005), 669-670; Johanna Louisa Nazro Diary, February 5, 1861, in Underwood Collection, Western Kentucky University.

3   *Louisville Journal*, March 6, 1861; Wilson Porter Shortridge, "Kentucky Neutrality in 1861," *Mississippi Valley Historical Review*, 9 (March 1923), 291-292.

4   *Louisville Journal*, March 11, 1861.

5   John Jefferson Diary, March 14 and 16, 1861, in John F. Jefferson Papers, Filson Club.

Harper's Weekly

GOVERNOR MAGOFFIN'S NEUTRALITY means holding THE COCK OF THE WALK (*Uncle Sam*) while THE CONFEDERATE CAT (*Jeff Davis*) kills off his Chickens.

The Southern rights clubs followed the *Louiseville Courier's* lead by challenging the *Louisville Journal* to justify its opposition to a convention. After all, the *Journal* had claimed that slavery was protected, yet it also acknowledged that Lincoln was elected on the grounds of opposing slavery. By the *Journal's* own analysis, how could Kentucky trust Lincoln? The North had broken its trust with Kentucky and violated the state's rights. Kentuckians must organize to reclaim those rights. The Southern rights clubs continued to support compromise in order to bring in more members, but it insisted that if the North rejected one more effort at compromise, Kentucky must seek secession. They also called for the Southern Rights Party to meet on March 20, the same day the legislature planned to return. To no one's surprise, the Democratic Union Party issued a call to meet as well.[6]

Before either party or the legislature had time to meet, several key events occurred that influenced future actions. First, the Confederate government met and officially created the new nation. Second, the last of the compromise efforts ended in Washington, with the Peace Convention and the Crittenden

---

6   *Louisville Courier*, March 15 and 19, 1861; Volz, "Party, State, and Nation: Kentucky and the Coming of the American Civil War," 418-420; Shortridge, "Kentucky Neutrality," 292-293.

Compromise both ending in failure. Neither of these events affected Kentucky in any great way because most people by that time expected compromise to fail.

The event that drew the most attention was the inauguration of Lincoln, on March 4. Responses to his speech spanned the full gamut of emotions and positions. Some said Lincoln had said what was needed, while others were so angry with his remarks that they called for his assassination. Unionists feared Lincoln's speech might give secessionists the ammunition needed to draw more support. One Kentuckian at first feared to read the speech, but rejoiced after he finally did so. He described it as straightforward, kind, and unsectional. Most Unionists reacted the same way. John Jefferson declared, "The address was conservative and constitutional and much milder than expected." Anna Dicken told her sweetheart Henry Rust, a member of the legislature, that she wrongly expected Lincoln's inaugural to be a declaration of war. She believed that the best thing about the speech was that it allowed most Kentuckians to remain in the Union and fight for their rights. Kentuckians had the guarantee they wanted: Lincoln said he would not touch slavery where it already existed. Now Unionists had to pray that nothing would happen to force the national government to use coercion against the seceded South.[7]

The States Rights clubs disagreed with the Unionists. The *Louiseville Courier* denounced Lincoln's address as a declaration of war. It condemned the president's policy of changing the Fugitive Slave Law to better protect free blacks from capture, but what most drew its ire was the president's policy toward the Confederacy. Refusing to recognize the legitimacy of the Confederate States, Lincoln insisted that Federal laws be enforced in all states, including the South, and announced that he would use all of his powers to maintain Union prerogatives in the South. The *Kentucky Statesman* agreed with the *Louisville Courier* that the speech was indeed a declaration of war. The paper went on to argue that it no longer mattered who started the war because Lincoln would take the blame. The *Louisville Courier* saw this policy as leaving no chance for peace because the Confederacy, acting as a sovereign nation, had the right to control military forts within its own territory. Both sides would have to play a

---

7   Volz, "Party, State, and Nation," 433-435; Cynthina [sic] to R. Breckinridge, March 8, 1861, in Breckinridge Family Papers, Library of Congress; G. Channey to H. Duncan, March 6, 1861, in Duncan Family Papers, University of Kentucky; Anna to Henry, March 17, 1861, in Dicken-Trout-Balke Papers, University of Kentucky; John Jefferson, Diary, March 15, 1861; John Caperton to Andrew Erskine, March 6, 1861, in Caperton Family Papers, Filson Club.

waiting game to see how Lincoln and the Confederacy handled the problems of military forts, especially Fort Sumter in Charleston Harbor.[8]

When the States Rights convention, the Democratic Union convention, and the legislature finally met on March 20, nothing had changed since the legislature adjourned in February. Neither the formation of a new government, the defeat of the Crittenden Compromise, nor Lincoln's speech seemed to have changed anyone's opinion. The States Rights Party created a platform it hoped to push on the legislature. It wanted the legislators to recognize that the Union had lost its credibility by allowing its abolitionist leader to block any chance of compromise. It wanted Kentuckians to act quickly to protect themselves from any actions Lincoln might take toward the South. With the loss of so many Southern votes in Congress, it saw the Republicans as having too much power, and if Kentuckians did not act quickly they would see their slaves taken. The *Louisville Journal* countered by insisting that the States Rights convention meant to trick Kentuckians into secession by blaming Republicans for the collapse of compromise. Tricked or not, going into the March 20 session of the legislature, Kentucky could still go in either direction.[9]

The legislature picked up where it left off, very divided and not wanting to address any real issues. The States Rights Party, given its defeat in the last session and with no new strategy to make Unionists rethink their stance, avoided all talk of a state convention. Instead, it presented several other issues, although these were only tabled or sent to the Committee on Federal Relations. The House tried to call a border state convention at Frankfort, which would allow all border states to act in unison, but that bill was also sent to committee, as was a measure proposing the recall of all Union troops from the South. W. C. Richardson offered a resolution that would denounce Lincoln as an instigator of civil war if he attempted to hold Federal forts and collect taxes in the South. Again, the bill was sent to committee. Finally, it was proposed to set a time for receiving the committee's report, but the vote was 42 to 42, with a tie serving to defeat the recommendation.[10]

---

8 Volz, "Party, State, and Nation," 435; *Louisville Courier*, March 5, 1861; *Kentucky Statesman*, March 8, 1861.

9 *Kentucky Statesman*, March, 22, 1861; *Louisville Journal*, March 19, 1861; Volz, "Party, State, and Nation," 420-421.

10 *House Journal*, 318-319, 323, 364-366, 369; *Senate Journal*, 423; Volz, "Party, State, and Nation," 435-436.

Some people were angry with the lack of progress. Anna told Henry Rust, a legislator, that the legislature had wasted time with worthless discussion and that it was time for its members to step up and start working. An explanation for the legislature's lack of work came from Representative G. A. Lacy in a letter to Robert Breckinridge. Lacy believed that the legislature simply did not know what to do, and he thought the best course of action was to do nothing until national events unfolded completely. He feared that angry parties had formed to agitate the crisis, and insisted that the legislators did not want to act rashly. Evidence of this is that 72 percent of the legislators voted the same way their county did in the November presidential elections. The only noticeable detractors from the pattern were in the Jackson Purchase, where they all voted "no," and the southern mountain region, where they voted "yes." Once again, there were 20 counties whose legislators did not vote at all. No one was willing to leave their comfort zones and do anything that might be seen as rash.[11]

With so much importance placed on the secession issue, the legislature invited the state's two most esteemed politicians to speak: John Crittenden and John C. Breckinridge. Crittenden spoke on March 26 and delivered what one person called a "masterful effort." The crux of his speech was that secession was illegal, so any talk of leaving the Union meant revolution. He also insisted that the best place for Kentucky to ensure its rights was in the Union. The most interesting part of his speech showed that the leaders of the Democratic Union Party, such as he, were not unconditional Unionists. Crittenden hoped the North would not use military force to regain the South, and warned that to do so would prompt the border states to secede. He proposed that the Confederacy be allowed to leave the Union peacefully. At some time down the road, he predicted, the Confederacy would regret its decision; then the wayward states could be allowed to rejoin the Union peacefully.[12]

One reason for the delay in legislative action was that the States Rights Party had to hold off adjournment until Breckinridge had time to travel to Frankfort. Once he arrived, Breckinridge again insisted that he stood for the Union, but not for one that restricted freedom. Unlike Crittenden, he claimed that under certain circumstances a state had the right to secede. He blamed the

---

11 Anna to Henry, March 23, 1861, in Dicken-Trout-Balke Papers, University of Kentucky; B. Lacy to R. Breckinridge, March 21, 1861, in Breckinridge Family Papers, Library of Congress; Volz, "Party, State, and Nation," 435-436.

12 John Jefferson, Diary, March 29, 1861; Kirwan, *John J. Crittenden*, 432.

Republicans for rejecting the best chance the nation had for peace, but insisted that Kentucky continue to work toward the goals stated in the Crittenden Compromise. Like Crittenden, Breckinridge believed that the only chance left for peace was for the Union to allow the South to go its separate way and to pull all Union troops out of the South before something happened that could not be reversed. Lastly, Breckinridge called for a convention of the border states to propose a unified plan of action. If the North then rejected that plan, Kentucky should align itself with the Confederacy. Breckinridge wanted his speech to sound pro-Union, but he came off as pro-secession. Unionists called his address treasonous, while Jefferson Davis received a report that Breckinridge was clearly on the Confederate side.[13]

Before the legislature adjourned for the second time in 1861, it was able to pass two resolutions. First, by a vote in the House of 94 to one, it ratified the proposed Thirteenth Amendment, which, had it passed, would have protected slavery in the states. Interestingly, the one "no" vote came from the legislator who represented Hickman and Fulton Counties in the Jackson Purchase. He possibly feared the amendment might hurt his state's chance of secession. Second, and more importantly, on March 29, by a vote of 37 to zero, the Senate agreed to call a convention of border states to meet at Frankfort on May 27. The House endorsed its action. The first Saturday in May was set for electing twelve delegates to the convention, one from each congressional district and two at large.[14]

The vote in the House on the border state convention was not recorded, but, according to the *Louisville Journal*, it was much more contested. Each side had reasons both to oppose and support a convention. The States Rights Party viewed a convention as positive because it could be used to endorse the Crittenden Compromise as an ultimatum. If the North accepted the Compromise, maybe the South would return; but if the North rejected compromise again, it would give the party the strength needed to pull Kentucky out of the Union. The negative side of the convention for them was that if the old Bell and Douglas coalitions remained intact under the new Democratic Union Party label, they could win a majority of the delegates to the convention

---

13 *Louisville Journal*, April 2, 1861; Davis, *Breckinridge*, 262-262; Harrison and Klotter, *A New History of Kentucky*, 187; Samuel Haycraft Journal, April 2, 1861, Filson Club.

14 *Senate Journal*, 362-269; Volz, "Party, State, and Nation," 436.

and seize the momentum going into a summer when Kentuckians would vote for new state legislators.[15]

For the Democratic Unionists, the pros and cons were reversed. They saw themselves as the stronger party, with the potential to mold the border states convention their way. Yet, at the same time, they feared that something drastic could change the loyalties of the other border states, something like the North trying to coerce the South or the South attacking a Union fort. They also did not want to issue an ultimatum to the North, because if it was rejected, they would have no further viable argument against secession.[16]

One plus for the Democratic Union Party was its choice of candidates. Its at-large candidates were Crittenden and James Guthrie, two men prominent enough to be considered for the presidential nomination, Crittenden by the Constitutional Union Party and Guthrie by the Democrats. The men running in the congressional districts were also very well known men. They included former governor Charles Morehead as well as Joshua Bell and Archibald Dixon, who had both run for governor.[17]

One member of the legislature, Blanton Duncan, did not have much hope in the success of a border states convention. He believed the Southern rights ticket was not strong enough to win, but that in the end it would not matter. He called the proposed border states convention "child's play" because no matter who won the elections in May, it would be too late to save the nation; and when the split was made permanent, Kentucky would have to join the Confederacy. He expected every day that some event would propel the divided nation into war. And when in mid-April Confederate guns forced the surrender of Fort Sumter, an election victory in May did, indeed, seem irrelevant.[18]

Fort Sumter placed Kentucky Unionists in a difficult position. They had hoped to avoid war, but the attack seemed to make war inevitable. Their worst fears came true when Lincoln called for 75,000 volunteers from all loyal states to put down the rebellion in the South. Even worse, he asked for four regiments from Kentucky. The only thing the *Louisville Journal* could do now was

---

15 *Louisville Journal*, April 2, 1861; Shortridge, "Kentucky Neutrality," 293, Volz, "Party, State, and Nation," 436-437.

16 D. Bedinger to Crittenden, April 11, 1861, in Crittenden Papers, Library of Congress.

17 Volz, "Party, State, and Nation," 137-138.

18 Blanton Duncan to C. Breckinridge, April 6, 1861, in Breckinridge Family Papers, Library of Congress.

denounce both sides. It blamed the Confederacy for deliberately starting a war, but it also called for the impeachment of Lincoln. The *Louisville Journal* believed Lincoln's plan to retaliate was wrong, but still did not see it as a reason to rush into secession.[19]

Oddly, it was Magoffin who came to the Unionists' aid, although unintentionally. When Lincoln requested four regiments from Kentucky, Magoffin replied, "I say, emphatically, Kentucky will furnish no troops for the wicked purpose of subduing her sister Southern States." The Unionists supported Magoffin's response, which went with their own stance of anti-coercion; but they took his position a step farther. Unionists feared that, with Sumter and Lincoln's call for troops, the States Rights Party might gain the strength needed to pull Kentucky out of the Union. To counter them, the Democratic Union Party insisted that neutrality remained the state's best course.[20]

Neutrality, even in the midst of war, seemed a very attractive alternative to the Unionists. Under the banner of neutrality, they could continue to oppose coercion without having to side with either the Union or the Confederacy. If neutrality had earlier been a way to avoid secession, it now offered the best chance to keep the war out of Kentucky. The *Louisville Journal* maintained that if Kentucky remained neutral its rights would have to be respected, and that neither side would dare enter the state. This brand of neutrality could also be a way to gain more support from the fence-sitters in Kentucky. Unionists could now claim the mantle of peace, and if the Southern Rights Party opposed them, they would label it the war party. They believed that being the peace party would appeal to self-interested people, yet make patriots still feel good about their stance. On April 18, the party endorsed Magoffin's refusal to send troops, and warned Lincoln that war did not justify invading or sending an army through the state. If such a violation did occur, it continued, Kentucky would have to protect itself by seeking alliance with the Confederate States.[21]

19 Fellman, Gordon, and Sutherland, *This Terrible War: The Civil War and its Aftermath*, 80-81; Harrison and Klotter, *A New History of Kentucky*, 187; Volz, "Party, State, and Nation," 439-440; *Louisville Journal*, April 15 and 16, 1861.

20 Harrison and Klotter, *A New History of Kentucky*, 187; Volz, "Party, State, and Nation," 439-440; *Louisville Courier*, April 13, 1861.

21 Harrison and Klotter, *A New History of Kentucky*, 187; William T. McKinney, "The Defeat of the Secessionists in Kentucky," *Journal of Negro History*, 1 (October 1916), 384-86; Guthrie speech, Frank Moore, ed., *Rebellion Record*, 12 vols. (New York: G. P. Putman, multiple dates),

In the beginning, the States Rights Party recoiled from the idea of wartime neutrality. The *Louiseville Courier* insisted that those who wanted neutrality secretly meant to give power to the North. The paper insisted that neutrality would only draw the anger of both sides, and argued that for Kentucky to reject the Confederacy was the same as suicide. It did not believe the Union would allow Kentucky to remain neutral. If Kentuckians did not provide the four regiments required, the United States would view them as enemies, and Kentucky without the aid of the Confederacy would be vulnerable. The *Kentucky Statesman* did not believe Kentuckians would stand for neutrality while war raged around them, claiming it would be worse than absurd. According to the paper, the only thing stopping Kentucky men from rushing to fight along with the Confederacy was that they were waiting for their state to make up its mind. In a bit of foreshadowing, the *Statesman* wrote that our men want to fight, but remember our first duty is to the state.[22]

Politically, adherents of the States Rights Party also disapproved of wartime neutrality because it threatened their goal of holding a state convention; but after the attack on Fort Sumter and Lincoln's call for troops, they saw a new way to achieve their aims. The states of Virginia, Tennessee, North Carolina, and Arkansas all cited coercion to justify their switch to secession, and States Rights Kentuckians hoped they could ride the same wave of discontent out of the Union. If Kentuckians had to decide between the two obvious choices, to fight either for the Union or the Confederacy, the States Rights Party had a good chance of success if the Union could be portrayed as actively trying to coerce them to fight against the Confederacy.[23]

However, this new third approach, that of wartime neutrality—an approach that might allow the state to avoid bloodshed and destruction—had the power to derail States Righters' hopes of secession. They understood the appeal of neutrality and feared it would rob them of the momentum built toward secession in the border states. States Righters knew with neutrality they would have to change their tactics away from instant secession to a new plan whose success would require patience. Their power could be hurt if they were labeled the war party, so to retain their relatively equal political power in the

---

Vol. 1, Doc. 63, 72-76; Volz, "Party, State, and Nation," 441-442; Speed, *The Union Cause in Kentucky*, 57-59; *Louisville Journal*, April 16, 18, and 19, 1861.

22 *Louisville Courier*, April 17 and 18, 1861; *Kentucky Statesman*, April 16 and 19, 1861.

23 Harrison and Klotter, *A New Kentucky History*, 187-188.

state they needed to be seen as embracing neutrality as their own policy; they would have to hope for future events to justify secession. This approach is seen within the pages of the *Kentucky Statesman*. The paper had supported secession all along, but beginning in May it claimed that all Kentuckians wanted to avoid war and that they only wanted to be left alone. It did add that Kentuckians refused to be a conquered people and would fight if invaded, but hoped to avoid any confrontation.[24]

Neutrality set Kentucky apart from every other slave state still in the Union. Before Fort Sumter, the eight states (seven, if not counting Delaware, which never wanted to secede) were being watched closely to see which side they would join. Of the seven, only Kentucky chose neutrality. All seven states had similar views on secession. They all professed love and loyalty for the Union but warned that any attempt to force the upper South into the war would change that loyalty. Apparently, a majority of the white population of all seven states also strongly supported the institution of slavery. Most of the seven, excluding Arkansas, still retained a vibrant two-party political system that had helped keep them in the Union.

Yet, after the attack on Sumter and the call to arms, four of the states seceded while two sided with the Union. Missouri had discussed neutrality, but ultimately only Kentucky practiced it. With all their similarities, why did Kentucky declare itself neutral, and why did states such as Virginia and Tennessee not also follow that course?

There are several possible reasons why Kentucky was the only state to declare itself neutral. According to Speed, Kentucky had stronger Unionist feelings than other border states. But Speed does not accurately explain the source of this sentiment. Besides that, it is impossible to measure degrees of unionism in the upper South. Kentuckians, generally, do not appear to have been more devoted to the Union than Virginians or Arkansans.[25]

Historian E. Merton Coulter suggested a more convincing approach. Using an economics argument, he demonstrated that all trade involving the Mississippi River Valley in one way or another touched Kentucky. Neutrality, he insisted, allowed Kentucky to continue its trade relationship with both sides. Additionally, the existence of the Louisville and Nashville Railroad, whose

---

24 Speed, *The Union Cause in Kentucky*, 53; Volz, "Party, State, and Nation," 443; *Kentucky Statesman*, May 7, 1861.

25 Speed, *The Union Cause in Kentucky*, 21.

president was James Guthrie, allowed trade between those two cities. That trade had slowed during the time before the formation of the Confederate States, but the secession of the South opened new opportunities for Kentucky to prosper. From February to June 1861, for example, profits by both river and rail increased from $23,000 to $68,000.[26]

Both the North and the South allowed Kentucky to continue to trade, holding out hope that it would abandon neutrality and join their side. On February 25, 1861, the Confederate government passed a law allowing free navigation of the Mississippi River in an attempt to maintain the friendship of Kentucky and other border states. At the same time, the Northern government allowed Kentucky to trade with the South. When some citizens of Cincinnati, upset at Kentucky for aiding the Confederacy, stopped river traffic to Louisville, the people of Louisville stopped a steamer full of supplies heading north. Passions on both sides ran high, and each side threatened to invade the other, until Lincoln intervened on May 2 to insist on open trade across the Ohio River so as to avoid driving Kentucky into the Confederacy.[27]

Another possible explanation for Kentucky neutrality was suggested in a previous chapter. The four states of the upper South that seceded all had a slave state directly above them to serve as a buffer in case of war; the four that remained loyal to the Union all bordered free states. The four that bordered free states had more to fear from secession, knowing that if they joined the Confederacy they would be the immediate battleground between the two nations. Both Virginia and Kentucky legislators addressed the issue of the destruction of their state, but the debates in both states suggested that Kentucky, which bordered free states, worried much more about its 700-mile border with the North and the resultant likely dangers of war. Virginia, which had a slave state, Maryland, above it, did not discuss the issue to the same extent as Kentucky.[28]

There is one last plausible explanation for neutrality. The best way of explaining the theory is by again comparing Kentucky to Virginia. The differences between the two states are apparent. The Virginia legislature voted 140 to 0 to hold a state convention, and when the people of Virginia voted for

---

26 Coulter, *The Civil War and Readjustment in Kentucky*, 57-64.

27 *Ibid.*, 57-64.

28 For more information about the concerns of secession, see the debate records located in the *Kentucky Senate Journal, Kentucky House Journal,* and *Proceedings of the Virginia State Convention.*

delegates to the convention, they overwhelmingly voted for Unionists. The Kentucky legislature rejected a convention by 20 votes, and so, without a chance to vote for delegates, members of the legislature could not know which side Kentuckians would favor. In Virginia, both Unionists and secessionists in the legislature voted for a state convention, while in Kentucky, Unionists and secessionists divided on the issue. Virginia Unionists apparently felt confident they would win the majority of the convention delegates and defeat secession, while Kentucky Unionists did not feel so confident about the outcome of a convention.[29]

After the election of delegates, Virginia Unionists, having won the day, could relax, knowing their side held popular support. With so many Unionist delegates and so few secessionists, the secessionists were seen as outsiders and radicals. The Virginia convention on April 4 defeated secession by a two-to-one margin. The president of the Virginia convention, John Janney, had told his wife at the end of March that he was confident about the outcome of the vote. Some people still wanted to secede, he said, "but they can't move old Virginia yet awhile." Kentucky Unionists did not have the same luxury. Between February and April, they battled every day to keep their slight edge over the States Rights Party, never knowing what event might reverse their role as the majority. With the two sides so evenly matched, the secessionists in Kentucky were not seen as being particularly radical. Neither side could take an extreme stance without putting badly needed support at risk.[30]

Kentucky Unionists needed to support the Union without looking like submissionists, so they proposed to serve as mediators between the North and South. The idea was for Kentucky, as a neutral power, to broker a peace. Virginians adopted a different stance when dealing with the North. They claimed they stood for the Union, but only as long as the Union did not try to coerce the South. Virginians could afford to be referred to as submissionists because they were strong enough politically to suffer minor losses within the state. Kentucky Unionists made the same claim of being pro-Union, but they could not speak as boldly as the Virginians because Kentucky Unionists could

---

29 Henry T. Shanks, *The Secession Movement in Virginia* (New York: Ams Press, 1971), 143-50; *Proceedings of the Virginia State Convention*, 4 vols. (Richmond: Virginia State Library, 1965), 3: 112-168; 4:144.

30 John Janney to Alice Janney, March 30 and 31, 1861, in John Janney Collection, Virginia Tech University.

not afford the loss of any votes. Therefore, negotiating a path of neutrality seemed the safest course of action.

Lincoln's call for troops left Virginia and Kentucky Unionists in different situations. Virginia Unionists, having never considered neutrality, and with no popular support for it, found it easier, if discouraging, to reverse themselves on secession. When only given the option of fighting for the Union or Confederacy, the attack on Sumter was enough to convince Virginians to support the Confederacy. However, in Kentucky, such a transformation did not occur. Kentucky Unionists remained ready to negotiate. They still believed any form of coercion to be wrong; but, knowing the strong sentiment for neutrality within the state, they continued to promote that policy, even in war. Kentuckians believed they did not have to choose one side or the other. Neutrality gave them a third option, one that proved very appealing. Even States Righters, sensing popular opinion, were forced to support neutrality—for the moment.[31]

This same comparison could be made to other states in the upper South. Arkansans followed the same pattern as Virginians. They voted 53 to 11 to hold a convention and elected a large majority of Unionist or cooperationist delegates. They remained firmly Unionist—until after Fort Sumter. The Tennessee and North Carolina legislatures both agreed to hold conventions, but the people of those states were so strongly Unionist that they rejected them. Then, after Sumter, they too reversed themselves. Maryland and Missouri both called conventions, Missouri by a vote of 105 to 18. Before either of these states could decide their own fate, it was decided for them. Lincoln arrested anyone supporting secession in Maryland, and General Nathaniel Lyon ensured that Missouri remained loyal. Kentucky was the one holdout, the one state that fought against a convention, and the only state to declare itself neutral. No other state was so equally polarized, and it was the effect of that polarization that led Kentuckians to embrace neutrality. Unionists elsewhere knew they could win; neutrality could only hurt them. In Kentucky, Unionists were not confident of victory, so neutrality became attractive.

When the Kentucky legislature resumed its session on May 6, 1861, it was flooded by petitions from across the state in support of neutrality. One petition came from 143 women of Larue County. They had opposed secession and did not now want war to leave them fatherless and widowed. On May, 16, the

---

31 Coulter, *Civil War and Readjustment,* 52.

House acknowledged the depth of these feelings and voted to remain neutral by a count of 69 to 25. The Unionists voted unanimously for neutrality and were joined by about half of the states rights members. Those from the Jackson Purchase voted unanimously "no" and were joined by a scattering from elsewhere throughout the state.[32]

The legislators were even more unified in their support of Magoffin's decision not to send troops to Lincoln's army. That vote was 89 to four, the City of Louisville and Jefferson County being the only ones to oppose.[33]

On May 20, Magoffin, acting by the will of the legislature, announced that Kentucky would be neutral in the upcoming struggle. He warned both sides against breaching that neutrality, and urged Kentuckians to do nothing that could be considered a violation of neutrality. He warned both the Union and the Confederacy that under no circumstances should they try to march an army through the state. In fact, he called for Kentuckians to arm themselves and repel any incursion.[34]

Anna Dicken applauded the decision to declare neutrality; it would protect the people of the state from the horrors and destruction of the war. So said most people in Kentucky. But their struggle for neutrality was far from over: with people on both sides hoping to have Kentucky join with them, several key events would test the state's resolve.[35]

32 *Ibid.*, 54-56; Volz, "Party, State, and Nation," 449-450.

33 *Kentucky Senate Journal*, 81.

34 Speed, *The Union Cause in Kentucky*, 47-49; Magoffin's Proclamation, *Rebellion Record*, vol. I, Doc. 181, 264.

35 Anna to Henry, May 20, 1861, in Dicken-Troutman-Balke Papers, University of Kentucky.

C hapter 7

Border Conventions and Lincoln Guns:

April to May 1861

B etween the time of the attack on Fort Sumter and the legislature's official declaration of neutrality, the most pressing issue facing Kentuckians was the election of delegates to serve at a border states convention. Fort Sumter had changed things since the legislature originally called for a meeting. By May 4, 1861, voting day for delegates to the convention, Virginia had already seceded, and Arkansas, Tennessee, and North Carolina seemed likely to follow.

Originally, the States Righters' biggest complaint was that the legislature had scheduled election day too early for them to put together a platform and nominate quality men. After Fort Sumter, their new concern was whether they should persist in having the convention at all, with those four crucial additional states gone to the Confederacy. Even with their concerns, the States Rights Party met and hammered out a platform and chose men to run on its ticket. The platform called for passage of the Crittenden Amendment as a way of bringing the Confederacy back into the Union, as well as continued work toward maintaining the peace. If the Union sent troops into the South, Kentucky should side with the Confederacy, and the party would accept no compromise effort that gave blacks the right to vote in federal elections. If peace could not be achieved under these conditions, Kentucky should call a state convention and prepare to secede. The party's candidates—one from each congressional district plus two at-large—did not have the political clout of the Unionists, but they hoped that Sumter and the secession of four more states would give them the votes needed to win. They chose as their two at-large candidates William Butler of Carol County and James Clay of Fayette County.[1]

On April 26, James Clay addressed a crowd of supporters. He denounced the Unionists for suggesting that preserving the Union was worth any compromise. Only the Crittenden Amendment would suffice, he insisted. The Unionists wanted to force Kentucky to follow the will of a border states convention, while he believed Kentuckians should be free to decide their own path. Clay told his supporters that he would do all in his power to save the nation, but he did not believe a Union without honor was worth saving. Lastly, he did not believe neutrality was a viable option. Kentucky needed to secure its rights in either the Union or the Confederacy.[2]

Before the day for voting came, Clay and other States Rights candidates were forced to change their views. In fact, the *Louisville Journal* reported on May 2 that one secessionist candidate from the ninth ward, realizing that the people did not want secession, now stood for neutrality.[3]

Having organized campaign efforts back in early April, the Democratic Unionist Party got the jump on the States Rights Party and ran a much stronger group of candidates. As noted previously, its two at-large candidates were John Crittenden and James Guthrie. The Democratic Unionists, like the States Righters, endorsed the Crittenden Amendment. The difference between the two parties was that the Unionists really wanted the amendment, whereas the States Rights Party wanted to use it as an ultimatum. The *Louisville Journal* reported on the day of the election that a vote for the Democratic Union Party meant neutrality and peace, while a vote for the State Rights Party meant secession and war. Most Kentuckians saw it the same way.[4]

---

1 *Louisville Courier*, April 13 and 19, 1861. The other men on the States Rights ticket were Henry Burnett, J. Crockett, George Ewing, A. Talbott, J. Helm, M. Martin, Humphrey Harshal, Thomas Porter, Emory Whitaker, and Richard Stover.

2 *Louisville Courier*, April 27, 1861.

3 *Ibid.*; *Louisville Journal*, May 2, 1861.

4 Volz, "Party, State, and Nation: Kentucky and the Coming of the American Civil War," 436-438; Kirwan, *John J. Crittenden*, 437; *Louisville Journal*, April 5 and May 4, 1861.

On May 4, Kentuckians demolished the States Rights Party at the polls by overwhelmingly voting for the Democratic Unionists 106,863 to 4,262. Both Speed and Coulter used the results to illustrate that secession was not an option in Kentucky, and with such a landslide it is easy to see how they could come to that conclusion. But, as seen in the presidential election, numbers do not always tell the entire story. When examining who did not vote and what the Democratic Unionists' platform entailed, it becomes clear the election was not as overwhelming a victory as Speed and Coulter suggested. Something both men addressed but did not dwell upon was the position the States Rights Party took right before the election and the opposing platforms. As the *Louisville Courier* put it, the States Rights Party thought the time for peace had come and gone, so the party saw no point in holding a border state convention, especially with Virginia not attending. Even if the rest of the upper South supported the Crittenden Amendment, those states would never get enough national support to pass it. Most of the States Rights candidates had, in fact, pulled out of the election and declared that Kentucky should call a state convention to secede.[5]

A closer analysis of the election results further undermines the Speed-Coulter argument. Over 106,000 registered voters—the same number that voted for the Democratic Unionist candidates—did not vote in the May election. Seventy-nine percent of the counties dropped in voter turnout between the presidential election and the May election. Of the 29 counties that increased voter turnout, only three had voted Democratic in the presidential election, and all three were from the eastern mountain region, where historian Harry Volz has demonstrated that they voted Democratic to fight against the planter elite, not because they favored secession. All 29 counties that increased their turnout were already Democratic Union Party strongholds. The lowest percentage of Democratic Unionist voters in those counties was 82 percent, and turnout in 26 of the counties was 99 to 100 percent.[6]

The drop in voters came in counties that had voted for Breckinridge in the presidential election. Every county that voted for Breckinridge, except for the three in the mountains, dropped in voter turnout, with an average of only 58 percent of the voters who voted in November returning to the polls in May. If

5 Secretary of State Election results, 1855-1872, Kentucky State Archives; *Louisville Courier,* May 3, 1961; Speed, *The Union Cause in Kentucky,* 87.

6 Secretary of State election results,1855-1872, Kentucky State Archives; Volz, "Party, State, and Nation," 445-448.

the mountain counties are excluded, the average drops to 50 percent. In other words, since Breckinridge voters constituted the majority of the States Rights Party, then members of the States Rights Party did not vote. The best example of States Righters' lack of turnout came in the Jackson Purchase. The purchase was the most pro-secessionist area of the state, and less than 23 percent of its residents who had voted in the presidential election participated in the border states convention vote. If all of the States Rights Party adherents had voted in May, Kentucky's Unionist image would be far less impressive.[7]

County	Pres	Border	% of voters
Adair	D-1105	U-1185	107.24%
Allen	BE-1140	U-1079	94.65%
Anderson	BR-1098	U-569	51.82%
Ballard	BE-1204	U-11	0.91%
Barren	BE-1181	U-1312	111.09%
Bath	BR-1735	U-1246	71.82%
Boone	BE-1768	U-1386	78.39%
Bourbon	BE-1753	U-930	53.05%
Boyd	BR-1197	U-855	71.43%
Boyle	BE-1084	U-1777	163.93%
Bracken	BE-1775	U-156	8.79%
Breathitt	BR-572	U-1342	234.62%
Breckinridge	BE-1622	U-971	59.86%
Bullitt	BE-988	U-1045	105.77%
Butler	BE-945	U-898	95.03%

7   Secretary of State election results, 1855-1872.

County	Pres	Border	% of voters
Caldwell*	D-1551	U-483	31.14%
Calloway*	BR-1296	U-133	10.26%
Campbell	BE-2648	U-3037	114.69%
Carroll	BR-1722	U-568	32.98%
Carter	BR-1063	U-1084	101.98%
Casey	BE-927	U-1189	128.26%
Christian	BE-832	U-1407	76.80%
Clarke	BE-1410	U-1051	74.54%
Clay	BR-806	U-578	71.71%
Clinton	BE-711	U-710	99.86%
Crittenden	BE-750	U-1010	134.67%
Cumberland	BE-865	U-844	97.57%
Daviess	BE-2265	U-1403	61.94%
Edmonson	BE-516	U-496	96.12%
Estill	BR-1030	U-994	96.50%
Fayette	BR-5566	U-1589	28.55%
Fleming	BE-1836	U-1529	83.28%
Floyd	BR-673	S-271	40.27%
Franklin	BR-1734	U-842	48.56%
Fulton*	BR-714	S-274	38.38%
Gallatin	BR-837	U-469	56.03%

County	Pres	Border	% of voters
Garrard	BE-1091	U-1213	111.18%
Grant	BR-1498	U-1158	77.30%
Graves*	BR-2025	U-599	29.58%
Grayson	BE-1111	U-1173	105.58%
Green	BE-977	U-851	87.10%
Greenup	BE-1238	U-1412	114.05%
Hancock	BR-892	U-388	43.50%
Hardin	BE-2091	U-2016	96.41%
Harlan	BE-599	U-626	104.51%
Harrison	BR-2321	U-862	37.14%
Hart	BE-1439	U-1445	100.42%
Henderson	BE-1560	U-1069	68.53%
Henry	BR-1837	U-1256	68.37%
Hopkins	BE-2570	U-940	36.58%
Hickman*	BR-968	0	0.00%
Jackson	BE-390	U-318	81.54%
Jefferson	BE-9565	U-9977	104.31%
Jessamine	BE-1202	U-839	69.80%
Johnson	BR-666	U-535	80.33%
Kenton	BE-3558	U-3673	103.23%
Knox	BE-877	0	0.00%
Larue	D-886	U-1116	125.96%

County	Pres	Border	% of voters
Laurel	BE- 773	U-612	79.17%
Lawrence	BE-958	U-685	71.50%
Letcher	BR-373	U-349	93.57%
Lewis	BE-1111	U-1344	120.97%
Lincoln	BE-1199	U-1030	85.90%
Livingston*	BE-906	U-284	31.35%
Logan	BE-2004	U-995	49.65%
Lyon*	BR-746	U-93	12.47%
Madison	BE-2093	U-1378	65.84%
Magoffin	BR-508	U-402	79.13%
Marion	BE-1660	U-1561	94.04%
Marshall*	BR-1080	0	0.00%
Mason	BE-2377	U-2209	92.93%
McGracken*	BE-1242	U-201	16.18%
McLean	BE-536	U-888	165.67%
Meade	BE-1101	U-853	77.48%
Mercer	BR-1826	U-1543	84.50%
Metcalf	BE-805	U-994	123.48%
Monroe	BE-973	U-1183	122.85%
Montgomery	BE-1078	U-636	59.00%
Morgan	BR-965	U-373	38.65%
Muhlenburg	BE-1353	U-1378	101.85%

County	Pres	Border	% of voters
Nelson	BE-1179	U-1226	103.99%
Nicholas	BR-1704	U-1179	69.19%
Ohio	BE-1409	U-1799	127.68%
Oldham	BE-936	U-711	75.96%
Owens	BR-2342	S-1467	62.64%
Owsley	BR-705	U-613	86.95%
Pendleton	BR-1800	U-1357	75.39%
Perry	BR-370	U-299	80.81%
Powell	BR-558	U-270	48.39%
Pulaski	BE-1172	U-2117	180.63%
Pike	BR-792	U-460	58.08%
Rockcastle	BE-698	U-764	109.46%
Rowan	BR-333	U-291	87.39%
Scott	BR-1954	U-757	38.74%
Shelby	BE-1998	U-1464	73.27%
Simpson	BE-917	0	0.00%
Spencer	BE-732	U-610	83.33%
Taylor	D-920	U-977	106.20%
Todd	BE-1067	U-906	84.91%
Trigg*	BR-1146	U-430	37.52%
Trimble	BR-923	U-502	54.39%
Union	BE-1580	U-869	55.00%

County	Pres	Border	% of voters
Warren	BE-1926	U-1916	99.48%
Washington	BE-1218	U-1662	136.45%
Wayne	BR-1310	U-671	51.22%
Whitley	BR-1089	U-933	85.67%
Woodford	BE-1196	0	0.00%
Wolfe	BR-461	U-275	59.65%
Webster	BR-956	U-592	61.92%

Table Notes

Column 1: County name.

Column 2: Winner of the 1860 Presidential election (BR: Breckinridge; BE: Bell; D: Douglas) and the total number of voters.

Column 3: Winner of the 1861 Border State Convention vote (U: Unionists; S: States Rights) and total number of voters.

Column 4: Percentage of voters from the Presidential election who voted in the border state election.

* Part of the Jackson Purchase.

*   *   *

Another point worth emphasizing is that when voters went to the polls in May, their choice was not between the Union and the Confederacy. As shown earlier, a vote for the Democratic Union Party was a vote for neutrality and continued work toward compromise, whereas a vote for the States Rights Party was a vote for the Crittenden Amendment. Only if the Amendment failed would secession be an issue. The Democratic Union Party was comprised mostly of Bell and Douglas supporters, and, as seen earlier, a vote for Bell did not mean a vote for unconditional unionism. If Kentuckians had voted for secession or a convention, the votes might have looked much different. Instead, the border states convention was portrayed as a vote for either war or peace.

Kentuckians overwhelmingly chose neutrality and peace by voting for the Democratic Union Party.[8]

Two days after the Unionist electoral victory, the legislature reconvened at Frankfort. According to the *Louisville Courier*, no test for secession was taken because both sides feared the other's strength, showing that those who wanted the Union and those who wanted secession were still fairly evenly divided. Both sides realized that the people had spoken at the polls, and even the strongest of secessionists had to admit that support for neutrality was too strong to pull Kentucky out of the Union. The *Louiseville Journal* confirmed that the people had answered the question of their allegiance on May 4. It was clear that they did not want to join either side, but instead decided to remain neutral and arm the Commonwealth to protect against invasion. The paper acknowledged that many secessionists sat in the legislature, but after the election they would not dare go against neutrality.[9]

Governor Magoffin was the first to address the legislature. Although a strong supporter of secession, his tone softened a bit after the States Rights defeat; but he still wanted the legislature to call a state convention. Magoffin believed Lincoln had killed the Constitution when he raised a standing army in one section to fight against another section. Kentuckians had three choices, according to Magoffin: stay in the Union and pay their share of the "enormous"

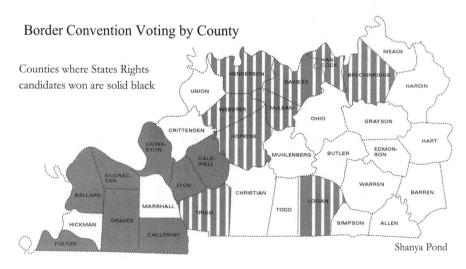

Border Convention Voting by County

Counties where States Rights
candidates won are solid black

Shanya Pond

---

8   *Louisville Journal*, April 18 and 19, 1861.

9   *Ibid.*, May 6, 1861.

war debt to come; declare independence and go it alone; or ally themselves with the Confederacy. He reminded the legislature that its duty was to protect the state, and with Lincoln declaring war on the South and slavery, it needed at least to prepare to fend off an invader. He had asked banks for loans to buy arms, but he now needed the legislature to provide money.[10]

The legislature agreed to Magoffin's request to arm the state, but it also wanted peace as long as honor would permit. Legislators refused to agree to the governor's request to hold a convention. They believed that neutrality was the best course, even though they would not officially declare neutrality until May 20. To guarantee the proposed neutrality of the state, the legislature asked Magoffin to inform neighboring states of its position and ask that they respect it. Some Unionists, not trusting Magoffin to support neutrality, also wanted him

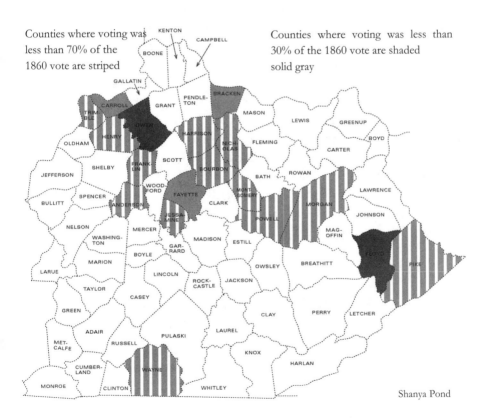

Counties where voting was less than 70% of the 1860 vote are striped

Counties where voting was less than 30% of the 1860 vote are shaded solid gray

Shanya Pond

10 *House Journal*, May 7; *Kentucky Statesman*, May 10, 1861.

to report any correspondence between himself and the Confederate government, but the Senate voted against this requirement 22 to 15.[11]

In order for the governor and the legislature to act as one, both parties agreed to create a six-man board, with three members from each side, which could generate a plan. The Unionists selected John Crittenden, Archibald Dixon, and Samuel Nicholas to serve. Dixon, from Henderson County, was first elected as a Whig to the legislature in 1830, serving on and off until 1843. In 1844, he was elected lieutenant governor but lost in his bid for the governorship in 1851. He took Henry Clay's seat in the U. S. Senate in 1852, when Clay resigned. Nicholas, of Lexington, was the first president of the University of Louisville, in 1846-47. Before the war, he was a successful lawyer and defender of the Union.[12]

The States Rights Party sent John C. Breckinridge, Governor Magoffin, and Richard Hawes. Hawes began his political career as a Whig state representative from 1828 to 1834. In 1837, he was elected to Congress and served until 1841. He joined the Democratic Party after the breakup of the Whigs in the 1850s, and during the secession crisis fought for neutrality.[13]

Pro-Confederates on the board still pushed for a state convention, but the Unionists, still barely holding the balance of power, blocked it. Both sides agreed to endorse neutrality and to arm the state against possible invasion. Democratic Unionists wanted to select a five-man military board. The States Righters agreed, but they wanted Magoffin to sit on the board as commander in chief. The Unionists so distrusted the governor that they refused. The proposed board thus failed, and the group only endorsed the call for neutrality.[14]

By May 16, the House had received the board's slight yet meaningful recommendation and decided to put it to a vote. Kentucky had already declared

---

11 *Louisville Journal*, May 7, 1861; *Senate Journal*, May 13, 1861; *House Journal*, May 10, 1861.

12 Davis, *Breckinridge*, 266-267; Kirwan, *John J. Crittenden*, 434-435; Coulter, *The Civil War and Readjustment in Kentucky*, 53; Margaret L. Merrick, "Samuel Nicholas," in Kleber, ed., *Kentucky Encyclopedia*, 681; Unknown author, "Archibald Dixon," in Kleber, ed., *Kentucky Encyclopedia*, 267-268.

13 William C. Davis, *Breckinridge: Statesman, Soldier, Symbol* (Baton Rouge: Louisiana State University Press, 1974), 266-267; Kirwan, *John J. Crittenden*, 434-435; E. Merton Coulter, *The Civil War and Readjustment in Kentucky* (Chapel Hill: University of North Carolina Press, 1926), 53; Elizabeth C. Hawes, "Richard Hawes," in John Kleber, ed., *The Kentucky Encyclopedia*, 418-419.

14 Davis, *Breckinridge*, 266-267; Kirwan, *John J. Crittenden*, 434-435; Coulter, *The Civil War and Readjustment*, 53.

itself (unofficially) neutral, but the legislature wanted to formalize its position. The first vote was on whether to approve of Magoffin's refusal to raise troops for the U. S. government. The House approved it 89 to four. A second vote, to endorse Kentucky neutrality, passed 69 to 26. A majority of both parties voted for neutrality, but it was almost exclusively States Rights Party members who voted no. The Unionists then proposed a new preamble to the neutrality resolution, which called for even stricter neutrality and sounded more pro-Union. The States Rights Party wanted to table the vote, but lost 47 to 48.[15]

Magoffin finally issued a formal statement declaring armed neutrality on May 20. Besides warning both warring nations not to enter the state, he also forbade citizens of Kentucky to make any war-like demonstration against either side. Party presses on both sides supported the declaration, yet both sides also took issue with it. While praising Magoffin for doing his duty, the *Louisville Courier* was upset with how the Democratic Unionists had restricted the governor's military power by rejecting the military board. The *Louisville Journal*, while agreeing with neutrality, did not want to forbid United States troops from entering the state. It saw Magoffin as trying to cause a conflict between Kentucky and the Union by denying the Union access to its own territory. Such a restriction also made it far too easy, should even a single U. S. soldier enter Kentucky, for Magoffin to claim a breach of neutrality and push for secession.[16]

The Democratic Unionists never trusted Magoffin when it came to neutrality, but from a letter he sent to Jefferson Davis the day before his proclamation, it seems clear that Magoffin meant to enforce neutrality against both sides. He told Davis that Kentucky wanted to remain neutral in the upcoming war and would not support either side. He knew that Lincoln was building up a force within Kentucky, but he had written to Lincoln and asked him to remove all troops from the state. He was writing to inform Davis that he expected the Confederacy also to respect Kentucky's neutrality. Magoffin was especially concerned with a large Confederate force being raised on the Tennessee border. He asked that these troops not cross into Kentucky and

---

15 *House Journal*, May 16, 1861; N. S. Shaler, *Kentucky: A Pioneer Commonwealth* (Boston: Houghton Mifflin Company, 1884), 244-246; *Louisville Courier*, May 17, 1861; Volz, "Party, State, and Nation," 450, footnotes.

16 *Louisville Courier*, May 21, 1861; *Louisville Journal*, May 21 and 22, 1861.

assured Davis that he would not let Lincoln invade the Confederacy through his state.[17]

The Border State Convention issued a call for all border states to assume neutrality when it met at Frankfort on May 27—not that the statement carried much weight. Two more states—Arkansas and North Carolina—had seceded by then. Only delegates from Kentucky, Missouri, and Tennessee attended, and they did not include all the men who had been selected for the meeting. Only nine of the twelve delegates from Kentucky participated, and only seven came from Missouri. One Unionist from Tennessee arrived. The Convention and its president, John Crittenden, issued an address to the people of the United States. They still held out hope that peace could be reached, but realized the problem of recognizing the sovereignty of the Confederate States. They endorsed the very pro-Union view that the Constitution did not permit secession, and so believed the Confederacy bore responsibility for finding common ground with the United States. They realized that war was upon the land, but expressed hope that their states would not be forced to participate in the conflict.[18]

The Kentucky members of the Convention also sent a proclamation to the people of their own state. They declared that the state must remain in the role of mediator. Kentuckians did not seek neutrality out of fear but from patriotism and to ensure their security. They accused both sides of wrongdoing: the fanaticism of the North and the defiant spirit of the South had produced this crisis. They wanted Kentucky to be an asylum for liberty.[19]

Still, not all Kentuckians agreed with neutrality, including John C. Breckinridge. He argued that Kentucky could not bury its head in the sand and pretend that nothing had happened. He believed the state must stand with one side or the other, and since Kentucky had already refused troops to the Union, they, too, were technically in rebellion and might as well join the Confederacy. The *Kentucky Statesman* did not even believe it was possible to declare neutrality

17 Magoffin to Jefferson Davis, May 19, 1861, OR Series 1, 52, pt. 2, 102-103.

18 Address of the Convention of the Border States to the People of the United States, Moore, *Rebellion Record*, Vol. 1, Doc. 241, 350-351; Wilson Porter Shortridge, "Kentucky Neutrality in 1861," *Mississippi Valley Historical Review*, 9 (March 1923), 293-294; Kirwan, *John J. Crittenden*, 437-438.

19 Address of the Convention of the Border States to the People of Kentucky, Moore, *Rebellion Record*, Vol. 1, Doc. 243, 353-356; Address to the People of Kentucky by the Delegates to the Border States Convention, Robert Carter Richards Papers, Filson Club.

without being sovereign. First, the paper said, we must declare our independence; then we can declare ourselves neutral.[20]

Other Kentuckians showed their disagreement by leaving the state to fight for the Confederacy. Before the attack on Fort Sumter, Jefferson Davis would not accept troops from Kentucky or any state outside the Confederacy. After the attack, he allowed Kentuckians to enlist in Louisiana regiments and eventually to form their own regiments in the state. As early as April 22, Magoffin received a request from the Confederacy to send troops to Harpers Ferry to help protect Virginia; Magoffin responded that he lacked the authority to comply.[21]

But that same day, John Jefferson declared in his diary that secessionist feeling in the state was growing stronger and that many men were forming military units to fight for the Confederacy. The *Louisville Journal* reported that officers were resigning their commissions in the U.S. Army in order to join the rebels. Crittenden wrote to his son, a lieutenant in the Army, that he knew several officers who were resigning their positions, but hoped he would not join them. Crittenden reasoned that Kentucky had not seceded, and with so many examples of "treachery and dishonor," he would be proud if his son stood by the Union. Just days after Fort Sumter, both Louisville newspapers reported a regiment being raised by Blanton Duncan, a member of the legislature, for the purpose of assisting the Confederacy. Duncan's regiment left for Virginia in time to fight in the first battle of Bull Run. In fact, on April 16, one official report had four companies of Kentucky troops already in Virginia prepared to fight, and William Preston Johnson informed Confederate Secretary of War Leroy Pope Walker on April 26 that four hundred men had left Kentucky for Virginia. Duncan told Walker that 480 troops had already joined the Confederacy and that he should expect three more companies in a few days. Four more companies had recently formed in the state. One observer reported that secessionists opened a recruiting office in Louisville on April 18.[22]

20 Davis, *Breckinridge*, 266; *Kentucky Statesman*, May 17, 1861.

21 Coulter, *The Civil War and Readjustment*, 48-49; *House Journal*, May 10.

22 *Louisville Courier*, April 15, 1861; Mrs. A. M. Colman, *Life of J. J. Crittenden* (Philadelphia: J. B. Lippincott and Co., 1871), 321-322; John Jefferson Diary, April 22, 1861, in John F. Jefferson Papers, Filson Club; *Louisville Journal*, April 16 and 18, 1861; Geo. Deas to R. S. Garnett, May 23, 1861, OR Series. 1, vol. 2, pt. 2, 867-868; Blanton Duncan to Walker, May 5, 1861, OR Series 1, vol. 51, pt. 2, 66; Absolom Johnson Diary, April 25, 1861, Filson Club.

On April 22, Lunsford Yandell, a prominent doctor at the Louisville Medical Institute, explained his decision to abandon Kentucky and fight for the Confederacy. Yandell looked upon armed neutrality with contempt and believed it a weak and dangerous folly. He believed the border states should pick a side and either fight "their brethren of the South, who are battling for their rights and for an institution in which Kentucky, Virginia, and Tennessee are intended, or they must fight the vandals of the North who are waging a war upon Southern institutions . . . who are determined to destroy slavery or to annihilate the people of the South . . . we must fight, and I choose to fight for Southern Rights." Yandell went on to declare why he was fighting: "I joined the army from a high sense of duty. I believe, the course of the South is a just and holy cause. I believe God is on our side and he will defend the right. I may not live to see our victory, but if I am killed, I shall die with the proud conviction of having done my duty."[23]

Other Kentuckians did not want to abandon their state. As one man said to his wife, Kentucky should remain neutral until better prepared, and that, with 700 miles of territory exposed to the North, all men should stay in the state to defend its border. Men who took his approach began to refer to it as armed neutrality. The challenge for such men, in both parties, was to try to arm themselves.[24]

The States Rights Party had the early advantage: it not only had the governor on its side, but it also controlled the State Guard. During the past decade, Kentuckians had seen the growing hostility between the two sections and, knowing they would be caught in the middle of any possible conflict, had decided to prepare themselves for defense. In March 1860, the legislature had created a new militia system. All men between 18 and 45 were enrolled, with some men chosen for a full-time militia known as the State Guard. Most of the men composing the State Guard were thought to have Southern loyalties, and during the secession crisis they acted distinctly pro-secession. At the time Fort Sumter was attacked, the State Guard consisted of 61 companies and controlled the state armory.[25]

---

23 Lunford Yandell to Pat, April 22, 1861, in Yandell Family Papers, Filson Club.

24 Henry to Sue, April 25, 1861, in Scrogin/Haviland Papers, Kentucky Historical Society.

25 Coulter, *The Civil War and Readjustment,* 82-83; Shortridge, "Kentucky Neutrality," 294-296; *Louisville Journal,* May 22, 1861.

The man placed in charge of the State Guard was General Simon Bolivar Buckner. A graduate from West Point, Buckner had served well under General Winfield Scott during the Mexican War. As inspector-general of the State Guard, Buckner's leanings were with the Confederacy, but he did respect Kentucky's neutrality and tried to keep Kentucky out of harm's way. Later, when Kentucky broke with neutrality in September 1861, he was offered a commission in the Union army, but he turned it down for a Confederate commission.[26]

Even with the state arsenal under his control, Magoffin did not have sufficient weapons to guard against an attack. Back in January, he had asked for money from the legislature to buy arms; but the Unionists, not wishing to supply secessionists with any more weapons, had granted him only $20,000, a portion of what he requested. After Sumter, Magoffin did not wait for the legislature to convene. Instead, he sent agents across the state to solicit private donations. The Bank of Kentucky donated $6,000, while the Bank of Louisville and the Commercial Bank each donated $10,000. On May 11, Confederate Secretary of War Walker received a letter explaining that Kentucky did not have enough money to buy weapons, and asking that the Confederate government donate 1,000 rifles. Walker was promised that, if properly armed, Kentucky would resist unto death any invasion from the north.[27]

On the same day that Walker received his letter, a bill was introduced in the Kentucky House to provide two and a half million dollars for the state militia. It was defeated 49 to 45. The *Louisville Courier* attributed the loss to the large amount requested. The bill also had lacked provisions for training men to fend off attacks by the armies of the Union and the Confederacy. Unionists opposed the bill, argued the editors at the *Courier*, because they wanted an equal split of state funds between the State Guard and the Home Guard, the latter being a new militia currently being raised by Unionists. On May 17, a new bill was proposed: $1,300,000 for arms, $150,000 for ammunition, and $600,000 for training. An amendment reduced these sums to $550,000 for arms, $40,000 for ammunition, and $300,000 for training. The bill then passed 49 to 46. *Courier* editors fumed because four members of the States Rights Party were absent for

26 Lowell H. Harrison, "Simon Bolivar Buckner," in Kleber, *The Kentucky Encyclopedia*, 136-137.

27 Coulter, *The Civil War and Readjustment*, 83-85; Shortridge, "Kentucky Neutrality," 296-297; Leslie Coombs to Green Adams, April 23, 1861, OR Series I, 52, pt. 1, 136; *Louisville Journal*, Apr. 19, 1861; A. P. Thompson to L. Walker, May 11, 1861, OR Series 1, 52, pt. 1, 94-95.

the vote on the original bill. Its editors also claimed that the original version would have passed had all four been in attendance. According to the newspaper, the States Rights Party lost even more strength when some secessionists left the legislature in disgust after passage of the amended bill.[28]

Further change had been made to the military bill by the time it passed the Senate on May 24. The final version was as follows: a five-man military board was given a budget of $1,600,000. Up to $750,000 of the money would be used to buy arms, which were to be equally distributed between the Home and State Guards. The board could also erect mills to make gunpowder; although, to avoid having them seized by either Union or Confederacy, the mills could not be built in a border county. The Home Guard could be officially recognized, but its members would not be excused from military duty in the state militia. Part of the money was to be used for training men, and before any man received arms he must take an oath to the state. The most controversial part of the bill was the creation of the five-man military board, which could not include the governor. Unionists still distrusted Magoffin, so the final bill effectively stripped him of his authority as commander in chief of the state militia, instead giving full military powers to the new board.[29]

As seen by the creation of the military board, the Democratic Unionists were uncomfortable with the way Magoffin was arming the state. They feared he might yet drive Kentucky out of the Union by force. Crittenden received a letter pleading with him to stop Magoffin before the governor grew too strong. The author of the letter also hoped that Unionists could be properly armed.[30]

He got his wish; and, as it turned out, anti-secessionists had a better source of weapons than the States Rights Party. Lieutenant William Nelson of the U.S. Navy met with Lincoln in May to offer his services. Lincoln used Nelson, a native Kentuckian, to supply rifles to Kentucky Unionists. Nelson took 5,000 "Lincoln Guns" to Cincinnati, where he prepared to ferry them across the Ohio River and distribute them around the state. Nelson met with several prominent Unionists to decide the best way to do this. The group was composed of staunch union men whom Lincoln and Nelson could trust; they included James

---

28 *House Journal*, May 11, 17, and 23, 1861; *Louisville Courier*, May 14, 18, and 22, 1861.

29 *Acts of the Legislature of the Commonwealth of Kentucky, 1860-1861* (Frankfort: Kentucky Yeoman Office, 1866), 4-6; Coulter, *The Civil War and Readjustment*, 86-87.

30 R. M. R. to Crittenden, Apr. 20, 1861, in Crittenden Papers, Library of Congress.

Harlan, John J. Crittenden, Garret Davis, Charles Wickliffe, Thornton Marshall, James Speed, and one of Lincoln's closest friends, Joshua Speed.[31]

These men were all important statesmen. James Harlan had served as a Whig in the U.S. Congress from 1835 to 1839 and then in the Kentucky legislature for several more years. In 1851, he was elected attorney general of Kentucky, and after the secession crisis Lincoln appointed him district attorney of Kentucky. Garrett Davis had served in the U.S. Congress as a Whig from 1839 to 1847, after which he returned to the private sector. He turned down offers to run for governor in 1855 and for president in 1856. Charles Wickliffe was elected as a Whig lieutenant governor in 1836 and took over the state when the governor died in the final year of his term. From 1841 through1845, Wickliffe served as U.S. postmaster general, and in June of 1861 he was elected as a Unionist to Congress. James Speed was elected to the legislature in 1847 and the state senate in 1851.[32]

Of all the men at the meeting, the one Lincoln told Nelson he could most rely on was Joshua Fry Speed, considered to be Lincoln's closest and oldest friend. On April 15, 1837, Lincoln entered the Bell & Co. general store in Springfield to purchase bedding before securing lodging. The clerk who assisted him was Joshua Speed. After the two spoke awhile, and Lincoln confessed his financial difficulties, Speed offered to share his bed with his new customer and friend. From 1837 until 1841, the two shared a bed as well as hopes and dreams. According to Lincoln biographer David Donald, Lincoln had few true friends, but he considered Speed his most intimate. Both men were interested in politics and campaigned for the Whig Party, but what brought them closest was confiding in each other about love. Speed was there for Lincoln as the latter courted and proposed to Mary Owens and Sara Rickard, both of which fell through. Speed was also there when Lincoln called off his engagement to Mary Todd, then regretted his decision so much that he did not leave his bed for over a week. Speed kept a watchful eye over his friend, fearing he might commit suicide. That same year Speed moved back to Louisville, but

31 Speed, *The Union Cause in Kentucky,* 99-103; Coulter, *The Civil War and Readjustment,* 88-89; *Louisville Courier*, May 22, 1861.

32 Ross A. Webb, "Garrett Davis," in Kleber, *The Kentucky Encyclopedia*, 255-256; Charles R. Lee, Jr., "James Harlan," in Kleber, *The Kentucky Encyclopedia* , 406; James J. Holmberg, "James Speed," in Kleber, *The Kentucky Encyclopedia*, 840-841; Lowell H. Harrison, "Charles Anderson Wickliffe," in Kleber, *The Kentucky Encyclopedia*, 950-951.

Lincoln visited him for a month in the summer, still pining over the loss of Mary Todd.[33]

Speed and Lincoln did not see each other again until after Lincoln won the presidency, but they remained close through letters. Speed vowed never again to enter politics and settled down in his family home outside Louisville to begin the life of a farmer. In 1853, he was hired as president of the Louisville, Cincinnati, and Lexington Railroad. Included among Speed's possessions were fourteen slaves. Speed was brought up in a slave-owning family in Kentucky, but his father exemplified the necessary evil ideology in Kentucky by both owning slaves while at the same time being anti-slavery. Speed's brother James Speed took his father's ideas even further when he freed his own slaves in the 1850s. However, it was slavery where Joshua Speed and Lincoln diverged in their thinking. In an 1855 letter, Speed told Lincoln that they disagreed over slavery and that he thought the rights of slave ownership should be upheld. Lincoln wrote back expressing his disappointment with Speed, but reassuring him of their friendship.[34]

Their differences regarding slavery led the two friends to drift politically after the introduction of the Kansas-Nebraska Act. Lincoln joined the new Republican Party to stop the spread of slavery, whereas Speed joined with the Democrats and supported popular sovereignty. Their difference in opinion did not, however, hurt their friendship. In a May 19, 1860, letter, Speed congratulated Lincoln on his presidential nomination, reminding him they were still friends, yet informing him that he could not vote for him. Though the two men supported different parties, after the election they were like-minded in the belief of the importance of preserving the Union. Speed wrote to Lincoln after his victory offering his assistance, but acknowledging how many offers for help he would receive, and so understood if Lincoln declined his offer. But Lincoln did want the aid of his closest friend, and asked the Speeds to visit him in Chicago. At Chicago the two men discussed who might fill cabinet positions. Lincoln supposedly offered Speed the treasury position, which Speed declined. Lincoln was in need of a border state man in his cabinet, so Speed began his real assistance to Lincoln by being his eyes and ears in Kentucky. Lincoln asked

---

33 David Herbert Donald, *We Are Lincoln Men: Abraham Lincoln and His Friends* (New York: Simon & Schuster, 2003), xvi, 29-30, 44-45; Gary Lee Williams, "James and Joshua Speed: Lincoln's Kentucky Friends (Ph.D. diss., Duke University, 1971), 15-21.

34 Williams, "James and Joshua Speed," 37-63.

During the secession crisis, Simon Bolivar Buckner was appointed head of the Kentucky militia. He did all in his power to preserve the state's neutrality. Buckner joined the Confederacy when Kentucky sided with the Union, and led the Southern army into Kentucky—something he would do again in 1862. After the war he held a wide variety of positions, including governor of Kentucky from 1887 to 1891. *Library of Congress*

Speed to talk with James Guthrie and ascertain his willingness to take a post. When Guthrie also declined, Lincoln appointed Edward Bates of Missouri as Attorney General.[35]

It was this close relationship that Lincoln had with Speed that brought Nelson to Speed's home to ask for assistance with the guns. It was Speed who suggested they bring in the guns secretly so as not to hurt the Union cause and harm neutrality. Speed made assignments to deliver the weapons to Kentucky's Home Guard, the very existence of which gave further evidence of the balance of power between the Democratic Union and States Rights parties. General Buckner had fought against the creation of the Home Guard. He claimed that two armed militias in the state would lead to a civil war within the state. Nor did he see the need for another military unit, with the State Guard already pledged to keep the state neutral. The *Louisville Courier* denounced the distribution of the "Lincoln Guns," claiming that they threatened the state's profession of neutrality. Furthermore, it charged that General Garrett Davis, who commanded the Home Guard, wanted to make himself a military dictator over the state, and that as soon as his men were armed he would side with the Union. The *Kentucky Statesman* questioned the secrecy of the rifles; if Lincoln felt distributing weapons to private citizens was legitimate, why was it done in secrecy? The only answer was, Lincoln knew he was breaking neutrality.[36]

The States Rights Party suggested that an investigation was in order to decide whether either Lincoln or the Unionists had defied neutrality. The vote in favor of an investigation was 47 to 44, but a two-thirds vote being necessary for passage, the investigation failed. The States Righters continued to press the issue, but when Unionists suggested that any investigation should also explore alleged ties of the Knights of the Golden Circle to the Confederacy, the States Righters backed off.[37]

Buckner's worst fears of civil war almost came true when the State Guard tried to capture the Lincoln Guns or stop them from reaching their destinations. Joseph Breckinridge, son of Robert Breckinridge, told of one such incident on May 9. A shipment of arms was leaving Cincinnati for central Kentucky when the Unionists received word that secessionists planned an

---

35 Donald, *We Are Lincoln Men*, 54-55; Williams, "James and Joshua Speed," 68-73.

36 Williams, "James and Joshua Speed," 86-88; *Louisville Journal*, May 22, 1861; *Louisville Courier*, May 22, 1861; Coulter, *The Civil War and Readjustment*, 88-89; *Kentucky Statesman*, May 21, 1861.

37 *House Journal*, May 20-23, 1861; *Louisville Courier*, May 25, 1861.

James Speed served in both houses of the Kentucky legislature. He strongly opposed slavery and joined the Republican Party, all of which hurt him politically at times in Kentucky. When Lincoln needed to appoint a new Attorney General, he wanted a Kentuckian, and for personal reasons and to thank him for his support Lincoln appointed Speed in 1864. Speed's brother Joshua Fry Speed is considered to have been Lincoln's closest friend and confidant.
Library of Congress

ambush. The shipment was returned to Cincinnati and rerouted by boat to Louisville and then by train to Lexington. Again, a group of states rights men learned of the shipment and planned to seize it at Lexington. Luckily for the Unionists, the train took a different route and so avoided the ambush; but when the pro-Confederate men realized their plan was ruined, they rushed to Lexington and started a fight with the Unionists. Blood would have been spilt if John C. Breckinridge had not stepped in and calmed the crowd.[38]

During the month after Fort Sumter, neutrality became an attractive idea to Kentuckians. As seen by voting practices, the Unionists held a majority over the States Righters, but it was the Unionists who proposed neutrality as the best way to defeat secession. If Kentucky was as pro-Union as some have suggested, it should have been the secessionists who pressed to keep Kentucky neutral. The equal strength of the two sides was further demonstrated by the way they scrambled to arm their respective militias. Unionists still believed secessionists were strong enough to carry Kentucky out of the Union. Even the massive defeat for the States Rights Party in the May election did not prove Kentucky's loyalty to the Union. If it were so, Unionists would not have blocked the call for a state convention in May or tried so desperately to create and arm its own Home Guard.

38 Joseph Breckinridge to Robert Breckinridge, May 9, 1861, in Breckinridge Family Papers, Library of Congress.

C hapter 8

The Struggle to Remain Neutral:
May to June 1861

I t was clear from the moment that Kentucky declared armed neutrality that its position would be hard to maintain. As noted, many secessionists disagreed with neutrality and left to join the Confederacy. Others believed that each side would support neutrality only until it was strong enough to force its views on the state. To achieve this, both sides raced to arm themselves and protect against an insurrection by the other. Unionists did not trust the States Rights Party, and now that neutrality had been declared some of them did not see it as a plausible solution. Elsewhere in the country, people thought Kentuckians were delusional.

James Headley, a Kentucky lawyer, who had been living in Kansas, reported that people there called neutrality the "silliest" idea in the conflict. They alleged that anyone not actively for the Union was against it. Headley summarized their thinking: "If the Kentuckians think that they can maintain any such position they are deceived." Headley himself believed that the Union would use any excuse to justify military occupation; "subjection of the State" and "Pillage and Plunder" would then surely follow. He continued, "Revolutions never go backward but when begun they push forward with the speed of the whirlwind, and woe to him to stand directly in the path neutral, armed or unarmed—for he will be crushed."

The problem for Kentucky, as Headley saw it, was that the North would not accept neutrality, and if Kentuckians were forced to choose a side, they had no good choice. If they joined the North, slavery was at risk. If they joined the Confederacy, Kentucky the Federals would invade the state. What made the situation even harder was that those who opposed neutrality had begun to fight openly against it.[1]

Even some unconditional Unionists, who had been content thus far to have at least maintained neutrality, began to resist it. In May, Simon Cameron, Lincoln's secretary of war, received letters from Kentucky Unionists both offering and asking for aid. Two of these letters resulted in the shipment of the "Lincoln Guns" to Kentucky. Garrett Davis asked Cameron for guns to arm men who were willing to stand by the Union. Davis believed that Governor Magoffin was attempting to raise a secessionist army, so he wanted the Union to raise 20,000 troops for the protection of Kentucky. He suggested that Robert Anderson, of Fort Sumter fame, command the army because only he had the moral fiber strong enough to counter John C. Breckinridge's influence. The next week, Cameron received a letter from another Kentuckian who pledged himself and the members of the Home Guard at Newport to fight for the Union even if Kentucky seceded. He reported that they had 800 men drilling every night, but they needed guns.[2]

The Union high command also became uneasy with Kentucky's neutral status. Because commanders saw secession as a distinct possibility, they prepared to defend Kentucky in case its neutrality was broken. George B. McClellan, the general responsible for Kentucky during this period, wrote letters to influential Kentuckians giving his opinions of the circumstances and recommending what he thought were appropriate actions. McClellan believed that Governor Magoffin was a traitor, and he accused General Simon B. Buckner of being under the governor's influence. McClellan feared a large force of secessionists were gathering at Gallipolis with the intention of attacking Cairo, Illinois. Also believing that Cincinnati might fall to a secessionist force, he proposed crossing into Kentucky with 40,000 men and occupying the heights across from the city. McClellan believed Kentucky's Union men would fight, but he feared that the state's secessionists were too strong for them. If that

---

1   McClellan to E. Townsend, May 10, 1861, *OR* Series I, 51, pt. 1, 374-376; James Headley to Father, May 7, 1861, in Thomas Henry Hines Papers, University of Kentucky.

2   Garrett Davis to Simon Cameron, May 3, 1861, *OR* Series I, 52, pt. 1, 137-139; C. Beyland to Simon Cameron, May 10, 1861, *ibid.*, 141-142.

George B. McClellan took over command of the Army of the Potomac in July 1862, a position in which he demonstrated outstanding organizational ability but questionable battlefield prowess. Before his initial triumphant entrance into the nation's capital, however, McClellan was put in command of the Department of Ohio, giving him responsibility over Kentucky. McClellan believed Kentucky's governor and many of its citizens were secessionists, so he built up troops on the state's northern border and tried to arm its citizens. *Library of Congress*

were the case, McClellan wanted to be in a position to help the Unionists, rather than see them crushed by those he viewed as traitors.[3]

Another concern for both sides was the Jackson Purchase. The Jackson Purchase was cut off from the rest of Kentucky by the Tennessee and Cumberland Rivers. The pro-Confederate Jackson Purchase had two strategic locations, Columbus and Paducah, situated along the Mississippi and Ohio Rivers. Whichever side controlled those two towns controlled the corresponding river. Because of their importance, both the United States and the Confederacy moved troops into the vicinity. Should Kentucky neutrality be broken, both sides meant to rush in and occupy them. General Ulysses S. Grant positioned himself at Cairo, Illinois, just across the river from Paducah. Panicked by the large Union buildup across the river, rebel sympathizers from Kentucky begged Confederates in Tennessee for assistance. On May 16, Confederate General Leonidas Polk asked Jefferson Davis for permission to move into Kentucky and occupy Columbus. Davis denied permission, but Polk remained poised to move. The State Guard also moved large portions of its men into the Purchase.[4]

On May 21, leaders in the first congressional district, made up of the Jackson Purchase, called for a district convention at Mayfield, in Graves County. The purpose of the convention was to sever ties with the rest of Kentucky and join like-minded men in Tennessee. Most Kentuckians thought secession of the Purchase was a forgone conclusion, but the *Louisville Journal* demanded that Magoffin do something to stop the meeting. McClellan informed Lincoln that the Purchase was on its way out and that Confederate troops would soon be moving in. The meeting began on May 27 with around 160 delegates from the Purchase and Tennessee.[5]

Unfortunately, most records of the meeting were destroyed, but some evidence of what occurred has survived. Several prominent men, most of them secessionists, addressed the convention, but not all thought that the district should secede at that time. Richard Gholsom believed that the states rights

---

3 McClellan to E. Townsend, May 10, 1861, OR Series I, 51, pt. 1, 374-376; McClellan to E. Townsend, May 17, 1861, *ibid.*, 380-381.

4 Berry Craig, "Jackson Purchase Considers Secession," *Register of Kentucky History Society*, vol. 99 (Autumn 2001), 339-344.

5 *Louisville Journal*, May 21, 1861; *Louisville Courier*, June 5, 1861; Craig, "Jackson Purchase Considers Secession," 344-348. Craig wrote that the Convention began on May 29.

theory of secession did not apply to a section within a state. In fact, he saw a danger in this approach. If one part of Kentucky seceded, there would be no chance of Kentucky as a whole ever seceding. Gholsom stressed that if Kentuckians exercised patience, Lincoln would eventually invade the state and give the whole state an excuse to secede. Lloyd Tilghman agreed with Gholsom. He insisted that Kentuckians should not leave the state to fight for the Confederacy because it would not be long before they could fight as Confederates within Kentucky. Other delegates, however, thought it was time for the Purchase to join the rebels. Henry Clay King asked Kentuckians to cross the border and enlist in the Confederacy. A delegate from Tennessee told them that it was their destiny to join the Confederacy and that neutrality was the same as secession. He promised that Tennessee had enough guns to arm the men of the Purchase if they chose to leave.[6]

After three days of debate, the Mayville Convention voted 130 to 30 to remain within the fold. The delegates condemned Lincoln for breaking the law and starting a war, and praised Magoffin for denying Lincoln troops from Kentucky. They renewed the call for a state convention to decide the issue of secession, and they urged Magoffin to shore up the state's defenses. The Mayville Convention showed that even the most strongly secessionist region of Kentucky was still loyal to the state over either side.[7]

The Mayville Convention also shows that both sides continued to fear invasion, and for good reason. Invasion would not only bring war, but it might drive the state to the opposite side of the invader. Anna Dicken still feared the Confederacy for just this reason. She knew thousands of people hoped General Polk might enter the state, but she believed that was exactly what the Union hoped Polk would do. A Confederate invasion would justify the Union doing the same, as it had in Maryland and Missouri. Anna believed the best course for Kentuckians, even those with Confederate loyalties, was to remain neutral.[8]

As seen by McClellan's letters and the buildup of troops at Cairo, Kentuckians had reason to fear a Union breach of neutrality as much as a rebel one. The *Louisville Courier*, for example, reported on June 8 that U.S. troops had entered Kentucky to break up a secessionist camp at Elliot's Mill. When

---

6 Craig, "Jackson Purchase Considers Secession," 348-351.

7 *Ibid.*, 349-353; *Louisville Courier*, June 5, 1861.

8 Anna to Henry, June 6, 1861, in Dicken-Troutman-Balke Papers, University of Kentucky.

Robert Anderson is most famous today as the commander of Fort Sumter at the beginning of the war. After his surrender of the fort, he was assigned to Kentucky to raise troops. Unionists did not see Anderson's actions as a breach of neutrality because he was a Kentuckian raising Kentucky troops for Kentucky. *Library of Congress*

Kentuckians protested the invasion, the Union commander responded that loyal Kentuckians had begged him for protection. The paper's editorial accused the "tories," or Unionist Kentuckians, of lying to the U.S. Army in an attempt to entice troops into the state.[9]

The most serious threat to neutrality from the Union came with the creation of the Military Department of Kentucky on May 28. General Robert Anderson was placed in command. The native Kentuckian had already made a name for himself in the North as the beleaguered commander of Charleston's Fort Sumter. Born in Jefferson County to a distinguished family that stretched back to the Revolutionary War, Anderson graduated from West Point in 1825 and went on to serve in the Black Hawk War, the Seminole War, and the Mexican War. He was not dispatched to Charleston until December of 1860, just a few months before Southern forces opened fire on the harbor bastion. The Federals did not consider Anderson's new department a violation of neutrality because it operated outside the state. Anderson's principal duty was to recruit Unionists for the army. He set up two training camps outside the state, just across the Ohio River. Camp Clay was established in Ohio, across from Newport, and Camp Joe Holt was in Indiana, across from Louisville. In the first week of June, the first Kentucky regiment left Kentucky for Camp Clay. By the beginning of July, several more companies had assembled at the two camps.[10]

Anderson's mission did have its complications. Secessionists claimed foul play when he began his work, even though a similar camp, Camp Boone, was established shortly after to recruit Kentuckians for the Confederate army. The *Louisville Courier* reported that Anderson arrived in Kentucky under the ruse of visiting his family, but his true intentions were to take over the military and subjugate Kentucky the way the Union had subjugated Missouri and Maryland. Even some Unionists had reservations. Lincoln's trusted friend and advisor in Kentucky, Joshua Speed, never saw a breech in neutrality with the Lincoln guns, but worried that Anderson's involvement in Kentucky might be seen as

---

9 *Louisville Courier*, June 8, 1861.

10 Richard Nelson Current, *Lincoln's Loyalists: Union Soldiers from the Confederacy* (Boston: Northeast University Press, 1992), 10; George H. Yater, "Robert Anderson," in John Kleber, ed., *The Kentucky Encyclopedia*, 21; Coulter, *The Civil War and Readjustment in Kentucky*, 100-101; Basler, ed., *The Collected Works of Abraham Lincoln*, 359, 368-369; *Louisville Courier*, May 25 and June 1, 1861.

aggressive. Speed felt they already had the Home Guard, which by then was well supplied, and he questioned the soundness of raising troops.[11]

The first complete unit to assemble at Camp Joe Holt was Rousseau's Louisville Legion. Lovell Harrison Rousseau, from Lincoln County, was a successful lawyer and had been a captain in the Mexican War. In 1860, he was elected to the Kentucky legislature and served until he resigned to fight for the Union during the secession crisis. On April 24, he helped to organize the first Home Guard unit in Louisville. On May 21, in a speech to the legislature, he declared that Kentucky was and should remain loyal to the Union and that neutrality was a false position that would hurt the state. He accused secessionists of acquiescing to neutrality only until they had the chance to use the military to force Kentucky out of the Union. He agreed to respect neutrality, because it was the will of the state, but he believed Kentuckians would eventually be forced to call upon the Union to protect them from the secessionists. A few days later, on May 24, he began to organize a regiment of volunteers. Rousseau was elected colonel and James Speed selected major. When Rousseau informed Lincoln that his regiment was ready for service, the president commissioned him a colonel of volunteers in the Union army and authorized him to raise an entire legion of infantry and cavalry. On July 1, Rousseau and his troops, named the Louisville Legion, marched from Louisville across the river. Most of his men were from Home Guard units. Rousseau left shortly thereafter for Washington to meet with Lincoln, whom he convinced to supply Camp Joe Holt.[12]

The camp had been named for Joseph Holt, one of the most outspoken unconditional Unionists in Kentucky. In a letter to Joshua Speed on May 31, which would be published in the papers, Holt defended his unconditional Unionism. Lincoln, according to Holt, had done everything he could to keep the peace, being especially keen to appease the border states and keep them loyal. But the Confederacy had wanted war, Holt insisted, and they saw Fort Sumter as an opportunity to draw the border states into the Confederacy. Lincoln had the constitutional duty to call for troops and put down the

11 *Louisville Courier*, May 25 and June 1, 1861; Gary Lee Williams, "James and Joshua Speed: Lincoln's Kentucky Friends" (Ph.D. diss., Duke University, 1971), 89-91.

12 *Louisville Commercial*, September 11, 1895; Rousseau's speech in the Kentucky Senate, May 21, 1861, in Moore, ed., *Rebellion Record*, Vol. 1, Doc. 227, 330-333; Jack DeBerry, "Lovell Harrison Rousseau," in Kleber, *The Kentucky Encyclopedia*, 783; *Louisville Courier*, June 21, 1861.

The first official Kentucky Union outfit was Rousseau's Louisville Legion, raised on July 1, 1861, and assembled across the Ohio River in Indiana at Camp Joe Holt. Its commander, Lovell H. Rousseau, was appointed colonel, but by that October he was appointed brigadier general. Rousseau, a native of Indiana, attorney, and Mexican War veteran, moved to Kentucky and won a state senate seat there in 1860. Rousseau performed well during the Civil War in many of the major Western Theater battles. He commanded the District of Louisiana during Reconstruction. *Library of Congress*

rebellion, Holt continued, and if the South saw this as subjugation, it must understand that the president was responsible for subjugating citizens who broke the law.[13]

Holt also emphasized the ill consequences of both secession and neutrality. If Kentuckians seceded, they would be leaving a government that had always protected them for a government that did not have the power to do so. They would legitimize a concept which, if successful, would not end with the Confederacy but would be seized upon by every radical movement that came along. They would expose themselves to attack along the border, their slaves would run away, and they would have no fugitive slave law to assist in their capture. If Kentuckians joined the Confederacy, their taxes would also be much higher; the Confederacy needed money to build its army and navy, and it would want to build forts along the border. Neutrality offered no better alternative, Holt said. Only complete loyalty to the Union could save the state from disaster. How could a man be neutral when his house was on fire?[14]

Holt's position is of particular interest because he had always been known as a firm supporter of Southern rights. Born in Breckinridge County, Holt had attended Centre College. By 1828, he had a successful law practice in Elizabethtown. During Andrew Jackson's 1828 presidential race, Holt became a strong supporter of the new Democratic Party, and won in 1832 position as prosecuting attorney in Louisville. In 1835, he moved to Vicksburg, Mississippi, where he made his fortune in the cotton trade. While in Vicksburg, he and his wife both caught tuberculosis. His wife died, but he returned to Louisville to recover from his sickness. That was in 1842, when he was only thirty-five years old.[15]

Once back in Kentucky, Holt met and married Margaret Wickliffe, the daughter of Governor Wickliffe. For the most part Holt stayed out of public life until 1856, when he came out as a stump speaker for the Democratic presidential ticket of James Buchanan and John C. Breckinridge. In return for

13 Joseph Holt, *The Fallacy of Neutrality: an Address by the Hon. Joseph Holt, to the People of Kentucky, Delivered at Louisville, July 13th, 1861*, also his letter to J. F. Speed, Esq. (New York: J. G. Gregory, 1861), 3-11.

14 Joseph Holt, *The Fallacy of Neutrality*, 6-19; *Louisville Courier*, June 15, 1861.

15 Roger Bartman, "Joseph Holt and Kentucky in the Civil War," *The Filson Club Quarterly*, Vol. 4 (April 1966), 106; Mary Allen Bernard, "Joseph Holt, Judge Advocate General, 1862-1875" (Ph.D. diss., University of Chicago, 1927), 47-50, 56-60; James D. Bennett, "Joseph Holt," in Kleber, *The Kentucky Encyclopedia*, 438.

helping Kentucky vote Democratic for the first time in years, he was summoned to Washington to serve as commissioner of patents. Two years later, he was appointed postmaster general. In that post, he showed his states rights views by supporting Virginia's right to halt the delivery of abolitionist mail into the state. In 1860, when John Floyd resigned as secretary of war, Holt was appointed to that office.[16]

It was during his time in the cabinet that Holt became a Unionist and developed his ideas about secession. Holt saw secession as a conspiracy by Southern leaders to gain more power. They had been seeking power since the days of John C. Calhoun, and they would not be satisfied until they had their own nation. It was Holt who took up the preparations to defend Fort Sumter and ordered Anderson to hold the fort at all costs. When accused of coercion by the South, Holt responded that protecting Federal property against rebels was entirely justified.[17]

It was after Fort Sumter that Lincoln, fearing the secession of the upper South, turned to men such as Anderson and Holt to help keep Kentucky loyal. Holt's name carried weight in Kentucky and Unionists respected him. However, some also found him to be a liability. His brand of Unionism was more uncompromising than their own, more flexible ideology. When Kentucky chose neutrality, Holt did not go along, but instead worked with other unconditional Unionists to keep Kentucky in the Union. He spent most of his efforts giving speeches to support Lincoln, but ultimately Holt found that he was out of step with Kentucky. During his time in Washington, he had lost touch with public opinion in the state. Unconditional Unionists and troops at Camp Joe Holt praised him, but most Kentuckians, including most Unionists, still held to neutrality as their best bet.[18]

So, with forces everywhere working against neutrality, Magoffin reached out to ensure that all sides respected Kentucky's status. With the governor's encouragement, Buckner worked out a plan with McClellan to keep Union troops out of the state. Buckner promised to protect Union property in Kentucky and to keep Confederate forces at bay. McClellan agreed not to interfere with the state, even if Confederate troops entered, as long as Buckner

---

16 Bernard, "Joseph Holt, Judge Advocate General," 50-52, 56; Bennett, "Joseph Holt," in Kleber, *The Kentucky Encyclopedia*, 438.

17 Bernard, "Joseph Holt, Judge Advocate General," 54, 60-66.

18 *Ibid.*, 67-73, 80-81; Bartman, "Joseph Holt and Kentucky," 108-109, 111-115.

forced them out. Governor Isham Harris of Tennessee informed General Gideon Pillow on June 13 of the arrangement between Buckner and McClellan and ordered Pillow to follow suit. Only if the North tried to subjugate Kentucky should his men enter the state to drive them out.[19]

By late June, the United States and Confederate States appeared to have accepted Kentucky neutrality, particularly so when Kentuckians reaffirmed their position yet again on June 20. When Lincoln called for a special session of Congress to meet on July 4, Magoffin announced that new congressmen were to be sent to Washington and called for elections. Once again, both sides supported neutrality. Typical of Democratic Unionist candidates, John Young Brown argued that the people had spoken in the May election for peace and neutrality, and that he planned to stand for the same. He added that he had no intention of helping Lincoln. Neither did T. L. Jones of Covington. He opposed sending money or men to help the Union war effort and went as far as to say that Lincoln should be impeached. Lastly, H. W. Bruce said that if elected he would not vote for even one dollar to support the war. He accused Lincoln of breaking the law with his suspensions of habeas corpus, and he believed the people of Kentucky wanted nothing more than peace. There were a few Unionist candidates who supported Lincoln, but the Union ticket generally stood solidly in favor of neutrality.[20]

The Democratic Union platform also emphasized its continued support for slavery. Unionists claimed that the Confederacy planned to reopen the African slave trade, which would hurt the Kentucky slave market. Their platform also tried to convince Kentuckians that the Confederacy only wanted to use their state as a buffer and battleground between the deep South and the North. The most difficult argument candidates had to make regarded how they could support the Union without supporting its leader, especially after Lincoln had imposed a new policy of restricting trade to the South (discussed below). They side-stepped this dilemma in part by emphasizing their true allegiance to neutrality, especially as contrasted to the States Rights Party. The Democratic Unionists claimed that their rivals endorsed neutrality only as an expedient; as

19 Buckner to Magoffin, June 10, 1861, Moore, ed., *Rebellion Record*, Vol. 1, Doc. 30, 163; Isham Harris to Gideon Pillow, June 13, 1861, OR Series IV, 1, 376-378.

20 *Louisville Courier*, May 15, June 3 and 15, 1861. President Abraham Lincoln had arrested several secessionists in Maryland and was holding them in prison without the benefit of habeas corpus.

soon as they had the power necessary to leave the Union, they would demand secession.[21]

Yet, in some ways, the States Rights Party had the easier campaign by blaming the nation's problems on Lincoln: he was the one leading the nation to war; he was the one about to restrict Southern trade; he had ignored Kentucky's desire for neutrality with his Lincoln Guns. States Righters tried to flip the roles of the Unionists from the May elections. The *Kentucky Statesman* claimed the June elections were not a question of North and South, but a question of war and peace. Unionists and Lincoln, they claimed, would fight to uphold the Union and bring war. A good example of this from the paper was the campaign for a "Mr. Simms." The angle taken was simple: If you oppose war, vote for Simms; if you condemn invasion, vote for Simms; if you oppose the army marching through Kentucky, vote for Simms; if you oppose quartering Lincoln's troops in your homes, vote for Simms; lastly, if you seek a peaceful separation, vote for Simms.[22]

The Democratic Union Party again dominated in the election, winning in nine of the ten congressional districts. A new pattern emerged. Coulter claimed the Democratic Unionists won because voters with Southern sympathies did not vote, and at first glance the statistics seem to support him. As in May, June voters did not turn out in the same numbers as for the 1860 presidential election. Turnout dropped by 18,825 participants, with 66 percent of the counties recording a lower turnout than in November. The more interesting statistic is that 72 percent of the counties increased voting between the May and June elections. Equally striking, 62 counties, or 60 percent, recorded lower numbers for Democratic Union candidates and higher tallies for States Rights candidates between May and June. Of the 62 counties, only 16 had voted for Breckinridge in November, Constitutional Unionist counties all and some of the state's strongest slaveholding regions. According to historian Harry Volz, the explanation is that former slaveholding Whigs who had sat out the May elections changed sides in June and voted for the States Rights Party.[23]

21 Harrison, *The Civil War in Kentucky*, 11; Volz, "Party, State, and Nation: Kentucky and the Coming of the American Civil War," 453-455; *Louisville Journal*, May 29, 1861.

22 *Louisville Courier*, May 4, 1861; Volz, "Party, State, and Nation," 451-452; Harrison and Klotter, *A New History of Kentucky*, 189; *Kentucky Statesman*, June 4 and 11, 1861.

23 Secretary of State Election Results, 1855-1872, Kentucky State Archives; Coulter, *Civil War and Readjustment*, 95-96; Volz, "Party, State, and Nation," 458-460.

June 1861 Congressional Elections by District		
1st District	*Trimble (U)*	*Burnett (SR)*
Fulton	38	631
Hickman	58	791
Ballard	177	689
McCracken	298	612
Livingston	304	261
Graves	610	1,270
Calloway	305	842
Marshall	299	793
Caldwell	633	530
Lyon	277	271
Trigg	611	631
Union	615	522
Crittenden	898	353
Hopkins	797	561
Webster	305	233
Total	6,225	8,990

June 1861 Congressional Elections by District		
2nd District	*Jackson (U)*	*Bunch (SR)*
Christian	1,193	528
Henderson	753	559

2nd District	Jackson (U)	Bunch (SR)
Daviess	779	973
Muhlenburg	965	147
Ohio	1,390	185
Hancock	407	378
Breckinridge	1234	309
Butler	1031	14
Grayson	855	108
McLean	674	163
Total	9,281	3,364

June 1861 Congressional Elections by District		
3rd District	Grinder (U)	Lewis (SR)
Todd	720	266
Logan	993	1,005
Simpson	531	273
Warren	1,717	269
Edmonson	545	117
Barren	1,283	695
Hart	1,347	127
Monroe	1,104	77
Allen	1,139	227
Metcalfe	1,013	57
Total	10,392	3,113

June 1861 Congressional Elections by District		
4th District	*Harding (U)*	*Talbott (SR)*
Cumberland	782	82
Clinton	534	49
Wayne	772	393
Russell	709	103
Pulaski	1,847	516
Lincoln	1,020	295
Boyle	772	313
Taylor	852	91
Green	812	323
Adair	1,065	272
Casey	1154	32
Total	10,319	2,469

June 1861 Congressional Elections by District		
5th District	*Wickliffe (U)*	*Read (SR)*
Meade	502	326
Hardin	1,169	325
Bullitt	716	153
Larue	894	34
Marion	1,248	183
Washington	1,056	182

5th District	Wickliffe (U)	Read (SR)
Nelson	776	395
Mercer	1,053	479
Anderson	341	471
Spencer	464	171
Total	8,219	2,719

June 1861 Congressional Elections by District		
6th District	Dunlap (U)	Smith (SR)
Garrard	957	0
Madison	1,013	14
Rockcastle	582	0
Laurel	502	22
Knox	833	1
Estill	653	0
Owsley	484	1
Clay	562	17
Perry	161	5
Pike	95	0
Letcher	209	7
Whitley	673	10
Harlan	654	44
Floyd	62	0
Johnson	265	31

6th District	Dunlap (U)	Smith (SR)
Breathitt	192	0
Jackson	353	0
Magoffin	151	0
Total	8,401	152

June 1861 Congressional Elections by District		
7th District	Malbury (U)	Bruck (SR)
Jefferson	8,005	1,381
Henry	1,139	619
Shelby	1,247	648
Oldham	644	214
Total	11,035	2,862

June 1861 Congressional Elections by District		
8th District	Crittenden (U)	Simms (SR)
Bourbon	1,010	657
Fayette	1,696	666
Jessamine	823	361
Woodford	722	379
Scott	879	985
Franklin	1,092	685
Harrison	1,000	1,159
Nicholas	1,040	816

8th District	Crittenden (U)	Simms (SR)
Total	8,262	5,708

June 1861 Congressional Elections by District		
9th District	Wadsworth (U)	Williams (SR)
Mason	2,023	513
Lewis	1,184	149
Greenup	1,066	108
Lawrence	761	195
Carter	877	366
Morgan	550	747
Montgomery	646	387
Clarke	925	192
Bath	1,153	493
Fleming	1,476	407
Powell	231	84
Rowan	236	127
Boyd	869	36
Magoffin	133	66
Total	12,130	3,870

June 1861 Congressional Elections by District		
10th District	Menfies (U)	Hogan (SR)
Trimble	319	154

10th District	Menfies (U)	Hogan (SR)
Carroll	417	116
Owen	145	1,104
Gallatin	341	166
Grant	757	578
Boone	Unrecorded	Unrecorded
Kenten	2,151	479
Campbell	2,071	415
Pendleton	925	580
Bracken	1,247	164
Total	8,373	3,756

The June elections suggest that Kentuckians still wanted neutrality, but that many slaveholders did not trust the Democratic Union Party to remain neutral. Voters had turned out for the States Rights Party in every county of the state outside the mountain regions. Likewise, the drop in Unionist votes suggested that many earlier supporters had lost faith in the party, though not to the extent of switching allegiance to the States Righters.

In the mountains, where people had always voted Democrat, voters did not want to back the States Rights Party. Unimpressed with the Democratic Unionists, however, they by and large declined to vote at all. The *Kentucky Statesman* suggested that the Union Party victory did not mean what these Unionists hoped that it did. The paper suggested that everyone it polled still hated and did not trust President Lincoln, and they in no way supported war. According to the *Kentucky Statesman*, Kentuckians still saw a vote for the States Rights Party as a vote for civil war. The newspaper agreed the election results constituted a win for neutrality.[24]

---

24 Secretary of State Election Results, 1855-1872, Kentucky State Archives; *Kentucky Statesman*, June 25, 1861.

The day after the election, and with the success of the Unionist victory, Federal customs agents announced that no shipments could be made south on the Louisville and Nashville Railroad without a permit. Lincoln had wanted to stop trading much sooner, and had even asked General Anderson to oversee it. Once again it was the influence of Joshua Speed that swayed Lincoln. Speed wrote to Lincoln warning him of the potential problems that trade restriction might present for Kentucky Unionists. He reminded Lincoln of the upcoming elections, and to not give the States Rights Party any more reasons to fear that Lincoln might interfere with neutrality. When the time came to act, Speed suggested that the Home Guard handle the trade restrictions. The Home Guard might not be as effective as the Federal army, but it would cause fewer problems.[25]

Speed knew the pulse of his state. The announcement of trade stoppages brought protest from Louisville, one of the strongest Unionist cities in Kentucky, which claimed that cutting off trade was as much a declaration of war as if the Union army had bombarded the city. Louisville had grown economically stronger since the secession crisis. As Southern states seceded from the Union, Northern states cut off trade with their former partners. Kentucky, however, continued trading with the South, and because the state also traded with the North, it became the principal hub between these Northern and Southern states. Because of its location on the Mississippi River and the presence of the Louisville and Nashville Railroad, Louisville quickly became the most important trade center in the entire state. All of this meant that Northern merchants would trade with Kentucky, and then Kentucky would trade with the Southern merchants outside its boundary. The amount of freight carried by the Louisville and Nashville Railroad demonstrates the economic growth. During 1860, freight declined every month, but starting in February 1861 volume picked up. In February, the railroad made $23,000 from freight to South states; in June, it made $68,000.[26]

James Guthrie, a man who had already played a major role in Kentucky politics as a Democratic Party leader and member of the Washington Peace Convention, grew in importance as the president of the Louisville and Nashville

---

25 Williams, "James and Joshua Speed," 93-94; Coulter, *Civil War and Readjustment*, 60-62, 73-75.

26 Williams, "James and Joshua Speed," 93-94; Coulter, *Civil War and Readjustment*, 60-64, 73-75.

Railroad. During the summer of 1861, the Louisville and Nashville was the only major line running between the two nations, leaving Guthrie in the difficult position of having to tiptoe between two belligerent countries. Neither side was pleased with the situation. For its part, the Confederacy did not like the thought of supplying the North, but allowed trade to continue because the large majority of rolling stock was moving from north to south. As early as 1860, Southern states had begun hoarding supplies in preparation for a coming conflict. After the firing upon Fort Sumter in April 1861, rumors circulated that people in Louisville would starve with all available foodstuffs going to Tennessee. What made the trade even more lopsided was that on May 21, the Confederacy passed a law restricting the trade of cotton, sugar, rice, tobacco, and naval stores to the Union.[27]

As long as the two sides remained peaceful, Northerners did not care about Kentucky trading with the Confederate states. President Lincoln, however, feared upsetting the border states more than he feared trade with the Confederacy. However, after the attack on Fort Sumter, individual towns saw such trade as supplying the enemy, even though the Federal government allowed it. Cincinnati acted by blockading all trade to Louisville down the Mississippi River. Louisville citizens countered by preparing to attack a steamer bound to Pittsburg from St. Louis, and to march on Cincinnati. Delegations from both cities met and peace was restored, but the situation remained tense. On June 12, Lincoln, under pressure from Northerners, declared that customs agents should use their best judgment as to what should or should not be shipped to Southern states. Northern states took this as an opportunity to pressure customs agents to stop all of Kentucky's trade southward. They wanted to halt all trade to Kentucky until it was clear to which side the state would give its allegiance.[28]

With Lincoln's announcement of restrictions on shipments to the South, Kentuckians had to be resourceful if they wanted to maintain their economic boom. If they could not ship by rail, they would ship by wagon. Agents only checked rail freight that was sent from Louisville; they could not know what

---

27 Maury Klein, *History of the Louisville and Nashville Railroad* (Lexington: University Press of Kentucky, 2003), 22-30; Robert S. Cotterill, "James Guthrie—Kentuckian, 1792-1869," in *Register of Kentucky Historical Society*, vol. 20 (1922), 290-294.

28 Coulter, *Civil War and Readjustment*, 60-62, 70-71; Klein, *History of the Louisville and Nashville Railroad*, 26-28.

cargo might be added down the line. Wagons would carry cargo to towns farther south along the track, where it would be loaded onto the freight cars. Even more simply, wagons could carry cargo the entire distance to towns along the border, such as Franklin, which became the new hub for shipments. For the Memphis trade, shipments were transported overland to the Mississippi River below Cairo, where merchants had free access to trade between Columbus and Memphis.[29]

As for the Confederacy, by July Tennessee Governor Isham Harris began putting agents on northbound trains to enforce the South's embargo. On July 4, Governor Harris, fearing the loss of trade and also that the Louisville & Nashville Railroad might be used as the means to invade his state, seized control of the part of the line within Tennessee, taking five engines, three passenger cars, and seventy freight cars. Harris still authorized some trade north, but Guthrie refused to send any more shipments into Tennessee out of fear of losing more rolling stock. This aggressive act on the part of the Confederacy drove a very powerful man within the state to change his formerly Southern sympathies to complete support for the Union. For men like Guthrie, the Confederacy pushed him away more than the Union pulled. This would not be the last time Tennessee would make such a tragic decision.[30]

29 Coulter, *Civil War and Readjustment*, 76-78.

30 Klein, *History of the Louisville and Nashville Railroad*, 28-30; Cotterill, "James Guthrie," 293-294.

C hapter 9

The End of Neutrality:
July to September 1861

July began the same way that June ended, with most Kentuckians claiming neutrality, but also with the failure of neutrality a growing possibility. Both Democratic Unionists and States Righters broke the spirit, if not the legal limits, of neutrality. Governor Magoffin declared that troops raised in Kentucky for the purpose of fighting for the Union defied the neutrality policy, but the *Louisville Journal* accused Magoffin of doing the same thing to help the Rebels. The paper justified Unionist actions by claiming these men were arming not for attack but to defend themselves against the small minority of men who hoped to take Kentucky out of the Union by force. In early July, the *Journal* continued with several complaints against the States Righters. The paper claimed that Unionists in Paducah were being forced out of their homes by secessionists, and that secession leaders in the legislature were meeting to discuss ways for the state to secede. The *Journal* believed that secessionists were trying to get the U.S. Army to invade the state, which would give them the excuse they needed to bring in Confederate troops.[1]

In response, States Rights Party members had their own complaints about Unionists. They claimed that the legislature was in the pocket of Lincoln, and

---

1 *Louisville Journal*, July 2, 16, 18, and 19, 1861.

that to reward the faithful legislators Lincoln had appointed one of them a colonel and another a captain in the Union army and made one legislator a U.S. marshal. They claimed a conspiracy existed among Union newspapers to undermine neutrality by telling lies about the loyalties of the State Guard. The *Kentucky Statesman* reported it had lists of the breaches of neutrality by the North, whereas it claimed not a single breach could be found amongst Southern supporters. The *Louisville Courier* published a long list of grievances involving the actions of Lincoln's government outside of Kentucky, too. It had suspended habeas corpus in Missouri and Maryland, limited freedom of speech in Maryland, denied the right to petition the government in New York City, disbanded a legally formed militia in Missouri, conducted illegal searches in Missouri and Maryland, and denied due process in Missouri.[2]

Such chaos and accusations caused many Kentuckians to agree with Judge Henry Haviland, who believed Kentucky was in the best position of any state in the Union—as long as it stayed neutral. Both political parties still officially endorsed neutrality, and he hoped they would continue to do so. He received a letter from troops in Virginia who described that state as a wasteland, and he did not want to see the same happen to Kentucky. Let the war be fought in Virginia and Tennessee, Haviland proclaimed, and spare Kentucky.[3]

Any hopes for such a happy outcome rested largely with Abraham Lincoln. When Buckner and Crittenden traveled to Washington in early July to speak with Lincoln, the president confirmed his desire to permit Kentucky neutrality. However, Lincoln also emphasized that his first duty was to suppress the rebellion. He hoped to do so with the least amount of disturbance, but nothing would stop him from fulfilling his duty.[4]

Undoubtedly, Lincoln faced a difficult situation when it came to Kentucky, but by most accounts, he handled it well. Lincoln had connections to Kentucky that he did not have with other loyal slave states, and so he treated his native state differently than Missouri and Maryland. Lincoln once said that "to lose Kentucky is to lose the whole game." Kentucky held a strategically important geographical position in the war, and Lincoln feared that if Kentucky seceded, so would Missouri and Maryland. In the other two states, he was accused of

2   *Kentucky Statesman*, June 28, 1861; *Louisville Courier*, July 1, 13, and 17, 1861.

3   Henry to Sue, July 15, 1861, in Scogin/Haviland Papers, Kentucky Historical Society.

4   Harrison and Klotter, *A New History of Kentucky*, 190-191; Crittenden to Magoffin, July 10, 1861, in Governor Beriah Magoffin Records, Kentucky State Archives.

acting hastily by sending in the army and arresting men he viewed as traitors; in Kentucky, he was far more patient. He supported Kentucky's neutrality because he knew any breach could cause Kentucky to secede. At the same time, he reserved the right to move troops into Kentucky if necessary. For the moment, he was content to marshal troops along its northern border, and he tried to recruit as many Kentuckians as possible from within the state.[5]

Most impressively, Lincoln enacted his policy toward Kentucky in the face of opposition from all sides. Northerners criticized him for allowing neutrality, or what they called half loyalty. They mostly disagreed with allowing a neutral Kentucky to trade with the Confederacy, and they accused him of allowing Magoffin too much freedom in his relations with the Confederacy. While Northerners attacked him for his leniency, Kentuckians attacked him for his severity. One Kentuckian declared that Lincoln had gone against everything he said in his inaugural address; he had claimed to want peace, but every presidential act pushed the country closer to war. One legislator told his wife that, after examining Lincoln's actions since Fort Sumter, he believed the president had prostituted the flag of the United States; Lincoln went his own way and called anyone who dared disagree with him a traitor.[6]

One man who did stand by Lincoln was Joseph Holt. On July 13, Holt addressed the people of Louisville. He did not understand why Kentucky wanted neutrality. The Federal government had done no wrong, the Constitution was intact, and the nation was economically prosperous. According to Holt, the only reason the South had seceded was because of the defeat of Breckinridge in the presidential election. He urged Kentuckians to drop neutrality and work with the Union. He hoped that the example of Virginia would help anyone who supported secession to realize the horrors of Rebellion. In Virginia, all the schools and courts were closed. The state's credit was destroyed and all its commerce gone. He asked whether Kentuckians wanted to be in the same situation. Holt wanted Kentuckians to know he was for the Union at all costs and proud to be called a submissionist. He was not a

---

5   Richard Carwardine, *Lincoln: A Life of Purpose and Power* (New York: Knopf, 2006), 175-176; Mary Allen Bernard, "Joseph Holt, Judge Advocate General, 1862-1875" (Ph.D. diss., University of Chicago, 1927), 68-69; Coulter, *The Civil War and Readjustment in Kentucky*, 54; N. S. Shaler, *Kentucky: A Pioneer Commonwealth* (Boston: Houghton Mifflin Company, 1884), 248-249.

6   Carwardine, *Lincoln,* 176-177; Father to Johnnie, May 12, 1861, in Green Family Papers, Filson Club; Henry to Anna, May 4, 1861, in Dicken-Troutman-Balke Papers, University of Kentucky; *Kentucky Statesman,* July 9, 1861.

coward, but just the opposite: he was brave enough to do his duty. He saw neutrality as an embarrassment to the state and did not understand how Kentuckians could sleep at night. Neutrality was a tool of Rebel sympathizers to stop them from doing their duty. What Lincoln did, he did from necessity. If Kentuckians saw an army marching to destroy the capital, would they not march out to meet it? That was all that Lincoln had done.[7]

Both sides criticized Holt's speech. The *Louisville Courier* had the easier task. It condemned Holt for defending Lincoln and trying to turn the state over to him. Its biggest complaint was that Holt owned no property in Kentucky, having made his residence in Washington, and so his interests were not the same as most Kentuckians. The *Louisville Courier* also criticized him for wanting Kentucky to pay some share of the war debt. The paper's editors had the difficult task of disagreeing with Holt without disagreeing with his passionate Unionism. It too condemned him for being absent during most of the struggle. When Holt said that Kentuckians should be ashamed of their position, the *Journal* believed he insulted thousands of brave and loyal people. Kentucky Unionists, argued the *Louisville Journal*, were not indifferent toward the war. They loved the Union, but they believed there was more than one way to end the Rebellion, and they did not believe violence was the answer. As noted earlier, most Unionists came to see Holt as a liability.[8]

Breckinridge, still a U.S. senator, criticized Holt for justifying Lincoln's extra-legal actions. In a speech to the Senate, he asked that Lincoln be sanctioned for his actions. It was not necessary for the president to suspend habeas corpus, to raise an army without approval of Congress, to blockade Southern ports, or to invade and imprison citizens in Missouri, Breckinridge insisted. Breckinridge, while still remaining loyal to the Union, became one of the few voices of opposition to Lincoln in the Congress. He spent much of his time fighting against resolutions that would further aid preparations for war. His peers questioned his loyalties more every day; but after July 21, doubts about his loyalties would increase.[9]

Kentucky had been laboring for months to mediate a peaceful settlement between North and South, but as cannons roared on the morning of July 21

---

7   Address of Joseph Holt at Louisville, in Frank Moore, ed., *Rebellion Record* (New York: G. P. Putman, multiple dates), Doc. 90, 297-302.

8   *Louisville Courier*, July 15, 1861; *Louisville Journal*, July 15, 1861.

9   Davis, *Breckinridge*, 269-273.

around Manassas Junction, Virginia, the chance for peace vanished. At the end of the day, and after a staggering loss of life, the Confederate Army claimed victory as the Union army retreated to Washington. The *Louisville Courier* celebrated the victory in the hope that the States Rights Party could now win some momentum in Kentucky. Once again it was the Democratic Unionists who clung to neutrality, fearing that the States Rights Party might gain more followers. The *Louisville Journal* informed readers that neutrality was still the state's best option. Kentuckians might not prosper during these terrible times, but they would be safe. The paper went on to say that it expected secessionists to use Manassas to push for secession, but it believed neutrality was rooted strongly enough in Kentucky to thwart them.[10]

Kentuckians feared that neutrality would come to an end after Manassas. One diarist proclaimed, "[The] Confederate Army victorious. The neutrality of [Kentucky] at this time is I fear only like the ominous calm before a great storm. We look to the future with anxiety and fear, least [sic] our state may become the battle ground for conflicting armies." As both sides expected, the number of men leaving the state increased after the battle. By July 25, it was reported that around fifty companies had assembled at Camp Boone in Tennessee. There were not enough arms for all the new men, so they stole weapons from Kentucky Unionists. The *Louisville Journal* reported on July 26 that 1,000 muskets and six cannons had been stolen at Maysville and sent to Tennessee. The paper suspected that both Magoffin and Senator George W. Johnson knew about the theft, but they would do nothing about it. The most prominent man to leave the state for Confederate service was Buckner. Lincoln had offered him a commission in the Union Army earlier that month, but on July 24 he resigned his position in the state to accept a generalship in the Confederate army.[11]

With the start of the fighting, Kentuckians remaining in the state and fearing they might yet be pulled into the contest had one more chance to confirm their position on neutrality in an August 5 election for a new state legislature. The Democratic Union Party had the clear advantage after victories in the preceding two elections, but fearing how Manassas might shift people's loyalties, the party did not rest on past achievements. As the *Louisville Journal*

10 *Louisville Courier*, July 23, 1861; *Louisville Journal*, July 23, 1861.

11 Wallace Diaries, July 28, 1861, in Wallace-Sterling Family Diaries, Kentucky Historical Society; *Louisville Journal*, July 26, 1861; Coulter, *Civil War and Readjustment,* 104-105; *Louisville Courier*, July 24, 1861.

stated, the future safety of Kentucky rested on staying out of the war, and staying out of the war rested on the August election. The paper believed that the only way to ensure safety was a crushing defeat of the secessionists. Unionists knew they would win, but the gains made by the States Rights Party in the June election might inspire their opponent. The outcome of this election was crucial, too, because the newly elected legislature could decide to call a secession convention. Also, the new legislature would need a large enough Democratic Unionist majority to override any effort by Magoffin to veto pro-Unionist legislation. The day of the election, the *Louisville Journal* stated how it defined the election: a vote for the Union Party meant neutrality and peace; a vote for the other side meant secession and war. This strategy had worked twice before; there was no reason to believe it would not work again.[12]

As for the States Rights Party, its members knew its chance for victory was slim. The *Louisville Courier* challenged every county to nominate a candidate for the election, even when their prospects looked dim. The paper reminded readers that things could happen before the election to sway voters to their side—especially if President Lincoln demanded more troops and money from Kentucky. The party platform had three planks: support for Governor Magoffin's proclamation of neutrality; U.S. recognition of the Confederate government as a means of ending the war; and, when the separation was completed and peace restored, secession for Kentucky and membership in the Confederacy. Such a platform makes it easy to see how the Democratic Union Party made the case that the States Rights Party was only pretending to support neutrality.[13]

However, the States Rights Party attributed similar ulterior motives to the Democratic Unionists. Their refusal to put secession to a direct vote showed that they really supported the Union. Their leaders had said that even if a majority of Kentuckians want secession, they would not allow it. They armed only those people who supported the Union, invited the governor of Indiana to send troops to Kentucky, organized an illegal army in Louisville, organized a secret society to help Lincoln, encouraged interference with trade to hurt the economy, tried to break up the State Guard, chased away Buckner, and

---

12 *Louisville Journal*, July 22 and August 5, 1861; Harrison and Klotter, *A New History of Kentucky*, 189.

13 *Louisville Courier*, June 17 and 27, July 5 and 22, 1861; *Louisville Journal*, August 3, 1861.

recruited troops to fight for the Union while they denounced men who went to Tennessee to fight for the Confederacy.[14]

Unfortunately, few records of the August election have survived. The secretary of state did not record the results and newspapers contain only a smattering of information. From the outcome it is clear that the Union party dominated. Only half the Senate seats and a portion of the House were open for election, but Democratic Unionists' control of the House grew to a margin of 76 to 24 and the Senate to 27 to 11. Speed judged that the August election verified that even if Kentucky had called a secession convention, the state would never have seceded.[15]

In retrospect, the election ended any chance of a convention. However, at the time, the threat of secession continued to haunt Unionists, as seen in a letter received by Congressman Brutus Clay. W. A. Dudley, a Unionist banker from Lexington, worried that electoral success might lead the Democratic Union Party to exceed its mandate and endorse the war. He insisted that Kentucky remain on its neutral course. In all three preceding elections, he said, the platform had been neutrality, and that stance had produced victories. If the party abandoned neutrality now, Dudley believed it would lose public confidence. If Kentucky aided the Union war effort now, Democratic Unionists would lose popular support and things could quickly change. Dudley claimed the party had, in fact, lost over 1,000 votes in the August election over the mere suspicion of breaking with neutrality. He believed that if either side abandoned neutrality, the people would swing to support the other side. The danger went beyond politics, too. Given divisions within the state, entrance into the war meant a terrible internal war between Kentuckians.[16]

The *Louisville Journal* unknowingly agreed with Dudley's assessment. It rejoiced in the Democratic Unionist victory, but urged caution among those who wished to use the triumph to justify support for the North. The newspapers agreed that even though the States Rights Party had lost in the election, it had gained ground. The increased support, surmised the *Louisville Journal*, was the result of many Union men being duped into believing it was the true party of neutrality. The *Louisville Courier* mourned the loss, but was

14 *Louisville Courier*, July 24, 1861.

15 Harrison and Klotter, *A New History of Kentucky*, 189; Thomas Speed, *The Union Cause in Kentucky* (New York: The Knickerbocker Press, 1907), 88.

16 W. A. Dudley to B. Clay, August 12, 1861, in Clay Family Papers, University of Kentucky.

encouraged by the final result. It saw States Rights numbers growing in every election, and attributed that success to Lincoln's unwise policies. The editors of the *Courier* offered as an example the election in Spencer County, where in June the Unionists won by 297 votes but in August by only six. The paper insisted that if the election had been held a month later, the States Rights Party might have won. The *Kentucky Statesman* gave the example of Fayette County, where in the June election the Unionists held a majority by 1,030 votes, whereas now it was only 667 votes. The paper claimed that even though the States Rights Party had lost, it gained more than one-fourth additional votes above the June election. The The *Louisville Courier* also thought the Democratic Unionist victory would encourage men like Holt who wanted to abandon neutrality. The inevitable backlash seemed the only hope now of giving the States Right Party the strength it needed to take the state into the Confederacy.[17]

The papers were correct in their assessment. Based on the results of the Kentucky election, Lincoln made a daring move on August 6 by ordering General William "Bull" Nelson to assemble Union troops at Camp Dick Robinson in Garrard County, near the heart of Kentucky. By the end of August, Camp Robinson was home to the 3rd, 4th, and 7th Kentucky Infantry regiments, the 1st Kentucky Cavalry regiment, Hewitt's Battery, and the 1st and 2nd Tennessee Infantry regiments.[18]

A frustrated Magoffin demanded that all Union troops be pulled from the state. He told the president that Kentucky had long since made clear its desire to take no part in the war. Lincoln responded that he did not know the details of the situation, but did not believe he had violated Kentucky neutrality since all of the men and officers were from Kentucky and had mustered close to their homes. Lincoln said, "In all I have done in the premises, I have acted upon the urgent solicitations of many Kentuckians, and in accordance with what I believed, and still believe, to be the wish of the majority of all the Union-loving people of Kentucky." He went on to rebuke Magoffin by saying, "I most cordially sympathize with your wish to preserve the peace of my own native state, Kentucky; but it is with regret I search and cannot find, in your not very short letter, any declaration or intimation, that you entertain desire for the

---

17 *Louisville Journal*, August 6 and 9, 1861; *Louisville Courier*, August 6 and 7, 1861; *Kentucky Statesman*, August 6 and 9, 1861.

18 Richard Sears, "Camp Dick Robinson," in Kleber, ed. *The Kentucky Encyclopedia*, 157-158; Harrison and Klotter, *A New History of Kentucky*, 191; Davis, *Breckinridge*, 280-281.

preservation of the Federal Union." Clearly, Lincoln had decided that Magoffin was not on his side, and he had no intention of pulling troops out of Kentucky.[19]

By August 7, Governor Magoffin also had to deal with reports that over fifteen thousand guns had been given to Kentucky loyalists. At the same time, under-armed Confederate units in Tennessee and the State Guard in Kentucky were stealing weapons. Magoffin demanded that the arms stolen in the 1st and 2nd congressional districts be returned. He also asked that artillery pieces taken from the State Guard and being held by the mayor of Hawkins be promptly returned.[20]

On August 20, a shipment of guns arrived at Lexington for use by Unionists. A band of Confederate troops under the leadership of John Hunt Morgan came into Kentucky with plans to seize the weapons. At the same time, two hundred Unionist cavalrymen from Camp Dick Robinson rode into Lexington to retrieve the guns and, as they claimed, "to pillage and reck havoc." The two sides almost came to blows. Luckily Breckinridge arrived, calmed everyone down, and the Unionists left with their weapons.[21]

The Union continued to push the boundary of neutrality. On August 22, a U.S. gunboat captured the steamer *W. B. Terry* near Paducah, which the Federals claimed was transporting goods for the new Confederacy. At the same time, Union troops crossed into Ballard County, captured two men suspected of being traitors, and held them at Cairo, Illinois. Other troops crossed over to Columbus, Kentucky, and captured a secessionist flag there. The *Louisville Courier* demanded to know why state officials allowed such blatant violations. It claimed that if Tennessee soldiers did the same, Lincoln would pour troops into the state. *Courier* editors blamed the Democratic Union Party for these incursions and charged it with breaking the agreement on neutrality. Tennessee troops occupying an island in the Mississippi River that belonged to Kentucky left when asked to do so, but the Union continued to breach neutrality with impunity.[22]

---

19 Magoffin to Lincoln, August 19, 1861, *House Journal;* Lincoln to Magoffin, August 24, 1861, ibid., *Louisville Courier,* September 5, 1861; Basler, ed., *The Collected Works of Abraham Lincoln,* IV: 497; Harrison and Klotter, *A New History of Kentucky,* 191; Davis, *Breckinridge,* 280-281.

20 *Louisville Courier,* August 6 and 7, 1861; Davis, *Breckinridge,* 280-281.

21 *Louisville Courier,* August 23, 1861; Davis, *Breckinridge,* 280-281.

22 Coulter, *Civil War and Readjustment,* 107; *Louisville Courier,* August 23, 1861.

General Gideon Pillow was the first to breach Kentucky's neutrality. Convinced that the purpose of the Union buildup in Missouri was to invade Kentucky, Pillow convinced his superiors of the need to invade first and establish Confederate forces in good position to repulse the Union. *Library of Congress*

By the end of August, and with the mounting breaches of neutrality, Kentuckians feared their days of peace were coming to an end. One diarist lamented from Hopkinsville, "The town this evening in great excitement. Secession flags flying, secession drums beating and secession men hurrahing. Our beloved Kentucky after a noble struggle for peace is, I greatly fear, about to be engulfed in the fearful strife. This country is now under going a terrible revolution, oh, when and how will peace ever be restored to this distracted nation."[23]

Kentuckians were not the only ones unnerved by this turn of events. Confederate General Gideon Pillow informed General Leonidas Polk on August 28 that U.S. forces occupied five counties in Kentucky and were planning to invade Tennessee. More arms and men entered Kentucky every day, and General John C. Frémont was preparing to capture Columbus from Missouri. Pillow pleaded with Polk to allow him to enter Kentucky first in order to protect Columbus. The recent breaches of neutrality, he said, were enough to justify the Confederate occupation of Kentucky.[24]

To help relieve some of the growing pressure, Magoffin asked Jefferson Davis once again to respect Kentucky neutrality. Magoffin acknowledged the presence of Union troops in the state, but guaranteed Davis that he had asked Lincoln to remove them. He insisted that Kentucky wanted troops from neither side. Magoffin thanked Davis for his restraint and agreed that the Confederacy, unlike the Federals, had not broken trust, but he warned Davis that many Kentuckians worried about the growing Confederate force on the Tennessee border. Davis responded that he had no intention of violating Kentucky's neutrality, but believed that he needed to mass troops on the Tennessee border for his country's protection. Davis pointed to Missouri and Maryland as evidence of what could happen without sufficient deterrent. He meant to guarantee that the Union did not invade the Confederacy through Kentucky.[25]

Unionists received another scare on August 30. On that day, John C. Frémont issued an order to free slaves in Missouri. The States Righters used the proclamation to prove that Lincoln had planned all along to abolish slavery. Joshua Speed wrote a panicked letter to Lincoln once again warning him that the government's actions had the potential to cause real harm in Kentucky. He argued against the legality of freeing slaves and insisted that Lincoln was only proving his enemies right. Slavery was so engrained in Kentucky that Speed insisted whites would kill their slaves rather than free them. Once again he pledged his allegiance to his old friend, but warned Lincoln that not all

---

23 Wallace Journal, August 28, 1861, in Wallace-Sterling Family Diaries, Kentucky Historical Society.

24 Pillow to Polk, Aug. 28, 1861, OR 3, pt. 1, 685-687.

25 Magoffin to Davis, no date, OR 4, pt. 1, 396-397; Davis to Magoffin, Aug. 28, 1861, ibid., pt. 1, 378.

Leonidas Polk, an ordained bishop in the Episcopal Church, was given the rank
of major general in the Confederate army by his friend and former West Point
classmate Jefferson Davis and sent to Tennessee's northern border. It was
Polk's decision to send General Gideon Pillow into Kentucky to occupy the
high ground before the Union army. His breach of neutrality was a major reason
the Kentucky state legislature abandoned neutrality and sided with the Union.
Library of Congress

Unionists were so loyal. Speed later wrote to Holt that Kentucky could survive many Bull Runs, but not Frémont. Happily for Speed and other Unionists, Lincoln saw the danger of pushing abolitionism at this delicate stage of the war, and he feared Frémont might cost him Kentucky. He ordered the rambunctious general to retract his proclamation.[26]

By the end of August, a major shift had occurred in Kentucky. Since January 1861, it had been the Democratic Unionists pushing neutrality, with the States Righters forced to go along. By late August, when it looked as though neutrality might disintegrate, the States Righters became the driving force to keep the state neutral.

Their last chance for success came from what they called the "peace movement." A group of peace supporters met on August 17 to call on all Kentuckians to wear white ribbons and fly white flags from their homes and businesses to show their support for peace. They called for a convention of all like-minded citizens to meet on September 10. In the meantime, the initial meeting passed a series of resolutions to reassert the devotion of Kentuckians to the Union. Kentucky had acted all through the secession crisis as the mediator to the nation, they said. Kentuckians believed that only peace brought trade, employment, and prosperity, while war yielded only destruction. The *Louisville Journal* saw the peace convention as a secessionist trick, but agreed that Unionists should send delegates to the proposed convention.[27]

However, before the peace convention could commence, Kentucky would be invaded by both sides. On September 2, Ulysses Grant, who commanded Union troops in southeast Missouri, sent Federal forces to occupy Belmont, Missouri, directly across the Mississippi River from Columbus. Confederate Generals Polk and Pillow, convinced that Grant clearly intended to take the city, decided to make the first move. Believing that the Union had already defied Kentucky neutrality by establishing Camp Robinson, Pillow invaded the state on September 3 and took the high ground above Columbus. Two days later, Grant crossed the Ohio River and occupied the town of Paducah. Over the

26 Gary Lee Williams, "James and Joshua Speed: Lincoln's Kentucky Friends" (Ph.D. diss., Duke University, 1971), 100-102; Wilson Porter Shortridge, "Kentucky Neutrality in 1861," *Mississippi Valley Historical Review*, 9 (March 1923), 298; Coulter, *Civil War and Readjustment,* 111-113; Lincoln to Fremont, September 2, 1861, OR, Series II, 1, pt. 1, 766-767.

27 *Louisville Journal,* August 15 and 24, 1861; Shortridge, "Kentucky Neutrality," 298; Seceders Resolutions, August 17, 1861, Moore, ed., *Rebellion Record,* Vol. II, Doc. 199, 533; *Louisville Courier,* August 21, 1861.

On August 6, 1861, President Lincoln ordered General William "Bull" Nelson to assemble Union troops in Garrard County at what would be called Camp Dick Robinson. The States Rights Party called the camp a breach of neutrality. However the Union disagreed, stating that all the troops were from Kentucky. *Library of Congress*

next few days, the Federal army occupied several more Kentucky towns along the Ohio River, including Louisville. Confederate General Felix Zollicoffer entered Kentucky through the Cumberland Gap to occupy towns along the state's Southern border. War had come to Kentucky. One diarist, admitting this fact, asked, "Is there anything for Kentuckians to do but fight with desperation until every presumptuous invader is driven from her soil?"[28]

Among the people most surprised and upset by the invasion were Governor Harris of Tennessee and Confederate Secretary of War Walker. Neither man had given the order to invade Kentucky, and both were concerned about the consequences. Walker ordered Pillow to withdraw his troops, but Jefferson Davis decided that necessity justified the invasion. The Federal troops were in Kentucky to stay, and so must the Rebels remain. Polk informed Magoffin that he would leave the state if Grant agreed to do the same. The *Louisville Journal* reported that Polk wanted Camp Robinson broken up as well.

---

28 Harrison and Klotter, *A New History of Kentucky*, 191-192; Coulter, *Civil War and Readjustment*, 106-108; Harrison, *The Civil War in Kentucky*, 1975, 12-13; Shaler, *Kentucky*, 250-253; Wallace Journal, September 8 and 18, 1861.

But with Union troops established in Kentucky and Federal leaders believing they were required there, Grant was not interested in giving up his position.[29]

The States Righters could see neutrality crumbling around them, and with it any hopes for secession. Seessionists, explained the *Louisville Journal*, were holding barbeques and picnics to try to rally support for neutrality. The last effort of the States Righters to keep Kentucky out of the war was the peace convention, held on September 10 and 11 in Frankfort. Delegates from seventy counties attended, most of them States Righters and men who would later join the Confederacy. After two days of debates, they issued a proclamation to the state: neutrality should be respected by both North and South, and both sides should disband their camps and pull their troops out of Kentucky. If only one side complied, Kentuckians should drive the other side out by force. They condemned the Union for starting the war and Frémont for his attempt to free slaves in Missouri. But unfortunately for the States Righters, the state had already passed the point where neutrality could be restored.[30]

Kentuckians now turned to the legislature to see how it would react to the new developments, but all they got was inactivity. The *Louisville Journal* said of the legislature, "They act in relation to the present exigency in the state as if their heads were filled with lead instead of brains and their veins with water instead of blood." Four days had passed since the invasion, announced the *Journal*, and yet the legislature had not responded. The legislators' sluggishness aided the Confederacy, the paper said, by giving the Rebels confidence. The *Journal* knew the question of loyalty in Kentucky had yet to be determined, and it worried that the Confederates might still tempt Kentuckians to join them. It wanted the legislature to renounce the invasions and call on all Kentuckians to forget party allegiance and join in common cause against all invaders. Failure to do so could only end in a divided Kentucky and an especially bloody internal war.[31]

After several days of addressing what the *Louisville Journal* called "trifling matters," the legislature on September 11 moved to embrace the Union. Both houses, the Senate by 23 to nine and the House by 71 to 26, passed resolutions that instructed Magoffin to order Confederate troops to abandon the state. A

---

29 Coulter, *Civil War and Readjustment,* 109-110; Harrison and Klotter, *A New History of Kentucky,* 191-192; *Louisville Journal,* September 13, 1861.

30 *Louisville Journal,* September 7 and 12, 1861; *Louisville Courier,* September 12, 1861; Harrison and Klotter, *A New History of Kentucky,* 192; Coulter, *Civil War and Readjustment,* 113-114.

31 *Louisville Journal,* September 10 and 11, 1861.

resolution was also proposed in the House to request the Federal army to leave, but it was rejected 68 to 29. The Senate entertained proposals to withhold state funds and tax revenues from the Union government, but it voted on neither proposal. Clearly, the political competition that once had existed in the legislature was gone and Unionists dominated the state.[32]

General Buckner responded to the legislature's action on September 12 in a public letter to the people of Kentucky. He could not understand why Unionists allowed the North to breach its neutrality, yet insisted that Confederate troops evacuate the state. Buckner accused the Union of being the worst of the two culprits. It was President Lincoln, he argued, who had insisted that Kentucky was either with him or against him. Indeed, Lincoln had lured Kentucky into a false sense of security by seeming to accept neutrality and promising not to send in troops, only to send secret shipments of arms to Unionists and actively recruit troops in the state. Lincoln had destroyed the Constitution and set himself up as a military dictator. Buckner claimed further that the legislature had abandoned the people, and he called on all true Kentuckians to show their mothers that they were still men and to let their wives know they would protect them.[33]

Despite Buckner's pleas, most Kentuckians believed it was the Confederacy that had first breached neutrality, and so they accepted the legislature's tilt toward the Union. But Magoffin tried to defy the shift. He insisted that the people of Kentucky had three times voted for the state to remain neutral. He told the legislature that he would only sign a resolution that required both belligerents to abandon the state. Yet, given the current makeup and stance of the legislature, Magoffin's veto did little good. On September 13, the Senate voted 25 to nine to override Magoffin's veto, and the House did the same, 68 to 26.[34]

On the same day, the Unionist-controlled House introduced a measure that acknowledged the power of the U.S. Congress to tax the people of Kentucky as part of the war effort. This was the same proposal the Senate had failed to move on two days earlier; momentum for the Union was building. The House further stated that the war had indisputably been started by the Rebels, and that the

---

32 *Louisville Journal*, September 10, 1861; *Senate Journal*, 85-89, *House Journal*, 81-84.

33 General Buckner's Address, Moore, ed., *Rebellion Record*, Vol. III, Doc. 44, 126-128.

34 *House Journal*, 101-104; *Senate Journal*, 99-101.

Union was only trying to protect Kentucky. The measure passed on September 17, 71 to 22.[35]

Finally, on September 18, the legislature took the ultimate step. In the House, five resolutions were put forward and passed. The first stated that all Confederates should be expelled from the state and Federal troops should be called on for assistance. It passed 73 to 23. Second, it was recommended that Robert Anderson should be placed in charge of all Kentucky troops and a call for volunteers be issued to help protect the state. It passed 69 to 27. A motion that no citizen should be molested for his political views or have his property confiscated passed 69 to three. A motion that Magoffin should ask Colonel Thomas Crittenden to move his Indiana troops into the state passed 72 to 24. Finally, every citizen was asked to assist in pushing out the enemy. This passed 73 to 24.[36]

Magoffin vetoed all five resolutions. He continued to insist that neutrality required both Confederates and Federals to pull out. He objected to giving Anderson power over the military forces in Kentucky. He, as governor, should be commander of Kentucky forces, not the military board and especially not an officer of the Federal government. If that role was taken over by Federal authorities, Kentuckians would lose all power to control the destiny of their state. Magoffin did not want anyone to interfere with his direction of the State Guard. He wanted to use the troops to enforce peace, while the Union wanted to use them for war.

Magoffin's veto of the resolutions was once again overridden, this time by a vote of 69 to 21. Magoffin then capitulated and, following the will of the legislature, sent a letter to the Confederacy demanding the withdrawal of its troops. He then issued a public proclamation that the Confederate army must leave and that Anderson should use state forces to drive them out if they did not leave on their own.[37]

After a long and difficult struggle, Kentucky's neutrality had come to an end. However, the struggle to control Kentucky had just begun. Neither

---

35 *House Journal*, 104-105.

36 *House Journal*, 153-158. The three voting "no" to the third resolution were A. B. Chambers from Gallatin County, E. F. Burns from Owen County, and George Silvertooth from Mercer County. Gallatin and Owen counties are in the extreme north of Kentucky and Mercer County is in the Bluegrass region.

37 *House Journal*, 175-177; *Louisville Journal*, September 23, 1861.

militarily nor politically were the States Rights men willing to concede defeat, and the issue of who would direct the ultimate course of the state had yet to be determined.

C hapter 10

After Neutrality:
September to December 1861

I n the wake of Kentucky's decision to throw its support with the Union, the political environment in the Commonwealth changed. Several important men in the state were arrested on September 19. Martin Bart, the telegraph agent for the Associated Press, was taken into custody because of his Confederate sympathies and for using his position to help the South. Reuben Durrett, editor of the *Louisville Courier*, was arrested for writing "treasonous" editorials. The *Courier* was closed on the same day of his arrest. Lastly, Charles Morehead, Kentucky's former governor, was arrested for actively promoting rebellion in the Commonwealth. Morehead had been a Whig and a Know-Nothing and was considered a Unionist until after the Rebels fired upon and captured Fort Sumter. Once that momentous event occurred, Morehead had come out for succession the following month. However, he also made it clear that if Northern troops invaded the South, Kentucky should defend its Southern friends. In July, the *Courier* reported that Morehead stood accused of meeting with Isham Harris, the governor of Tennessee, for the purpose of obtaining assistance from that state to help Kentucky secede—a charge Morehead flatly denied. But on September 19, the former governor of Kentucky was pulled from his home in the middle of the night and hauled away to the nearest judge to stand trial. Fortunately for Morehead, his friend Judge

Sneed took possession of the prisoner while en route and escorted him to an Indiana prison for protection.[1]

Morehead's arrest sparked a firestorm of debate. President Lincoln received a letter from a Unionist asking for his release. The author claimed that Morehead's arrest was not necessary. He acknowledged that Morehead had feelings for the South, but everyone knew that his greatest wish was for the restoration of the Union. Morehead had condemned secession, and had only criticized the government when it suspended habeas corpus. Other people thought all of the arrests were justified. Joseph Holt said that the men arrested could not be trusted. They fell to their knees and swore allegiance to the United States, then stabbed the government in the back as they stood up, he said. Still, General Robert Anderson asked William Henry Seward on October 2 to release the prisoners, worried that their arrest would have an injurious effect on the Union cause. After four months in a Northern prison, and after local Kentucky leaders had pleaded for his return, Morehead was released, but he left the country for the duration of the war.[2]

Also on September 19, the legislature issued a warrant of arrest for John C. Breckinridge. Troops were sent from Camp Robinson to Lexington to ensure his capture. People who knew Breckinridge knew he was not a traitor and had never supported secession. In his last speech to the Senate on August 3, he declared that he still hoped to end the war and save the Union. He still hoped there was a chance for compromise; but, if not, the North should allow the South to leave peacefully. He did not consider this a treasonous idea, but he agreed to resign his position as senator if Kentuckians disagreed with him. His biographer, William C. Davis, described Breckinridge's dilemma. His allegiance was divided between the two sides. In the Confederacy, explained Davis, he had close friends and family, including his sixteen-year-old son, who had run off to join the Confederate army. His sympathies rested with the South. Joining the Confederacy, however, would kill his political career in the North and force him

---

1   Case of Charles Morehead, *OR*, Series II, 2, pt. 1, 85; Mary Allen Bernard, "Joseph Holt, Judge Advocate General, 1862-1875" (Ph.D. diss., University of Chicago, 1927), 2-4; Kirwan, *John J. Crittenden*, 455; *Louisville Courier*, July 18, 1861; *Louisville Journal*, May 28, 1861. The "Judge Sneed" mentioned was Judge Joseph Sneed.

2   G. Prentice to Lincoln, September 24, 1861, *OR*, Series II, 2, pt. 1, 807; Bernard, "Joseph Holt," 3-5; Lowell H. Harrison, "Charles Slaughter Morehead," in Kleber, ed., *The Kentucky Encyclopedia*, 648; Robert Anderson to Will Seward, October 2, 1861, *OR* Series II, vol. II, pt. 886-887.

Joseph Holt was appointed both as postmaster general and secretary of war under President James Buchanan. With Abraham Lincoln's election, Holt returned to Kentucky and fought to keep the state loyal to the Union. He quickly became the voice of the unconditional Unionists. He was appointed judge advocate general in 1862, and is most famous today for his role in the trial of Lincoln's assassins in 1865. *Library of Congress*

to renounce the Constitution he so loved. In the North he also had friends and family, and Breckinridge believed he would be the lone voice of opposition to the Republicans and what he saw as an unholy war.[3]

In early September, when both armies invaded the Commonwealth, Breckinridge did not think either action justified the desertion of neutrality. He spent most of the month speaking around the state about the importance of remaining neutral. On September 9, he spoke to a crowd of 10,000 people. The next day, as rumors circulated that he would be arrested, Breckinridge ignored future engagements to avoid being captured. When the legislature then sided with the Union and began to arrest suspected traitors, Breckinridge knew he had to act. With the troops from Camp Robinson approaching Lexington, he snuck out of town and went to Tennessee to join the Confederate Army. He justified his action, not by embracing secession, but by saying he did not want to sit in prison like Morehead, without a trial and for a crime he had not committed. Breckinridge may have made a smart decision. On September 28, Anderson received a reply to his request to William Seward. The secretary of state told him to check with James Guthrie or James Speed, but that, in his opinion, habeas corpus should remain suspended and all men accused of disloyalty imprisoned in Indiana.[4]

While the legislature debated whether to side with the Union and men were being arrested, the Confederate army went into action. The army, under command of Buckner, moved into Kentucky and established itself at Bowling Green on September 18. Buckner found Bowling Green a strong Unionist town, as typified by one resident who exclaimed, "The Philistines are upon us." Buckner addressed the people of Kentucky in an open letter meant to justify his actions. He focused on the tyrannical Lincoln, who, Buckner claimed, had required Kentuckians to choose between despotism and liberty. He said that Lincoln had lied to Kentuckians. As in Virginia and Missouri, he had promised peace, but all the while he was organizing the army to invade. Buckner, by

---

3 Davis, *Breckinridge*, 274-278; James C. Klotter, "John Cabell Breckinridge," in Kleber, *The Kentucky Encyclopedia*, 117-118.

4 Davis, *Breckinridge*, 282-287; Klotter, "John Cabell Breckinridge," in Kleber, ed., *The Kentucky Encyclopedia*, 117-118; William Seward to Robert Anderson, September 28, 1861, *OR* Series II, 2, pt. 1, 885. Other men arrested for treason: September 24: William Grubbs, Henry Thurber, Frank Crow, Stephen Wooldridge, Joseph McFeal, Joseph Back, William Carney, Lewis Holclaw; October 2: William Casto, Isaac Nelson, George Foster, B. F. Thomas William Hunt, and James Hall.

contrast, declared himself a liberator, not an aggressor. He had come back to Kentucky to help the people protect their wives and mothers from savages. He still loved the Constitution, but he feared the Union was no longer governed by the Constitution. He called on Kentuckians to set aside their differences and unite to repulse the common enemy. The members of the legislature had sold their birthright to Lincoln, who wanted to enslave them. Only a united Kentucky could stop him.[5]

In reply, General Anderson wrote his own letter to the Commonwealth. He feared the Union invasion might, as Anna Dicken had told Henry Rust, unite every honest States Rights' man in Kentucky. Anderson reminded the Commonwealth that he had been appointed by the legislature and came to enforce their laws, not to make his own. He reminded Kentuckians that the Confederates had first invaded the state and broken neutrality, and that it was they who must be driven out. To counter Anderson's argument, General Albert Sidney Johnston proclaimed, as had Buckner, that the Confederates had not entered Kentucky as a hostile army, but to let the Commonwealth have the freedom to choose whom to support without pressure from the Federal army.[6]

With neutrality abandoned, both armies received eager recruits. A statistical review of who fought for whom would seem to be another convincing argument for the strength of Unionism in Kentucky. No one is certain of the exact numbers, but there is general agreement that 90,000 troops fought for the Union while only 30,000 to 40,000 troops fought for the Confederacy. If the number of men who fought is seen as a reflection of how a vote on secession might have ended, then the argument for Kentucky being overwhelmingly Unionist is a good one.[7]

However, more than simply the total numbers, the sequence of enlistments is interesting. When looking at when men signed up, around 2,062 Kentuckians enlisted with the Union before the invasion in September, while 6,311 men enlisted with the Confederacy. Noting the uneven results, General Thomas

---

5 Harrison, *The Civil War in Kentucky*, 16-19; "To the People of Kentucky from Simon Buckner," September 17, 1861, in Simon Buckner Family Papers, Kentucky Historical Society.

6 Anna to Henry, September 17, 1861, in Dicken-Troutman-Balke Papers, University of Kentucky; Proclamation of General Anderson, September 21, 1861, in Moore, ed., *Rebellion Record*, Vol. III, doc. 56, 145; Proclamation from A. S. Johnston, September 22, 1861, *OR*, Series I, vol. 4, pt. 420-421.

7 *House Journal*, 240-244; Coulter, *The Civil War and Readjustment in Kentucky*, 248; Harrison and Klotter, *A New History of Kentucky*, 195.

informed Simon Cameron that all the young men in Kentucky supported the Rebels, and many were joining their army. Only the old men, too old to fight, he said, supported the Union. William T. Sherman also complained about the lack of support for the Union. He had called for 42,000 volunteers but received only 29,000 as late as December 1861. Nor did the Federals apparently trust the allegiance of these recruits, as seen by their reluctance to give Union troops in Kentucky proper supplies. So before the end of neutrality, it seemed as if popular support was with the Confederacy as far as troop strength.[8]

Union Enlistments Before September 5, 1861				
Regiment	*Company*	*Strength*	*Enlistment Month*	*Location of Enlistment*
Infantry				
1st Kentucky				
	A	42	April	Clay, OH
	B	46	May	Clay, OH
	C	39	June	Clay, OH
	D	38	July	Clay, OH
	F	43	June	Clay, OH
	G	38	July	Clay, OH
	H	37	May	Clay, OH
	I	42	May	Clay, OH
	K	43	May	Clay, OH

8   Adjunct General, *Report of the Adjunct General of the State of Kentucky* (Frankfort: Harney Press, 1876), 3-768; Adjunct General, *Report of the Adjunct General of the State of Kentucky, Confederate Kentucky Volunteers, War 1861-1865* (Utica: Cook and McDowell, 1980), 2-486; L. Thomas to Simon Cameron, October 21, 1861, OR, Series 1, vol. 4, pt. 313-314; Harrison, *The Civil War in Kentucky*, 14-15; Coulter, *Civil War and Readjustment*, 128-130.

Regiment	Company	Strength	Enlistment Month	Location of Enlistment
2nd Kentucky				
	A	37	May	Pendleton, IN
	B	40	May	Pendleton, IN
	C	37	May	Pendleton, IN
	D	27	June	Pendleton, IN
	E	34	June	Pendleton, IN
	F	38	June	Pendleton, IN
	G	25	June	Pendleton, IN
	H	41	June	Pendleton, IN
	I	42	June	Pendleton, IN
	K	37	May	Pendleton, IN
3rd Kentucky				
	B	29	August	Dick Robinson, KY
	C	20	August	Dick Robinson, KY
	E	13	August	Dick Robinson, KY
	F	22	July	Dick Robinson, KY
	G	26	August	Dick Robinson, KY
	H	20	August	Dick Robinson, KY
	I	38	July	Dick Robinson, KY
	K	29	July	Dick Robinson, KY
6th Kentucky				
	A	29	July	Joe Holt, IN

Regiment	Company	Strength	Enlistment Month	Location of Enlistment
	B	30	July	Joe Holt, IN
	C	28	July	Joe Holt, IN
	D	18	July	Joe Holt, IN
	E	24	July	Joe Holt, IN
	F	25	July	Joe Holt, IN
	G	23	July	Joe Holt, IN
	H	30	July	Joe Holt, IN
	I	20	July	Joe Holt, IN
	K	25	July	Joe Holt, IN
7th Kentucky				
	A	35	August	Dick Robinson, KY
	B	24	August	Dick Robinson, KY
	C	7	August	Dick Robinson, KY
	D	43	August	Dick Robinson, KY
	E	26	August	Dick Robinson, KY
	F	26	August	Dick Robinson, KY
	G	19	August	Dick Robinson, KY
	H	31	August	Dick Robinson, KY
	I	23	August	Dick Robinson, KY
	K	16	August	Dick Robinson, KY

Regiment	Company	Strength	Enlistment	Location of Enlistment
1st Kentucky Cavalry				
	A	55	July	Dick Robinson, KY
	B	55	July	Dick Robinson, KY
	C	48	July	Dick Robinson, KY
	D	34	Sept	Dick Robinson, KY
	E	39	Sept	Dick Robinson, KY
	F	40	Sept	Dick Robinson, KY
	G	33	Sept	Dick Robinson, KY
	H	57	Sept	Dick Robinson, KY
	I	31	Sept	Dick Robinson, KY
	J	49	Oct	Dick Robinson, KY
2nd Kentucky Cavalry				
	A	74	Sept	Muldrough Hill, KY
	B	66	August	Muldrough Hill, KY
	C	61	August	Muldrough Hill, KY

Union Table Notes

The 4th, 5th, and 18th to 27th infantry regiments enlisted between September and December 1861; The 28th to 45th infantry regiments enlisted between 1862 and 1865; The 3rd to 6th cavalry regiments enlisted between September and December 1861; The 7th to 17th cavalry regiments enlisted between 1862 and 1865; No artillery units enlisted before September 5, 1861; Total number of Union Kentucky troops: 2,062.

Confederate Enlistments Before September 5, 1861				
Infantry				
Regiment	*Company*	*Strength*	*Enlistment Month*	*Location of Enlistment*
1st Kentucky				
	A	110	April	Louisville, KY
	B	79	April	Louisville, KY
	C	113	April	Louisville, KY
	D	94	April	Louisville, KY
	E	124	April	Nashville, TN
	F	104	April	Murray, KY
	G	101	June	Owensboro, KY
	H	125	June	Louisville, KY
	I	93	May	New Orleans, LA
	K	107	June	Keysburg, KY
2nd Kentucky				
	A	185	July	Boone, TN
	B	141	July	Boone, TN
	C	181	July	Boone, TN
	D	152	July	Boone, TN
	E	142	July	Boone, TN
	F	134	July	Boone, TN
	G	146	July	Boone, TN

Regiment	Company	Strength	Enlistment Month	Location of Enlistment
	H	174	July	Boone, TN
	I	152	July	Boone, TN
	K	148	July	Boone, TN
3rd Kentucky				
	A	181	July	Boone, TN
	B	237	July	Boone, TN
	C	132	July	Boone, TN
	D	173	July	Boone, TN
	E	156	July	Boone, TN
	G	91	July	Boone, TN
	H	161	July	Boone, TN
	I	118	July	Boone, TN
	K	159	July	Boone, TN
	L	144	July	Boone, TN
	M	162	July	Corinth, MS
4th Kentucky				
	A	129	August	Glasgow, KY
	B	141	August	Henderson, KY
	C	170	August	Burnett, TN
	D	171	August	Burnett, TN
	E	155	August	Burnett, TN
	F	133	August	Burnett, TN

Regiment	Company	Strength	Enlistment Month	Location of Enlistment
	G	139	August	Burnett, TN
	H	130	August	Burnett, TN
	I	203	August	KY and TN
	K	162	Sept	Burnett, TN
Artillery				
Bell's Battery		78		
Cobb's Battery		244		
B. T. White's Light Artillery		137		

Table Notes

No Confederate cavalry regiments enlisted before September 5, 1861. The total number of Confederate Kentucky troops: 6,311.

*   *   *

By the end of the war, Unionism would appear to have triumphed in Kentucky as far as enlistments, but again there is more to the numbers. To begin with, around 24,000 black troops made up over a quarter of the 90,000 Union troops from Kentucky. Without the black troops, that leaves 66,000 troops fighting for the North. That was still at least 26,000 more than the number fighting for the Rebels, but two other factors should be considered in judging Union sentiment. First, Kentucky was subject to the Union draft but not the Confederate, which leads to the conclusion that at least some men were forced to fight for the Union. Second, many historians suggest that elsewhere men fought for the Confederacy due to loyalty to their state. After the Confederates invaded Kentucky, the state sided with the Union, and floods of Kentuckians joined the Federal army. Historian Daniel Crofts and others explain how many Southerners in border states that seceded, such as Virginia,

North Carolina, and Tennessee, supported the Union but joined the
Confederacy out of loyalty to their states. The most famous example is Robert
E. Lee, whose biographer, Douglas Southall Freeman, has chronicled the story
of Lee's difficult decision to fight against the Union.[9]

When it comes to troops, even after the Commonwealth ended neutrality,
most of its citizens did not. The 90,000 men who fought only made up 29
percent of those eligible. Seventy-one percent of the men instead decided not to
fight, the highest percentage of all the slave states. It can be conjectured that
some Kentuckians were loyal to the South but could not fight against their state,
so instead chose not to fight at all. Others may have taken neutrality to heart.[10]

The same triumph of state loyalty over sectional beliefs may be seen in
politics. For example, after early compromise efforts failed, Governor Magoffin
took up the cause of neutrality as the best chance for peace in Kentucky. Only
after Fort Sumter and Lincoln's call for troops did Magoffin advocate
secession. However, Magoffin never abandoned Kentucky for the Confederacy
as many other secession proponents did. Even after the August elections, in
which the Democratic Union Party dominated, the invasion of Kentucky by the
Confederacy, and the official endorsement by Kentucky of the Union,
Magoffin stood by Kentucky. He did not agree with the decision to remain
loyal, but he believed in following the will of the people. The only loyalty men
like Magoffin held more strongly than their devotion to either North or South
was their loyalty to Kentucky.[11]

Something similar happened in Virginia and Arkansas. Both John Janney of
Virginia and David Walker of Arkansas, the presidents of their respective
secession conventions, were strong supporters of the Union. They did all in
their power during their tenures as convention presidents to keep their states
loyal. However, after a majority within their states decided to secede, both men
followed their states into the Confederacy. Janney never did vote for secession,
but Walker did, so as to present a unified front. Another example came from
Texas, where James Throckmorton stood when it came time for him to vote on
secession and said, "Mr. President, in view of the responsibility, in the presence
of God and my country—and unawed by the wild spirit around me, I vote no!"

---

9 Harrison and Klotter, *A New History of Kentucky,* 179, 195-196.

10 William Freehling, *The South vs. The South* (Oxford: Oxford University Press, 2001), 54.

11 Harrison and Klotter, *A New History of Kentucky,* 194, Lowell H. Harrison, "Beriah
Magoffin," in Kleber, *The Kentucky Encyclopedia,* 603-604.

He fought against secession until the time when Texas joined the Confederacy, at which point he joined the Confederate army, in which he eventually reached the rank of brigadier general.[12]

If men were reluctant to fight for the Confederacy but did so out of allegiance to their states, then the same is likely true of men reluctant to fight for the Union but who did so out of loyalty to the state. On October 8, one legislator received a letter from his sweetheart stating that men were claiming a higher allegiance to the state than to Washington. She understood such allegiance when men's states seceded, but because Kentucky had stayed with the Union, their Rebellion was inexcusable.[13]

By October, Kentucky was a state under siege; both armies were growing and preparing to fight. One Kentucky Confederate soldier wrote to his wife from Bowling Green, "I feel I am fighting for civil liberty and in that cause I feel that all men capable of bearing arms should be in the service." Another man wrote to his girlfriend in the same month to explain why he must fight for the Union. He did not want to leave her to fight, but his conscience required him to give up everything to protect his nation from the tyrannical oppressors who had invaded the state. "The confederate troops have been coming in all day," exclaimed another man of the buildup in his part of the state. "The Union men have disbanded and secreted their arms, their force being too small to risk an engagement." Josie Underwood, a strong Unionist, had plenty to say about Confederates occupying her town of Bowling Green. Her main complaint was that Rebel soldiers came to her home begging for food, which her mother gave to them. The family would not allow them in the house, however, after they tore down the U.S. flag. When an old friend who had become a Confederate soldier asked if he could call on her, Josie agreed, but warned that she would not receive him in a Southern uniform. Matters on the other side were not much better. One man described what he called a reign of terror in Kentucky, with Confederate supporters fearing for their lives. He believed Southerners were

---

12 James Finck, "Honor and Duty to God and State: John Janney and the Virginia Secession Convention" (M.A. thesis, Virginia Tech, 2002); Robert Childers, "The Secession Crisis and Civil War in Arkansas Through the Eyes of Judge David Walker, Conditional Southern Unionist from Fayetteville" (M.A. thesis, University of Arkansas, 2001); T. R. Fehrenback, *Lone Star: A History of Texas and the Texans* (New York: American Legacy Press, 1983), 344-348.

13 Anna to Henry, October 8, 1861, in Dicken-Troutman-Balke Papers, University of Kentucky.

taking the oath to the Union only to save their property, lest they lose everything they owned.[14]

By the end of October, secessionists, knowing the legislature was completely Unionist but still believing that most Kentuckians supported the Confederacy, met for a state convention to decide what their relationship should be to the Federal government. They met on October 29 and 30 at Russellville, in Logan County, behind Confederate lines. The meeting was led by Breckinridge and George Johnson. Johnson was born in Georgetown, Kentucky, educated at Transylvania University, and made his living as a farmer. His first public office came in 1838 when he was elected to the state legislature. He served for three years. After the election of Lincoln to the presidency, Johnson came out against secession; but after Sumter, he began supporting the Confederacy. After Kentucky officially endorsed the Union, Johnson fled the Commonwealth and, although fifty years old, became a military aide to Buckner.[15]

Representatives from 32 counties arrived for the meeting. None had been officially elected, merely self appointed. They condemned the state legislature for breaking with neutrality and blocking a vote of the people on a secession convention. They still wanted Magoffin to insist on a state convention, one held outside the Union army's sphere of influence. Since they knew the impossibility of their request being granted, they issued their own call for a convention, to be held in Russellville on November 18.[16]

In the meantime, the big issue for the Commonwealth was slavery. Anson McCook, commander of Camp Nevin, informed William T. Sherman on November 5 that runaway slaves had become a major annoyance. That day, ten blacks had arrived in his camp, and he expected more. All claimed that their masters were secessionist and that some had even joined the Confederate army.

14 Letter to James Davis, October 24, 1861, in Berie Cain Papers, Western Kentucky University; B.H. Helm to Emile, October 10, 1861, in Emile Todd Helm Papers, Kentucky Historical Society; Unknown, October 29, 1861, in Thomas Robert McBeath Papers, University of Kentucky; Wallace Journal, October 1 and 9, 1861, in Wallace-Sterling Family Diaries, Kentucky Historical Society; Josie Nazro Diary, September 20 and 22, 1861, in Underwood Collection, Western Kentucky University; W. Gass to W. Caswell, October 14, 1861, OR, Series I, Vol. 4, pt. 447-448.

15 Harrison, *The Civil War in Kentucky*, 20; Lowell H. Harrison, "George W. Johnson," in Kleber, *The Kentucky Encyclopedia*, 473.

16 Harrison, *The Civil War in Kentucky*, 20-22; Coulter, *Civil War and Readjustment*, 137.

McCook knew that to allow the slaves to remain in camp could hurt the Union cause in Kentucky, but wondered how much that mattered. He told Sherman, who had replaced Anderson as Union commander, that he had no faith in the loyalty of Kentucky and saw no reason to protect slavery. However, as a matter of policy, he wanted to know how to handle the slave issue. Sherman replied on November 8 that the property laws of Kentucky were still in place and that all refugee slaves should be returned to their owners. In fact, Henry Halleck, commander of the Western Theater, had received a communication the previous day from Washington stressing that political affairs in Kentucky were more important than military considerations. The army in Kentucky must not give Kentuckians the wrong impression; it was there to maintain the Union, not to free slaves. That this was clearly the expectation of slave owners in the state could be seen at a November 23 meeting of Unionist men. They sent a declaration to the Commonwealth to emphasize that the government had no power to interfere with slavery and that arming slaves was a violation both of civilized warfare and of the will of God. Arming slaves would lead to the murder and rape of whites by blacks.[17]

On November 18, the Russellville secession convention met. One hundred and fifteen men arrived at the convention from 68 counties. Willis Machen was elected president of the convention. Machen had been elected to the state Senate in 1854, and from 1856 to 1860 he served in the State House of Representatives. During the secession crisis, Machen had been a strong supporter of secession and the Confederacy. He, therefore, agreed with the delegates who now argued that the Constitution gave the government only certain powers, and that the U. S. government had overstepped those powers. Besides the offences of the Federal government, delegates also condemned Kentucky's legislature for deceiving the people, breaking its pledge of neutrality, and inviting an invading army into the Commonwealth.[18]

On December 4, the Committee on Federal Relations delivered its report to the convention. It insisted that the only thing binding Kentucky to the Union was the U.S. Constitution, and that since that Constitution had been violated,

---

17 A. McCook to W. Sherman, November 5, 1861, *OR*, Series II, vol. 1, pt. 776; Field, 520; Headquarters to Halleck, November 7, 1861, *OR*, Series I, vol. 5, pt. 38; Meeting in Kentucky of Union Men, November 23, 1861; Moore, *Rebellion Record*, Vol. III, Doc. 186, 415-416.

18 Harrison, *The Civil War in Kentucky*, 20-21; Ordinance of Secession, November 20, 1861; Moore, *Rebellion Record*, Vol. 1, Doc. 23, 164-165; Meeting of the Provisional Government at Russellville, November 20, 1861, typed transcript, Filson Club.

every state was free to choose its own association. The non-slave states had united to impose a "tyrannous military despotism" on Maryland, Delaware, and Missouri, but that should not deter Kentucky from siding with the Confederacy. On December 10, the delegates voted to secede from the Union and join the Confederate States. They were received into the Confederacy on the same day. The new provisional legislature was to be made up of one hundred members elected as soon as the state was freed from the enemy. Until elections could be held, the new government would be led by a governor and ten men, one from each district. They would retain and follow the same state constitution, changing only those provisions inconsistent with the laws of the convention. George Johnson was chosen as provisional governor; Bowling Green was made the capital. On December 28, the new government issued orders for 30 infantry regiments and five cavalry regiments to be formed to drive out the Federal invaders. All men between 18 and 40 were required to either volunteer or give up their weapons. Failure to comply meant arrest.[19]

Magoffin denounced the new government and claimed it did not represent the people. Magoffin had tried to protect Kentucky, but by the end of the year, sides had been chosen, armies raised, neutrality killed, and the political battle over the state's fate decided.[20]

Kentucky never became the battleground its people once feared. Most of the major fighting in the Western Theater occurred to the south, in Tennessee. However, Kentuckians were not completely spared, either. The first major battle in the state occurred on January 19, 1862, when Confederate forces were defeated at Mill Springs. In February, Ulysses S. Grant captured Fort Henry and Fort Donelson in Tennessee. With the loss at Mill Spring and the two forts, Confederate General Albert Sidney Johnston pulled his forces out of Kentucky, all the way back to Mississippi.

Hoping to "liberate" Kentuckians, Confederate forces entered the state in August of 1862 and captured Frankfort on September 3. Richard Hawes was sworn in on October 4 as the new provisional state governor. Four days later the main Confederate army under Gen. Braxton Bragg was fought to a stalemate at Perryville, the bloodiest battle waged on Kentucky soil. Bragg retreated back through the Cumberland Gap and out of the Commonwealth.

---

19 Proceedings of the Convention Held at Russellville, Dec. 4, 10, and 28, 1861, typed manuscript, Filson Club; Harrison, *The Civil War in Kentucky*, 20-21.

20 Harrison, *The Civil War in Kentucky,* 20-21.

General U. S. Grant eventually became commanding general of all Union troops and later president of the United States. When the war began, he served in the Western Theater, where he was ordered to take Belmont, Missouri, across the Mississippi River from Columbus, Kentucky. His thrust there prompted the Confederacy to invade Kentucky, under the assumption that Grant intended to invade first and occupy the high ground. *Library of Congress*

That was the last conventional battle in the state, and a Confederate army would never again enter it. However, Kentucky was subject to raids and guerrilla warfare throughout the conflict. Indeed, perhaps reflecting its fierce political division of 1861, its guerrilla war was one of the most bitter, bloody, and prolonged in the entire South.[21]

As for the provisional government of 1861, it was forced to abandon its capital when the Confederate army left Bowling Green. It thereafter traveled with the army. During the battle of Shiloh, Governor Johnson joined with the 4th Kentucky Infantry in an assault and was mortally wounded. Hawes was chosen as his successor. Once again, the provisional government was forced to follow the Confederate Army out of the state after the loss at Perryville. The government would remain in exile for the remainder of the war.[22]

Beriah Magoffin continued to serve as the governor of the legitimate state of Kentucky, even though Unionists in the legislature, never fully trusting him, slowly stripped him of his authority through legislation. Finally, in August of 1862, Magoffin reached a deal with the legislature. He agreed to resign if Senator James Robinson, a conservative Unionist, replaced him because Robinson would respect the rights of Southern sympathizers. Linn Boyd, Magoffin's former lieutenant governor, had died in office three years earlier, but Magoffin never filled the position because the Senate Speaker in 1859, John Fisk, would have been next in line for the governorship. Robinson was elected Speaker of the Senate on September 2, 1861, but had resigned a few days later. With Magoffin's blessing, he once again assumed that post on August 16, 1862. Two days later on the morning of August 18, Robinson succeeded Magoffin when he gave up the governorship. Magoffin returned to his law practice until 1867, when he was elected to the Kentucky House of Representatives. He urged Kentuckians to accept the outcome of the war and the Thirteenth Amendment. He died in 1885.[23]

---

21 Harrison and Klotter, *A New History of Kentucky*, 197-204. For information on the guerrilla war, see Benjamin F. Cooling, *Fort Donelson's Legacy: War and Society in Kentucky and Tennessee, 1862-1863* (Knoxville: University of Tennessee Press, 1977); Robert Mackey, *The Uncivil War: Irregular Warfare in the Upper South, 1861-1865* (Norman: University of Oklahoma Press, 2004); Daniel Southerland, *A Savage Conflict* (Chapel Hill: University of North Carolina Press, 2009).

22 Harrison and Klotter, *A New History of Kentucky*, 193-194.

23 Harrison and Klotter, *A New History of Kentucky*, 194; Lowell H. Harrison, "Beriah Magoffin," in Kleber, *The Kentucky Encyclopedia*, 603-604.

Crittenden continued to serve in the U.S. House of Representatives. In July 1861, he introduced a resolution stating that the war was not being fought to end slavery. It passed. He remained in office until his death in July 1863.[24]

Simon B. Buckner surrendered to U. S. Grant at Fort Donelson in February 1862, but was exchanged in time to take part in the invasion of Kentucky later that summer. He saw extensive action in the Western and Trans-Mississippi theaters and surrendered with Gen. Edmund Kirby Smith in 1865. In 1887, Buckner was elected as the Democratic governor of Kentucky and served until 1891. He left the Democratic Party in 1896 when it nominated William Jennings Bryan and ran for vice president on the Gold Democratic ticket. Buckner died in January 1914.[25]

After John C. Breckinridge resigned his position in the U.S. Senate, he was commissioned a Confederate general and commanded a corps in the battles of Shiloh, Murfreesboro, Chickamauga, and Chattanooga. Directing his own command, he was victorious at the battle of New Market, in Virginia, before joining Jubal Early in the 1864 raid on Washington. In February 1865, he was appointed Confederate secretary of war and held that position when the end came. Breckinridge escaped with the rest of the Confederate government after Appomattox. He made his way down to Florida and from there to Cuba. He remained an expatriate for four years, until receiving amnesty. He returned to Kentucky and worked as a lawyer and president of a local railroad. He died in May 1875.[26]

November 1860 to November 1861 was a trying year for Kentuckians. They watched the nation they loved fall apart around them, while they did all in their power to find a peaceful solution to its problems. Yet, no matter how hard they tried, they could not seem to heal the wounds. In compromise after compromise, they insisted that war could be avoided; yet war came. Kentuckians were left with just one option if they were to avoid the war: to remain neutral. Neutrality was first proposed in early January, but the legislature did not accept it until April, after the fall of Fort Sumter.

Kentucky's neutrality came about for several reasons. First, the state's geographical position placed it in grave danger if war came. It had a 700-mile

24 Lowell H. Harrison and Frank F. Mathias, "John Jordan Crittenden," in Kleber, *The Kentucky Encyclopedia*, 240-241.

25 Lowell H. Harrison, "Simon Bolivar Buckner," in Kleber, *The Kentucky Encyclopedia*, 136-137.

26 James C. Klotter, "John Cabell Breckinridge," in Kleber, *The Kentucky Encyclopedia*, 117-118.

border with three Union states, the population of any of which by itself outnumbered the population of Kentucky. States such as Maryland, Missouri, and Kentucky realized that if they seceded they would become the border and the first battlegrounds.

Second, Kentuckians had a strong Southern identity. After the election of Lincoln, all the upper South states remained loyal to the Union, even though most of them called for state conventions to debate secession. The legislatures in each of these states overwhelmingly approved elections to allow the people to decide whether to hold a convention, and representatives thereto. The lone holdout was Kentucky. Thomas Speed suggested almost a century ago that Kentuckians rejected a convention out of loyalty to the Union. A new investigation suggested the opposite, that it was the strength of the Southern sympathizers in Kentucky that led to strong fear of the secession movement. Realizing their vulnerability, Unionists created a third option for their state, neither secession nor Union, but neutrality. After the attack on Fort Sumter, when other slave states joined the Confederacy, the majority of Kentuckians saw the merits of this course.

Kentucky held three elections in 1861. In all three, the Democratic Union Party defeated the States Rights Party, seeming to prove the dominance of Unionism in the Commonwealth. However, the Democratic Union Party ran on a platform of neutrality in all three elections, and it was this middle road that accounted for its success.

During the Civil War, Kentucky was a Union state, but Kentucky never fully embraced the Union cause. Many Kentuckians fought for the Confederacy, and many fought for the Union; but all did so, in a strange way, because of their loyalty to their state. Kentucky's difficult relationship with the Union would continue throughout the remainder of the war, and beyond into Reconstruction. It is easy to see why Kentucky struggled in this way: its economic and social interests were connected to the South, yet the Commonwealth had always been and remained deeply loyal to the United States. In the end, however, and in the hearts of its people, Kentucky meant more than either the Union or the Confederacy.

Appendix
Proclamations, Speeches, Party Platforms, and Other Documents

Magoffin Proclamation, April 24, 1860

RECENT events are of so startling a character as to render it imperatively necessary that the Legislature of Kentucky be again convened in extraordinary session. It is now apparent that the most energetic measures are being resorted to by the Government at Washington to prosecute a war upon an extended scale with the seceded States. Already large sums of money and supplies of men are being raised in the Northern States for that purpose. The tread of armies is the response which is being made to the measures of pacification which are being discussed before our people; whilst up to this moment we are comparatively in a defenseless attitude.

Whatever else should be done, it is, in my judgment, the duty of Kentucky, without delay, to place herself in a complete position for defense. The causes for apprehension are new certainly grave enough to impel every Kentuckian to demand that this be done, and to require of the Legislature of the State such additional action as may be necessary for the general welfare. To this end, I now call upon the members of the General Assembly to convene at the Capitol in Frankfort, on the 6th day of May, 1861.

In testimony whereof I, Beriah Magoffin, Governor of the Commonwealth of Kentucky, have hereunto subscribed my name and caused the seal of the

Commonwealth to be affixed. Done at the city of Frankfort, the 24th day of April, 1861, and in the sixty-ninth year of the Commonwealth.

B. MAGOFFIN.
By the Governor

THOS. B. MONROE, Secretary of State.
By JAS. W. TATE, Assistant Secretary.

*   *   *

Excerpt of a Speech given by John Bell of Tennessee on Slavery in the United States on July 5, 1850

Sir, no man who loves his country; no man who has any just pride in the reflection that he is an American citizen, but must desire that these dissensions should cease. For, sir, it is not a mere question whether we shall preserve the Union; for that may be, and yet prove no great boon either to ourselves or to posterity. The question is, not whether these States shall continue united according to the letter of the covenant by which they are bound together. It is, whether they shall continue to be united in heart; whether they shall continue to be practically and efficiently co-operative in carrying out the great ends of the association. The question is, whether mutual trust and confidence shall continue to animate and encourage mutual efforts in promoting and multiplying common benefits; or whether mutual hatred and distrust shall step in to check all progress; to distract and confound all joint endeavors for the common welfare; in fine, to entail upon the country all the evils of endless discord. That is the question. And when you present that issue to me, I say at once give me separation; give me disunion; give me anything in preference to a Union sustained only by power; by constitutional and legal ties, without reciprocal trust and confidence. If our future career is to be one of eternal discord, of angry crimination and recrimination, give me rather separation with all its consequences. If I am to be at peace, let it be peace in reality; and if I am to be at war, let me know it at once, that I may put my house in order, and be ready to meet the consequences. So, sir, if I could dictate the course of Congress in the pending difficulties, I would say, let the adjustment be made in the real spirit of concession, compromise, and conciliation. Let us have some assurance that the promised harmony shall be permanent. Stay this agitation; allay this burning fever that threatens to consume the system. Terminate this painful suspense, which is more intolerable than an open rupture. If we of the South have made up our minds to yield nothing, to endure nothing; or if a better spirit actuates us, and we are prepared both to yield something and endure something, and yet, cannot bring our Northern brethren to any terms of just and equitable arrangement, and they will continue to vex and harass us, now and forever, let us resolve, and let them suffer us, to manage our own affairs in our own way. But I trust it will never come to this issue.

*   *   *

Lincoln's "House Divided" speech

Mr. President and Gentlemen of the Convention:

If we could first know where we are and whither we are tending, we could better judge what to do and how to do it. We are now far into the fifth year since a policy was initiated with the avowed object and confident promise of putting an end to slavery agitation. Under the operation of that policy, that agitation has not only not ceased but has constantly augmented. In my opinion, it will not cease until a crisis shall have been reached and passed. "A house divided against itself cannot stand." I believe this government cannot endure, permanently, half slave and half free. I do not expect the Union to be dissolved; I do not expect the house to fall; but I do expect it will cease to be divided. It will become all one thing, or all the other. Either the opponents of slavery will arrest the further spread of it and place it where the public mind shall rest in the belief that it is in the course of ultimate extinction, or its advocates will push it forward till it shall become alike lawful in all the states, old as well as new, North as well as South.

Have we no tendency to the latter condition?

Let anyone who doubts carefully contemplate that now almost complete legal combination — piece of machinery, so to speak — compounded of the Nebraska doctrine and the Dred Scott decision. Let him consider, not only what work the machinery is adapted to do, and how well adapted, but also let him study the history of its construction and trace, if he can, or rather fail, if he can, to trace the evidences of design and concert of action among its chief architects, from the beginning.

The new year of 1854 found slavery excluded from more than half the states by state constitutions and from most of the national territory by congressional prohibition. Four days later commenced the struggle which ended in repealing that congressional prohibition. This opened all the national territory to slavery and was the first point gained.

But, so far, Congress *only* had acted; and an endorsement by the people, real or apparent, was indispensable to save the point already gained and give chance for more.

This necessity had not been overlooked, but had been provided for, as well as might be, in the notable argument of "squatter sovereignty," other-wise called "sacred right of self-government," which latter phrase, though expressive of the only rightful basis of any government, was so perverted in this attempted use of it as to amount to just this: That if any *one* man choose to enslave *another*, no *third* man shall be allowed to object. That argument was incorporated into the Nebraska Bill itself, in the language which follows:

It being the true intent and meaning of this act not to legislate slavery into an territory or state, nor to exclude it therefrom, but to leave the people there-of perfectly free to form and regulate their domestic institutions in their own way, subject only to the Constitution of the United States.

Then opened the roar of loose declamation in favor of "squatter sovereignty" and "sacred right of self-government." "But," said opposition members, "let us amend the bill so as to expressly declare that the people of the territory may exclude slavery." "Not we," said the friends of the measure; and down they voted the amendment.

While the Nebraska Bill was passing through Congress, a law case, involving the question of a Negro's freedom, by reason of his owner having voluntarily taken him first into a free state and then into a territory covered by the congressional prohibition, and held him as a slave for a long time in each, was passing through the United States Circuit Court for the district of Missouri; and both Nebraska Bill and lawsuit were brought to a decision in the same month of May 1854. The Negro's name was Dred Scott, which name now designates the decision finally made in the case. Before the then next presidential election, the law case came to, and was argued in, the Supreme Court of the United States; but the decision of it was deferred until after the election. Still, before the election, Senator Trumbull, on the floor of the Senate, requested the leading advocate of the Nebraska Bill to state his opinion whether the people of a territory can constitutionally exclude slavery from their limits; and the latter answers: "That is a question for the Supreme Court."

The election came. Mr. Buchanan was elected, and the endorsement, such as it was, secured. That was the second point gained. The endorsement, however, fell short of a clear popular majority by nearly 400,000 votes, and so, perhaps, was not overwhelmingly reliable and satisfactory. The outgoing President, in his last annual message, as impressively as possible echoed back upon the people the weight and authority of the endorsement. The Supreme Court met again, did not announce their decision, but ordered a reargument.

The presidential inauguration came, and still no decision of the Court; but the incoming President, in his inaugural address, fervently exhorted the people to abide by the forthcoming decision, whatever it might be. Then, in a few days, came the decision.

The reputed author of the Nebraska Bill finds an early occasion to make a speech at this capital endorsing the Dred Scott decision, and vehemently denouncing all opposition to it. The new President, too, seizes the early occasion of the Silliman letter to endorse and strongly construe that decision, and to express his astonishment that any different view had ever been entertained!

At length a squabble springs up between the President and the author of the Nebraska Bill, on the mere question of *fact*, whether the Lecompton constitution was or was not in any just sense made by the people of Kansas; and in that quarrel the latter declares that all he wants is a fair vote for the people, and that he cares not whether slavery be voted *down* or voted *up*. I do not understand his declaration, that he cares not whether slavery be voted down or voted up, to be intended by him other than as an apt definition of the policy he would impress upon the public mind — the principle for which he declares he has suffered so much and is ready to suffer to the end. And well may he cling to that principle! If he has any parental feeling, well may he cling to it. That principle is the only shred left of his original Nebraska doctrine.

Under the Dred Scott decision, "squatter sovereignty" squatted out of existence, tumbled down like temporary scaffolding; like the mold at the foundry, served through one blast and fell back into loose sand; helped to carry an election and then was kicked to the winds. His late joint struggle with the Republicans against the Lecompton constitution involves nothing of the original Nebraska doctrine. That struggle was made on a point — the right of a people to make their own constitution — upon which he and the Republicans have never differed.

The several points of the Dred Scott decision, in connection with Senator Douglas' "care not" policy, constitute the piece of machinery in its present state of advancement. This was the third point gained. The working points of that machinery are:

First, that no Negro slave, imported as such from Africa, and no descendant of such slave can ever be a citizen of any state in the sense of that term as used in the Constitution of the United States. This point is made in order to deprive the Negro, in every possible event, of the benefit of that provision of the United States Constitution which declares that "the citizens of each state shall be entitled to all the privileges and immunities of citizens in the several states."

Second, that, "subject to the Constitution of the United States," neither Congress nor a territorial legislature can exclude slavery from any United States territory. This point is made in order that individual men may fill up the territories with slaves, without danger of losing them as property, and thus enhance the chances of permanency to the institution through all the future.

Third, that whether the holding a Negro in actual slavery in a free state makes him free, as against the holder, the United States courts will not decide, but will leave to be decided by the courts of any slave state the Negro may be forced into by the master. This point is made, not to be pressed immediately but, if acquiesced in for awhile, and apparently endorsed by the people at an election, then to sustain the logical conclusion that what Dred Scott's master might lawfully do with Dred Scott in the free state of Illinois, every other master may lawfully do with any other one, or 1,000 slaves, in Illinois or in any other free state.

Auxiliary to all this, and working hand in hand with it, the Nebraska doctrine, or what is left of it, is to educate and mold public opinion, at least Northern public opinion, not to care whether slavery is voted down or voted up. This shows exactly where we now are; and partially, also, whither we are tending.

It will throw additional light on the latter to go back and run the mind over the string of historical facts already stated. Several things will now appear less dark and mysterious than they did when they were transpiring. The people were to be left "perfectly free," "subject only to the Constitution." What the Constitution had to do with it, outsiders could not then see. Plainly enough, now, it was an exactly fitted niche for the Dred Scott decision to afterward come in and declare the perfect freedom of the people to be just no freedom at all.

Why was the amendment expressly declaring the right of the people voted down? Plainly enough, now, the adoption of it would have spoiled the niche for the Dred Scott decision. Why was the Court decision held up? Why even a senator's individual opinion withheld till after the presidential election? Plainly enough, now, the speaking out then would have damaged the "perfectly free" argument upon which the election was to be carried. Why the outgoing President's felicitation on the endorsement? Why the delay of a reargument? Why the incoming President's advance exhortation in favor of the decision? These things look like the cautious patting and petting of a spirited horse preparatory to mounting him when it is dreaded that he may give the rider a fall. And why the hasty after-endorsement of the decision by the President and others?

We cannot absolutely know that all these exact adaptations are the result of preconcert. But when we see a lot of framed timbers, different portions of which we know have been gotten out at different times and places and by different workmen — Stephen, Franklin, Roger, and James, for instance — and when we see these timbers joined together and see they exactly make the frame of a house or a mill, all the tenons and mortises exactly fitting, and all the lengths and proportions of the different pieces exactly adapted to their respective places, and not a piece too many or too few, not omitting even scaffolding, or, if a single piece be lacking, we see the place in the frame exactly fitted and prepared yet to bring such piece in — in such a case, we find it impossible not to believe that Stephen and Franklin and Roger and James all understood one another from the beginning, and all worked upon a common plan or draft drawn up before the first blow was struck.

* * *

Republican Party Platform, 1860

Resolved, That we, the delegated representatives of the republican electors of the United States, in convention assembled, in discharge of the duty we owe to our constituent and our country, unite in the following declarations:

FIRST. That the history of the nation during the last four years has fully established the propriety and necessity of the organization and perpetuation of the republican party, and that the causes which called it into existence are permanent in their nature, and now more than ever before demand its peaceful and constitutional triumph.

SECOND. That the maintenance of the principles promulgated in the declaration of independence and embodied in the Federal constitution, "That all men are created equal; that they are endowed by their Creator with certain inalienable rights; that among these are life, liberty, and the pursuit of happiness; that to secure these rights, governments are instituted among men, deriving their just powers from the consent of the governed," is essential to the preservation of our republican institutions; and that the Federal constitution, the rights of the states, and the Union of the states, must and shall be preserved.

THIRD. That to the Union of the states this nation owes its unprecedented increase in population; its surprising development of material resources; its rapid augmentation of wealth; its happiness at home and its honor abroad; and we hold in abhorrence all schemes for disunion, come from whatever source they may; and we congratulate the country that no republican member of congress has uttered or countenanced the threats of disunion so often made by democratic members, without rebuke and with applause from their political associates; and we denounce those threats of disunion, in case of a popular overthrow of their ascendency, as denying the vital principles of a free government, and as an avowal of contemplated treason, which it is the imperative duty of an indignant people sternly to rebuke and forever silence.

FOURTH. That the maintenance inviolate of the rights of the states, and especially the right of each state, to order and control its own domestic institutions according to its own judgment exclusively, is essential to that balance of power on which the perfection and endurance of our political fabric depends, and we denounce the lawless invasion by armed force of the soil of any state or territory, no matter under what pretext, as among the gravest of crimes.

FIFTH. That the present democratic administration has far exceeded our worst apprehension in its measureless subserviency to the exactions of a sectional interest, as is especially evident in its desperate exertions to force the infamous Lecompton constitution upon the protesting people of Kansas—in construing the personal relation between master and servant to involve an unqualified property in persons—in its attempted enforcement everywhere, on land and sea, through the intervention of congress and of the Federal courts, of the extreme pretensions of a purely local interest, and in its general and unvarying abuse of the power entrusted to it by a confiding people.

SIXTH. That the people justly view with alarm the reckless extravagance which pervades every department of the Federal government; that a return to rigid economy and accountability is indispensable to arrest the systematic plunder of the public treasury by favored partisans; while the recent startling developments of frauds and corruptions at the Federal metropolis, show that an entire change of administration is imperatively demanded.

SEVENTH. That the new dogma that the constitution of its own force carries slavery into any or all of the territories of the United States, is a dangerous political heresy, at variance with the explicit provisions of that instrument itself, with cotemporaneous exposition, and with legislative and judicial precedent, is revolutionary in its tendency and subversive of the peace and harmony of the country.

EIGHTH. That the normal condition of all the territory of the United States is that of freedom; that as our republican fathers, when they had abolished slavery in all our national territory, ordained that no "person should be deprived of life, liberty or property, without due process of law," it becomes our duty, by legislation, whenever such legislation is necessary, to maintain this provision of the constitution against all attempts to violate it; and we deny the authority of congress, of a territorial legislature, or of any individuals, to give legal existence to slavery in any territory of the United States.

NINTH. That we brand the recent reopening of the African slave trade, under the cover of our national flag, aided by perversions of judicial power, as a crime against humanity, and a burning shame to our country and age, and we call upon congress to take prompt and efficient measures for the total and final suppression of that execrable traffic.

TENTH. That in the recent vetoes by the Federal governors of the acts of the legislatures of Kansas and Nebraska, prohibiting slavery in those territories, we find a practical illustration of the boasted democratic principle of non-intervention and popular sovereignty, embodied in the Kansas-Nebraska bill, and a demonstration of the deception and fraud involved therein.

ELEVENTH. That Kansas should of right be immediately admitted as a state, under the constitution recently formed and adopted by her people, and accepted by the house of representatives.

TWELFTH. That while providing revenue for the support of the general government by duties upon imports, sound policy requires such an adjustment of these imposts as to encourage the development of the industrial interests of the whole country, and we commend that policy of national exchanges which secures to the workingmen liberal wages, to agriculture remunerating prices, to mechanics and manufacturers an adequate reward for their skill, labor and enterprise, and to the nation commercial prosperity and independence.

THIRTEENTH. That we protest against any sale or alienation to others of the public lands held by actual settlers, and against any view of the free homestead policy which regards the settlers as paupers or suppliants for public bounty, and we demand the passage by congress of the complete and satisfactory homestead measure which has already passed the house.

FOURTEENTH. That the republican party is opposed to any change in our naturalization laws, or any state legislation by which the rights of citizenship hitherto accorded by emigrants from foreign lands shall be abridged or impaired; and in favor of giving a full and efficient protection to the rights of all classes of citizens, whether native or naturalized, both at home and abroad.

FIFTEENTH. That appropriation by congress for river and harbor improvements of a national character, required for the accommodation and security of an existing commerce, are authorized by the constitution and justified by the obligation of government to protect the lives and property of its citizens.

SIXTEENTH. That a railroad to the Pacific ocean is imperatively demanded by the interests of the whole country; that the Federal government ought to render immediate and efficient aid in its construction; and that, as preliminary thereto, a daily overland mail should be promptly established.

SEVENTEENTH. Finally, having thus set forth our distinctive principles and views, we invite the cooperation of all citizens, however differing on other questions who substantially agree with us in their affirmance and support.

*   *   *

Constitutional Union Party Platform, 1860

Whereas, Experience has demonstrated that Platforms adopted by the partisan conventions of the country have had the effect to mislead and deceive the people, and at the same time to widen the political divisions of the country, by the creation and encouragement of geographical and sectional parties; therefore,

Resolved, That it is both the part of patriotism and of duty *to recognise* no political principle other than THE CONSTITUTION OF THE COUNTRY, THE UNION OF THE STATES, AND THE ENFORCEMENT OF THE LAWS, and that as representatives of the Constitutional Union men of the country in National Convention assembled, we hereby pledge ourselves to maintain, protect, and defend, separately and unitedly, these great principles of public liberty and national safety, against all enemies at home and abroad, believing that thereby peace may once more be restored to the country, the rights of the People and of the States re-established, and the Government again placed in that condition, of justice, fraternity and equality, which under the example and Constitution of our fathers, has solemnly bound every citizen of the United States to maintain a more perfect union, establish justice, insure domestic tranquility, provide for the common defence, promote the general welfare, and secure the blessings of liberty to ourselves and our posterity.

*   *   *

Northern Democrat Party Platform, 1860

1. *Resolved,* That we, the Democracy of the Union in Convention assembled, hereby declare our affirmance of the resolutions unanimously adopted and declared as a platform of principles by the Democratic convention at Cincinnati, in the year 1856, believing that Democratic principles are unchangeable in their nature, when applied to the same subject matters; and we recommend, as the only further resolutions, the following:

2. Inasmuch as difference of opinion exists in the Democratic party as to the nature and extent of the powers of a Territorial Legislature, and as to the powers and duties of Congress, under the Constitution of the United States, over the institution of slavery within the Territories,

Resolved, That the Democratic party will abide by the decision of the Supreme Court of the United States upon these questions of Constitutional law.

3. *Resolved,* That it is the duty of the United States to afford ample and complete protection to all its citizens, whether at home or abroad, and whether native or foreign born.

4. *Resolved,* That one of the necessities of the age, in a military, commercial, and postal point of view, is speedy communication between the Atlantic and Pacific States; and the Democratic party pledge such Constitutional Government aid as will insure the construction of a Railroad to the Pacific coast, at the earliest practicable period.

5. *Resolved,* That the Democratic party are in favor of the acquisition of the Island of Cuba on such terms as shall be honorable to ourselves and just to Spain.

6. *Resolved,* That the enactments of the State Legislatures to defeat the faithful execution of the Fugitive Slave Law, are hostile in character, subversive of the Constitution, and revolutionary in their effect.

7. *Resolved,* That it is in accordance with the interpretation of the Cincinnati platform, that during the existence of the Territorial Governments the measure of restriction, whatever it may be, imposed by the Federal Constitution on the power of the Territorial Legislature over the subject of the domestic relations, as the same has been, or shall hereafter be finally determined by the Supreme Court of the United States, should be respected by all good citizens, and enforced with promptness and fidelity by every branch of the general government.

*   *   *

Southern Democrat Party Platform

Resolved, That the platform adopted by the Democratic party at Cincinnati be affirmed, with the following explanatory resolutions:

1. That the Government of a Territory organized by an act of Congress is provisional and temporary, and during its existence all citizens of the United States have an equal right to settle with their property in the Territory, without their rights, either of person or property, being destroyed or impaired by Congressional or Territorial legislation.

2. That it is the duty of the Federal Government, in all its departments, to protect, when necessary, the rights of persons and property in the Territories, and wherever else its constitutional authority extends.

3. That when the settlers in a Territory, having an adequate population, form a State Constitution, the right of sovereignty commences, and being consummated by admission into the Union, they stand on an equal footing with the people of other States, and the State thus organized ought to be admitted into the Federal Union, whether its constitution prohibits or recognizes the institution of slavery.

Resolved, That the Democratic party are in favor of the acquisition of the Island of Cuba, on such terms as shall be honorable to ourselves and just to Spain, at the earliest practicable moment.

Resolved, That the enactments of State Legislatures to defeat the faithful execution of the Fugitive Slave Law are hostile in character, subversive of the Constitution, and revolutionary in their effect.

Resolved, That the Democracy of the United States recognize it as the imperative duty of this Government to protect the naturalized citizen in all his rights, whether at home or in foreign lands, to the same extent as its native—born citizens.

WHEREAS, One of the greatest necessities of the age in a political, commercial, postal and military point of view, is speedy communication between the Atlantic and Pacific coasts. Therefore be it

Resolved, that the National Democratic party do hereby pledge themselves to use every means in their power to secure the passage of some bill, to the extent of the constitutional authority of Congress, for the construction of a Pacific Railroad from the Mississippi River to the Pacific Ocean, at the earliest practicable moment.

*   *   *

Stephen Hale to Gov Magoffin, Dec. 27, 1860

His Excellency B. Magoffin,
Governor of the Commonwealth of Kentucky:

I have the honor of placing in your hands herewith, a Commission from the Governor of the State of Alabama, accrediting me as a Commissioner from that State to the sovereign State of Kentucky, to consult in reference to the momentous issues now pending between the Northern and Southern States of this Confederacy. Although each State, as a sovereign political community, must finally determine these grave issues for itself, yet the identity of interest, sympathy, and institutions, prevailing alike in all the slaveholding States, in the opinion of Alabama, renders it proper that there should be a frank and friendly consultation, by each one, with her sister Southern States, touching their common grievances, and the measures necessary to be adopted to protect the interest, honor, and safety of their citizens.

I come, then, in a spirit of fraternity, as the Commissioner on the part of the State of Alabama, to confer with the authorities of this Commonwealth, in reference to the infraction of our Constitutional rights, wrongs done and threatened to be done, as well as the mode and measure of redress proper to be adopted by the sovereign States aggrieved, to preserve their sovereignty, vindicate their rights and protect their citizens. In order to a clear understanding of the appropriate remedy, it may be proper to consider the rights and duties, both of the State and citizen, under the Federal Compact, as well as the wrongs done and threatened.

I therefor submit, for the consideration of your Excellency, the following propositions, which I hope will command your assent and approval:

1. The people are the source of all political power; and the primary object of all good Governments is to protect the citizen in the enjoyment of life, liberty and property; and whenever any form of Government becomes destructive of these ends, it is the inalienable right, and the duty of the people to alter or abolish it.

2. The equality of all the States of this Confederacy, as well as the equality of rights of all the citizens of the respective States under the Federal Constitution, is a fundamental principle in the scheme of the Federal Government. The Union of these States under the Constitution, was formed "to establish justice, insure domestic tranquility, provide for the common defense, promote the general welfare, and secure the blessings of liberty to her citizens and their posterity;" and when it is perverted to the destruction of the equality of the States, or substantially fails to accomplish these ends, it fails to achieve the purposes of its creation, and ought to be dissolved.

3. The Federal Government results from a Compact entered into between separate sovereign and independent States, call the Constitution of the United States, and Amendments thereto, by which these sovereign States delegated certain specific powers to be used by that Government, for the common defense and general welfare of all the States and their citizens; and when these powers are abused, or used for the destruction of the rights of any State or its citizens, each State has an equal right to judge for itself, as well of the violations and infractions of that instrument, as of the mode and measure of redress; and if the interest or safety of her citizens demands it, may resume the powers she had delegated, without let or hindrance from the Federal Government, or any other power on earth.

4. Each State is bound in good faith to observe and keep, on her part, all the stipulations and covenants inserted for the benefit of other States in the Constitutional Compact — the only bond of Union by which the several States are bound together; and when persistently violated by one party to the prejudice of her sister States, ceases to be obligatory on the States so aggrieved, and they may rightfully declare the compact broken, the Union thereby formed dissolved, and stand upon their original rights, as sovereign and independent political communities; and further, that each citizen owes his primary allegiance to the State in which he resides, and hence it is the imperative duty of the State to protect him in the enjoyment of all his Constitutional rights, and see to it that they are not denied or withheld from him with impunity, by any other State or Government.

If the foregoing propositions correctly indicate the objects of this Government, the rights and duties of the citizen, as well as the rights, powers and duties of the State and Federal Government under the Constitution, the next inquiry is, what rights have been denied, what wrongs have been done, or threatened to be done, of which the Southern States, or the people of the Southern States, can complain?

At the time of the adoption of the Federal Constitution, African slavery existed in twelve of the thirteen States. Slaves are recognized as property, and as a basis of political power, by the Federal Compact, and special provisions are made by that instrument for their protection as property. Under the influences of climate, and other causes, slavery has been banished from the Northern States, the slaves themselves have been sent to the Southern States, and there sold, and their price gone into the pockets of their former owners at the North. And in the meantime, African Slavery has not only become one of the fixed domestic institutions of the Southern States, but forms an important element of their political power, and constitutes the most valuable species of their property — worth, according to recent estimates, not less than four thousand millions of dollars; forming, in fact, the basis upon which rests the prosperity and wealth of most of these States, and supplying the commerce of the world with its richest freights, and furnishing the manufactories of two continents with the raw material, and their operatives with bread. It is upon this gigantic interest, this peculiar institution of the South, that the Northern States and their people have been waging an unrelenting and fanatical war for the last quarter of a century. An institution with which is bound up, not only the wealth and prosperity of the Southern people, but their very existence as a political community.

This war has been waged in every way that human ingenuity, urged on by fanaticism, could suggest. They attack us through their literature, in their schools, from the hustings, in their legislative halls, through the public press, and even their courts of justice forget the purity of their judicial ermine, to strike down the rights of the Southern slave-holder, and over-ride every barrier which the Constitution has erected for his protection; and the sacred desk is desecrated to this unholy crusade against our lives, our property, and the Constitutional rights guaranteed to us by the Compact of our Fathers. During all this time the Southern States have freely conceded to the Northern States, and the people of those States, every right secured to them by the Constitution, and an equal interest in the common Territories of the Government; protected the lives and property of their citizens of every kind, when brought within Southern jurisdiction; enforced through their courts, when necessary, every law of Congress passed for the protection of Northern property, and submitted, ever since the foundation of the Government, with scarcely a murmur, to the protection of their shipping, manufacturing and commercial interest, by odious bounties, discriminating tariffs, and unjust navigation-laws, passed by the Federal Government to the prejudice and injury of their own citizens.

The law of Congress for the rendition of fugitive slaves, passed in pursuance of an express provision of the Constitution, remains almost a dead letter upon the Statute Book. A majority of the Northern States, through their legislative enactments, have openly nullified it, and impose heavy fines and penalties upon all persons who aid in enforcing this law; and some of those States declare the Southern slave-holder, who goes within their jurisdiction to assert his legal rights under the Constitution, guilty of a high crime, and affix imprisonment in the penitentiary as the penalty. The Federal officers who attempt to discharge their duties under the law, as well as the owner of the slave, are set upon by mobs, and are fortunate if they escape without serious injury to life or limb; and the State authorities, instead of aiding in the enforcement of this law, refuse the use of their jails, and by every means which unprincipled fanaticism can devise, give countenance to the mob, and aid the fugitive to escape. Thus, there are annually large amounts of property actually stolen away from the Southern States, harbored and protected in Northern States, and by their citizens. And when a requisition is made for the thief by the Governor of a Southern State upon the

Executive of a Northern State, in pursuance of the express conditions of the Federal Constitution, he is insultingly told that the felon has committed no crime — and thus the criminal escapes, the property of the citizen is lost, the sovereignty of the State is insulted — and there is no redress, for the Federal Courts have no jurisdiction to award a mandamus to the Governor of a sovereign State, to compel him to do an official Executive act, and Congress, if disposed, under the Constitution has no power to afford a remedy. These are wrongs under which the Southern people have long suffered, and to which they have patiently submitted, in the hope that a returning sense of justice would prompt the people of the Northern States to discharge their Constitutional obligations, and save our common country. Recent events, however, have not justified their hopes; the more daring and restless fanatics have banded themselves together, have put in practice the terrible lessons taught by the timid, by making an armed incursion upon the sovereign State of Virginia, slaughtering her citizens, for the purpose of exciting a servile insurrection among her slave population, and arming them for the destruction of their own masters. During the past summer, theAbolition incendiary has lit up the prairies of Texas, fired the dwellings of the inhabitants, burned down whole towns and laid poison for her citizens — thus literally executing the terrible denunciations of fanaticism against the slave-holder — "Alarm to their sleep, fire to their dwellings, and poison to their food."

The same fell spirit, like an unchained demon, has for years swept over the plains of Kansas, leaving death, desolation and ruin in its track. Nor is this the mere ebullition of a few half-crazy fanatics, as is abundantly apparent from the sympathy manifested all over the North, where, in many places, the tragic death of John Brown, the leader of the raid upon Virginia, who died upon the gallows a condemned felon, is celebrated with public honors, and his name canonized as a martyr to liberty; and many, even of the more conservative papers of the Black Republican school, were accustomed to speak of his murderous attack upon the lives of the unsuspecting citizens of Virginia, in a half-sneering and half-apologetic tone. And what has the Federal Government done in the meantime to protect slave property upon the common Territories of the Union? Whilst a whole squadron of the American Navy is maintained on the coast of Africa, at an enormous expense, to enforce the execution of the laws against the slave trade — and properly, too — and the whole navy is kept afloat to protect the lives and property of American citizens upon the high seas, not a law has been passed by Congress, or an arm raised by the Federal Government, to protect the slave property of citizens from the Southern States upon the soil of Kansas — the common Territory and common property of the citizens of all the States — purchased alike by their common treasure, and held by the Federal Government, as declared by the Supreme Court of the United States, as the trustee for all their citizens; but, upon the contrary, a Territorial

Government, created by Congress, and supported out of the common treasury, under the influence and control of Emigrant Aid Societies and Abolition emissaries, is permitted to pass laws excluding and destroying all that species of property within her limits — thus ignoring, on the part of the Federal Government, one of the fundamental principles of all good Governments, the duty to protect the property of the citizen, and wholly refusing to maintain the equal rights of the States and the citizens of the States upon their common Territories.

As the last and crowning act of insult and outrage upon the people of the South, the citizens of the Northern States, by overwhelming majorities, on the 6th day of November last, elected Abraham Lincoln and Hannibal Hamlin, President and Vice President of the United States. Whilst it may be admitted that the mere election of any man to the Presidency, is not, per se, a sufficient cause for a dissolution of the Union; yet, when the issues upon, and circumstances under which he was elected, are properly appreciated and understood, the question arises whether a due regard to the interest, honor, and safety of their citizens, in view of this and all the other antecedent wrongs and outrages, do not render it the imperative duty of the Southern States to resume the powers they have delegated to the Federal Government, and interpose their sovereignty for the protection of their citizens.

What, then are the circumstances under which, and the issues upon which he was elected? His own declarations, and the current history of the times, but too plainly indicate he was elected by a Northern sectional vote, against the most solemn warnings and protestations of the whole South. He stands forth as the representative of the fanaticism of the North, which, for the last quarter of a century, has been making war upon the South, her property, her civilization, her institutions, and her interests; as the representative of that party which overrides all Constitutional barriers, ignores the obligations of official oaths, and acknowledges allegiance to a higher law than the Constitution, striking down the sovereignty and equality of the States, and resting its claims to popular favor upon the one dogma, the Equality of the Races, white and black.

It was upon this acknowledgment of allegiance to a higher law, that Mr. Seward rested his claim to the Presidency, in a speech made by him in Boston, before the election. He is the exponent, if not the author, of the doctrine of the Irrepressible Conflict between freedom and slavery, and proposes that the opponents of slavery shall arrest its further *expansion, and by Congressional Legislation exclude it from the common Territories of the Federal Government, and place it where the public mind shall rest in the belief that it is in the course of ultimate extinction.*

He claims for free negroes the right of suffrage, and an equal voice in the Government — in a word, all the rights of citizenship, although the Federal

Constitution, as construed by the highest judicial tribunal in the world, does not recognize Africans imported into this country as slaves, or their descendants, whether free or slaves, as citizens.

These were the issues presented in the last Presidential canvass, and upon these the American people passed at the ballot-box.

Upon the principles then announced by Mr. Lincoln and his leading friends, we are bound to expect his administration to be conducted. Hence it is, that in high places, among the Republican party, the election of Mr. Lincoln is hailed, not simply as a change of Administration, but as the inauguration of new principles, and a new theory of Government, and even as the downfall of slavery. Therefore it is that the election of Mr. Lincoln cannot be regarded otherwise than a solemn declaration, on the part of a great majority of the Northern people, of hostility to the South, her property and her institutions — nothing less than an open declaration of war — for the triumph of this new theory of Government destroys the property of the South, lays waste her fields, and inaugurates all the horrors of a San Domingo servile insurrection, consigning her citizens to assassinations, and her wives and daughters to pollution and violation, to gratify the lust of half-civilized Africans. Especially is this true in the cotton-growing States, where, in many localities, the slave outnumbers the white population ten to one.

If the policy of the Republicans is carried out, according to the programme indicated by the leaders of the party, and the South submits, degradation and ruin must overwhelm alike all classes of citizens in the Southern States. The slave-holder and non-slave-holder must ultimately share the same fate — all be degraded to a position of equality with free negroes, stand side by side with them at the polls, and fraternize in all the social relations of life; or else there will be an eternal war of races, desolating the land with blood, and utterly wasting and destroying all the resources of the country.

Who can look upon such a picture without a shudder? What Southern man, be he slave-holder or non-slave-holder, can without indignation and horror contemplate the triumph of negro equality, and see his own sons and daughters, in the not distant future, associating with free negroes upon terms of political and social equality, and the white man stripped, by the Heaven-daring hand of fanaticism of that title to superiority over the black race which God himself has bestowed? In the Northern States, where free negroes are so few as to form no appreciable part of the community, in spite of all the legislation for their protection, they still remain a degraded caste, excluded by the ban of society from social association with all but the lowest and most degraded of the white race. But in the South, where in many places the African race largely predominates, and, as a consequence, the two races would be continually pressing together, amalgamation, or the extermination of the one or the other, would be inevitable. Can Southern men submit to such degradation and ruin? God forbid that they should.

But, it is said, there are many Constitutional, conservative men at the North, who sympathize with and battle for us. That is true; but they are utterly powerless, as the late Presidential election unequivocally shows, to breast the tide of fanaticism that threatens to roll over and crush us. With them it is a question of principle, and we award to them all honor for their loyalty to the Constitution of our Fathers. But their defeat is not their ruin. With us it is a question of self-preservation — our lives, our property, the safety of our homes and our hearthstones — all that men hold dear on earth, is involved in the issue. If we triumph, vindicate our rights and maintain our institutions, a bright and joyous future lies before us. We can clothe the world with our staple, give wings to her commerce, and supply with bread the starving operative in other lands, and at the same time preserve an institution that has done more to civilize and Christianize the heathen than all human agencies beside — an institution alike beneficial to both races, ameliorating the moral, physical and intellectual condition of the one, and giving wealth and happiness to the other. If we fail, the light of our civilization goes down in blood, our wives and our little ones will be driven from their homes by the light of our own dwellings. The dark pall of barbarism must soon gather over our sunny land, and the scenes of West India emancipation, with its attendant horrors and crimes (that monument of British fanaticism and folly), be re-enacted in our own land upon a more gigantic scale.

Then, is it not time we should be up and doing, like men who know their rights and dare maintain them? To whom shall the people of the Southern States look for the protection of their rights, interests and honor? We answer, to their own sons and their respective States. To the States, as we have seen, under our system of Government, is due the primary allegiance of the citizen; and the correlative obligation of protection devolves upon the respective States — a duty from which they cannot escape, and which they dare not neglect without a violation of all the bonds of fealty that hold together the citizen and the sovereign.

The Northern States and their citizens have proved recreant to their obligations under the Federal Constitution; they have violated that Compact, and refused to perform their covenants in that behalf.

The Federal Government has failed to protect the rights and property of the citizens of the South, and is about to pass into the hands of a party pledged for the destruction, not only of their rights and property, but the equality of the States ordained by the Constitution, and the heaven-ordained superiority of the white over the black race. What remains, then, for the Southern States, and the people of these States, if they are loyal to the great principles of civil and religious liberty, sanctified by the sufferings of a seven-year's war, and baptized with the blood of the Revolution? Can they permit the rights of their citizens to be denied and spurned? their property spirited away, their own sovereignty violated, and themselves degraded to the position of mere dependencies, instead of sovereign States? or shall each for itself, judging the infractions of the Constitutional Compact, as well as the mode and measure of redress, declare that the covenants of that sacred instrument, in their behalf, and for the benefit of their citizens, have been willfully, deliberately, continuously and persistently broken and violated by the other parties to the compact, and that they and their citizens are therefore absolved from all further obligations to keep and perform the covenants thereof, resume the powers delegated to the Federal Government, and, as sovereign States, form other relations for the protection of their citizens and the discharge of the great ends of Government? The Union of these States was one of fraternity as well as equality; but what fraternity now exists between the citizens of the two sections? Various religious associations, powerful in numbers and influence, have been broken asunder, and the sympathies that bound together the people of the several States, at the time of the formation of the Constitution, has ceased to exist, and feelings of bitterness, and even hostility, have sprung up in its place. How can this be reconciled, and a spirit of fraternity established? Will the people of the North cease to make war upon the institution of Slavery, and award to it the protection guaranteed by the Constitution? The accumulated wrongs of many years, the late action of the members in Congress in refusing every measure of justice to the South, as well as the experience of all the past, answers, *No, never!*

Will the South give up the institution of slavery, and consent that her citizens be stripped of their property, her civilization destroyed, the whole land laid waste by fire and sword? It is impossible; she can not, she will not. Then why attempt any longer to hold together hostile States under the stipulations of a violated Constitution? It is impossible; disunion is inevitable. Why then wait longer for the consummation of a result that must come? Why waste further time in expostulations and appeals to Northern States and their citizens, only to be met, as we have been for years past, by renewed insults and repeated injuries? Will the South be better prepared to meet the emergency when the North shall be strengthened by the admission of the new territories of Kansas, Nebraska, Washington, Jefferson, Nevada, Idaho, Chippewa, and Arizonia, as non-slaveholding States, as we are warned from high sources will be done within the next four years, under the administration of Mr. Lincoln? Can the true men at the North ever make a more powerful or successful rally for the preservation of our rights and the Constitution, than they did in the last Presidential contest? There is nothing to inspire a hope that they can.

Shall we wait until our enemies shall possess themselves of all the powers of the Government? until Abolition Judges are on the Supreme Court bench, Abolition Collectors at every port, and Abolition Postmasters in every town, secret mail agents traversing the whole land, and a subsidized Press established in our midst to demoralize the people? Will we be stronger then, or better prepared to meet the struggle, if a struggle must come? No, verily! When that time shall come, well may our adversaries laugh at our folly, and deride our impotence. The deliberate judgment of Alabama, as indicated by the Joint Resolutions of her General Assembly, approved February 24, 1860, is, that prudence, patriotism, and loyalty to all the great principles of civil liberty incorporated in our Constitution, and consecrated by the memories of the past, demand that the Southern States should now resume their delegated powers, maintain the rights, interests and honor of their citizens, and vindicate their own sovereignty. And she most earnestly, but respectfully, invites her sister sovereign State, Kentucky, who so gallantly vindicated the sovereignty of the States in 1798, to the consideration of these grave and vital questions, hoping she may concur with the State of Alabama in the conclusions to which she has been driven by the impending dangers that now surround the Southern States. But if, on mature deliberation, she dissents on any point from the conclusions to which the State of Alabama has arrived, on behalf of that State I most respectfully ask a declaration by this venerable Commonwealth of her conclusions and position on all the issues discussed in this communication; and Alabama most respectfully urges upon the people and authorities of Kentucky the startling truth that *submission or acquiescence on the part of the Southern States, at this perilous hour, will enable Black Republicanism to redeem all its nefarious pledges, and accomplish its flagitious ends;* and that hesitation or delay in their action will be misconceived and misconstrued by their adversaries, and ascribed, not to that elevated patriotism that would sacrifice all but their honor to save the Union of their Fathers, but to division and dissension among themselves, and their consequent weakness; that prompt, bold and decided action is demanded alike by prudence, patriotism and the safety of their citizens.

Permit me, in conclusion, on behalf of the State of Alabama, to express my high gratification, at the cordial manner in which I have been received, as her Commissioner, by the authorities of the State of Kentucky, as well as the profound personal gratification which, as a son of Kentucky, born and reared within her borders, I feel, at the manner in which I, as the Commissioner from the State of my adoption, have been received and treated by the authorities of the State of my birth. Please accept assurances of the high consideration and esteem of,

Your obedient servant, &c.,

S. F. HALE,
Commissioner from the State of Alabama

*   *   *

Magoffin to S. F. Hale, Dec. 28, 1860

Ky., December 28, 1860.

Hon. S. F. HALE, Commissioner from the State of Alabama:

Your communication of the 27th instant, addressed to me by authority of the State of Alabama, has been attentively read. I concur with you in the opinion that the grave political issues yet pending and undetermined between the slave-holding and non-slave-holding States of the Confederacy are of a character to render eminently proper and highly important a full and frank conference on the part of the Southern members, identified, as they undoubtedly are, by a common interest, bound together by mutual sympathies, and with the whole social fabric resting on homogeneous institutions. And coming as you do in a spirit of fraternity, by virtue of a commission from a sister Southern State, to confer with the authorities of this State in reference to the measures necessary to be adopted to protect the interests and maintain the honor and safety of the States and their citizens, I extend you a cordial welcome to Kentucky.

You have not exaggerated the grievous wrongs, injuries, and indignities to which the slave-holding States and their citizens have long submitted with a degree of patience and forbearance justly attributable alone to that elevated patriotism and devotion to the Union which would lead them to sacrifice well-nigh all save honor to recover the Government to its original integrity of administration and perpetuate the Union upon the basis of equality established by the founders of the Republic. I may even add that the people of Kentucky, by reason of their geographical position and nearer proximity to those who seem so madly bent upon the destruction of our constitutional guarantees, realize yet more fully than our friends farther south the intolerable wrongs and menacing dangers you have so elaborately recounted. Nor are you, in my opinion, more keenly alive than are the people of this State to the importance of arresting the insane crusade so long waged against our institutions and our society by measures which shall be certainly effective. The rights of African slavery in the United States and the relations of the Federal Government to it, as an institution in the States and Territories, most assuredly demand at this time explicit definition and final recognition by the North. The slave-holding States are & now impelled by the very highest law of self-preservation to demand that this settlement should be concluded upon such a basis as shall not only conserve the institution in localities where it is now recognized, but secure its expansion, under no other restrictions than those which the laws of nature may throw around it. That unnecessary conflict between free labor and slave labor, but recently inaugurated by the Republican party as an element in our political struggles, must end, and the influence of soil, of climate, and local interests left unaided and unrestricted save by constitutional limitations to control the extension of slavery over the public domain. The war upon our social institutions and their guaranteed immunities waged through the Northern press, religious and secular, and now threatened to be conducted by a dominant political organization through the agency of State Legislatures and the Federal Government must be ended. Our safety, our honor, and our self-preservation alike demand that our interests be placed beyond the reach of further assault.

The people of Kentucky may differ variously touching the nature and theory of our complex system of government, but when called upon to pass upon these questions at the polls I think such an expression would develop no material variance of sentiment touching the wrongs you recite and the necessity of their prompt adjustment. They fully realize the fatal result of longer forbearance, and appreciate the peril of submission at this juncture. Kentucky would leave no effort untried to preserve the union of the States upon the basis of the Constitution as we construe it, but Kentucky will never submit to wrong and dishonor, let resistance cost what it may. Unqualified acquiescence in the administration of the Government upon the Chicago platform, in view of the movements already inaugurated at the South and the avowed purposes of the representative men of the Republican party, would, I feel assured, receive no favor in this State. Whether her citizens shall, in the last resort, throw themselves upon the right of revolution as the inherent right of a free people never surrendered, or shall assert the doctrine of secession, can be of little practical import. When the time of action comes (and it is now fearfully near at hand) our people will be found rallied as a unit under the flag of resistance to intolerable wrong, and being thus consolidated in feeling and action, I may well forego any discussion of the abstract theories to which one party or another may hold to cover their resistance.

It is true that as sovereign political communities the States must determine, each for itself, the grave issues now presented; and it may be that, when driven to the dire extremity of severing their relations with the Federal Government, formal, independent, separate State action will be proper and necessary. But resting, as do these political communities, upon a common social organization, constituting the sole object of attack and invasion, confronted by a common enemy, encompassed by a common peril in a word, involved in one common cause, it does seem to me that the mode and manner of defense and redress should be determined in a full and free conference of all the Southern States, and that their mutual safety requires full co-operation in carrying out the measures there agreed upon. The source whence oppression is now to be apprehended is an organized power, a political government in operation, to which resistance, though ultimately successful (and I do not for a moment question the issue), might be costly and destructive. We should look these facts in the face, nor close our eyes to what we may reasonably expect to encounter. I have therefore thought that a due regard to the opinions of all the slave-holding States would require that those measures which concern all alike and must ultimately involve all should be agreed upon in common convention and sustained by united action.

I have before expressed the belief and confidence, and do not now totally yield the hope, that if such a convention of delegates from the slave-holding States be assembled, and, after calm deliberation, present to the political party now holding the dominance of power in the Northern States and soon to assume the reins of national power, the firm alternative of ample guarantees to all our rights and security for future immunity or resistance, our just demands would be conceded and the Union be perpetuated stronger than before. Such an issue, so presented to the Congress of the United States and to the Legislatures and people of the Northern States (and it is practicable, in abundant time before the Government has passed into other hands) would come with a moral force which, if not potent to control the votes of the representative men, might produce a voice from their constituents which would influence them. But if it fail, our cause would emerge, if possible, stronger fortified by the approbation of the whole conservative sentiment of the country and supported by a host of Northern friends who would prove, in the ultimate issue, most valuable allies. After such an effort every man in the slave-holding States would feel satisfied that all had been done which could be done to preserve the legacy bequeathed us by the patriots of 76 and the statesmen of 89, and the South would stand in solid, unbroken phalanx a unit. In the brief time left it seems to me impracticable to effect this object through the agency of commissioners sent to the different States. A convention of authorized delegates is the true mode of bringing about co-operation among the Southern States, and to that movement I would respectfully ask your attention; and through you solicit the co-operation of Alabama.

There is yet another subject upon which the very highest considerations appeal for a united Southern expression. On the 4th of March next the Federal Government, unless contingencies now unlooked for occur, will pass into the control of the Republican party. So far as the policy of the incoming administration is foreshadowed in the antecedents of the President elect, in the enunciations of its representative men and the avowals of the press, it will be to ignore the acts of sovereignty thus proclaimed by Southern States, and of coercing the continuance of the Union. Its inevitable result will be civil war of the most fearful and revolting character. Now, however the people of the South may differ as to the mode and measure of redress, I take it that the fifteen slave holding States are united in opposition to such a policy, and would stand in solid column to resist the application of force by the Federal authority to coerce the seceding States. But it is of the utmost importance that before such a policy is attempted to be inaugurated the voice of the South should be heard in potential, official, and united protest. Possibly the incoming Administration would not be so dead to reason as after such an expression to persist in throwing the country into civil war, and we may therefore avert the calamity. An attempt to enforce the laws by blockading two or three Southern States would be regarded as quite a different affair from a declaration of war against 13,000,000 of freemen; and if Mr. Lincoln and his advisers be made to realize that such would be the issue of the force policy, it will be abandoned. Should we not realize to our enemies that consequence and avert the disastrous results? But if our enemies be crazed by victory and power and madly persist in their purpose, the South will be better prepared to resist.

You ask the co-operation of the Southern States in order to redress our wrongs. So do we. You have no hope of a redress in the Union. We yet look hopefully to assurances that a powerful reaction is going on at the North. You seek a remedy in secession from the Union. We wish the united action of the slave States, assembled in convention within the Union. You would act separately; we unitedly. If Alabama and the other slave States would meet us in convention, say at Nashville or elsewhere, as early as the 5th day of February, I do not doubt that we would agree in forty-eight hours upon such reasonable guarantees, by way of amendment to the Constitution of the United States, as would command at least the approbation of our numerous friends in the free States, and by giving them time to make the question with the people there, such a reaction in public opinion might yet take place as to secure us our rights and save the Government. If the effort failed the South would be united to a man, the North divided, the horrors of civil War would be averted (if anything can avert the calamity). And if that be not possible we would be in a better position to meet the dreadful collision. By such action, too, if it failed to preserve the Government, the basis of another confederacy would have been agreed upon, and the new government would in this mode be launched into operation much more speedily and easily than by the action you propose.

In addition to the foregoing, I have the honor to refer you to my letter of the 16th ultimo to the editor of The Yeoman and to my letter to the Governors of the slave States, dated the 9th of December, here- with transmitted to you, which, together with what I have said in this communication, embodies, with all due deference to the opinions of others, in my judgment, the principles, policy, and position which the slave States ought to maintain. The Legislature of Kentucky will assemble on the 17th of January, when the sentiment of the State will doubtless find official expression. Meantime, if the action of Alabama shall be arrested until the conference she has sought can be concluded by communication with that department of the government, I shall be pleased to transmit to the Legislature your views. I regret to have seen in the recent messages of two or three of our Southern sister States a recommendation of the passage of laws prohibiting the purchase by the citizens of those States of the slaves of the border slave-holding States. Such a course is not only liable to the objection so often urged by us against the abolitionists of the North of an endeavor to prohibit the slave-trade between the States, but it is likewise wanting in that fraternal feeling which should be common to States which are identified in their institutions and interests. It affords me pleasure, however, to add, as an act of justice to your State, that I have seen no indication of such a purpose on the part of Alabama. It would certainly be considered an act of injustice for the border slave-holding States to prohibit, by their legislation, the purchase of the products of the cotton-growing States, even though it be founded upon the mistaken policy of protection to their own interests. I cannot close this correspondence without again expressing to you my gratification in receiving you as the honored commissioner from your proud and chivalrous State, and at your courteous, able, dignified, and manly bearing in discharging the solemn and important duties which have been assigned to you.

I have the honor to be, with sentiments of high consideration, your friend and obedient servant,

B. MAGOFFIN.

*   *   *

Crittenden Compromise

A joint resolution (S. No.50) proposing certain amendments to the Constitution of the United States.

Whereas serious and alarming dissensions have arisen between the northern and southern States, concerning the rights and security of the rights of the slaveholding States, and especially their rights in the common territory of the United States; and whereas it is eminently desirable and proper that these dissensions, which now threaten the very existence of this Union, should be permanently quieted and settled by constitutional provisions, which shall do equal justice to all sections, and thereby restore to the people that peace and good-will which ought to prevail between all the citizens of the United States: Therefore,

Resolved by the Senate and House of Representatives of the United States of America in Congress assembled, (two thirds of both Houses concurring,) That the following articles be, and are hereby, proposed and submitted as amendments to the

Constitution of the United States, which shall be valid to all intents and purposes, as part of said Constitution, when ratified by conventions of three fourths of the several States:

Article 1. In all the territory of the United States now held, or hereafter acquired, situate north of 36 degrees 30 min, slavery or involuntary servitude, except as a punishment for crime, is prohibited while such territory shall remain under territorial government. In all the territory south of said line of latitude, slavery of the African race is hereby recognized as existing, and shall not be interfered with by Congress, but shall be protected as property by all the departments of the territorial government during its continuance. And when any territory, north or south of said line, within such boundaries as Congress may prescribe, shall contain the population requisite for a member of Congress according to the then Federal ratio of representation of the people of the United States, it shall, if its form of government be republican, be admitted into the Union, on an equal footing with the original States, with or without slavery, as the constitution of such new State may provide.

Art. 2.Congress shall have no power to abolish slavery in places under its exclusive jurisdiction, and situate within the limits of States that permit the holding of slaves.

Art. 3.Congress shall have no power to abolish slavery within the District of Columbia, so long as it exists in the adjoining States of Virginia and Maryland, or either, nor without the consent of the inhabitants, nor without just compensation first made to such owners of slaves as do not consent to such abolishment. Nor shall Congress at any time prohibit officers of the Federal Government, or members of Congress, whose duties require them to be in said District, from bringing with them their slaves, and holding them as such during the time their duties may require them to remain there, and afterwards taking them from the District.

Art. 4. Congress shall have no power to prohibit or hinder the transportation of slaves from one State to another, or to a Territory, in which slaves are by law permitted to be held, whether that transportation be by land, navigable rivers, or by the sea.

Art. 5. That in addition to the provisions of the third paragraph of the second section of the fourth article of the Constitution of the United States, Congress shall have power to provide by law, and it shall be its duty so to provide, that the United States shall pay to the owner who shall apply for it, the full value of his fugitive slave in all cases when the marshall or other officer whose duty it was to arrest said fugitive was prevented from so doing by violence or intimidation, or when, after arrest, said fugitive was rescued by force, and the owner thereby prevented and obstructed in the pursuit of his remedy for the recovery of his fugitive slave under the said clause of the Constitution and the laws made in pursuance thereof. And in all such cases, when the United States shall pay for such fugitive, they shall have the right, in their own name, to sue the county in which said violence, intimidation, or rescue was committed, and to recover from it, with interest and damages, the amount paid by them for said fugitive slave. And the said county, after it has paid said amount to the United States, may, for its indemnity, sue and recover from the wrong doers or rescuers by whom the owner was prevented from the recovery of his fugitive slave, in like manner as the owner himself might have sued and recovered.

Art. 6. No future amendment of the Constitution shall affect the five preceding articles; nor the third paragraph of the second section of the first article of the Constitution; nor the third paragraph of the second section of the fourth article of said Constitution; and no amendment shall be made to the Constitution which shall authorize or give to Congress any power to abolish or interfere with slavery in any of the States by whose laws it is, or may be, allowed or permitted.

And whereas, also, besides those causes of dissension embraced in the foregoing amendments proposed to the Constitution of the United States, there are others which come within the jurisdiction of Congress, and may be remedied by its legislative power; and whereas it is the desire of Congress, as far as its power will extend, to remove all just cause for the popular discontent and agitation which now disturb the peace of the country, and threaten the stability of its institutions: Therefore,

1. In Congress assembled, That the laws now in force for the recovery of fugitive slaves are in strict pursuance of the plain and mandatory provisions of the Constitution, and have been sanctioned as valid and constitutional by the judgement of the Supreme Court of the United States; that the slaveholding States are entitled to the faithful observance and execution of those laws, and that they ought not to be repealed, or so modified or changed as to impair their efficiency; and that laws ought to be made for the punishment of those who attempt by rescue of the slave, or other illegal means, to hinder or defeat the due execution of said laws.

2. That all State laws which conflict with the fugitive slave acts of Congress, or any other constitutional acts of Congress, or which, in their operation, impede, hinder, or delay the free course and due execution of any of said acts, are null and void by the plain provisions of the Constitution of the United States; yet those State laws, void as they are, have given color to practices, and led to consequences, which have obstructed the due administration and execution of acts of Congress, and especially the acts for the delivery of fugitive slaves, and have thereby contributed much to the discord and commotion now prevailing. Congress, therefore, in the present perilous juncture, does not deem it improper, respectfully and earnestly to recommend the repeal of those laws to the several States which have enacted them, or such legislative corrections or explanations of them as may prevent their being used or perverted to such mischievous purposes.

3. That the act of the 18th of September, 1850, commonly called the fugitive slave law, ought to be so amended as to make the fee of the commissioner, mentioned in the eighth section of the act, equal in amount in the cases decided by him, whether his decision be in favor of or against the claimant. And to avoid misconstruction, the last clause of the fifth section of said act, which authorizes the person holding a warrant for the arrest or detention of a fugitive slave, to summon to his aid the posse comitatus, and which declares it to be the duty of all good citizens to assist him in its execution, ought to be so amended as to expressly limit the authority and duty to cases in which there shall be resistance or danger of resistance or rescue.

4. That the laws for the suppression of the African slave trade, and especially those prohibiting the importation of slaves in the United States, ought to be made effectual, and ought to be thoroughly executed; and all further enactments necessary to those ends ought to be promptly made.

*   *   *

Magoffin Proclamation, April 24, 1860

RECENT events are of so startling a character as to render it imperatively necessary that the Legislature of Kentucky be again convened in extraordinary session. It is now apparent that the most energetic measures are being resorted to by the Government at Washington to prosecute a war upon an extended scale with the seceded States. Already large sums of money and supplies of men are being raised in the Northern States for that purpose. The tread of armies is the response which is being made to the measures of pacification which are being discussed before our people; whilst up to this moment we are comparatively in a defenseless attitude.

Whatever else should be done, it is, in my judgment, the duty of Kentucky, without delay, to place herself in a complete position for defense. The causes for apprehension are new certainly grave enough to impel every Kentuckian to demand that this be done, and to require of the Legislature of the State such additional action as may be necessary for the general welfare. To this end, I now call upon the members of the General Assembly to convene at the Capitol in Frankfort, on the 6th day of May, 1861.

In testimony whereof I, Beriah Magoffin, Governor of the Commonwealth of Kentucky, have hereunto subscribed my name and caused the seal of the Commonwealth to be affixed. Done at the city of Frankfort, the 24th day of April, 1861, and in the sixty-ninth year of the Commonwealth.

B. MAGOFFIN

*   *   *

Governor Magoffin to Jefferson Davis

COMMONWEALTH OF KENTUCKY, Executive DEPARTMENT,
Frankfort, May 19, 1861.

Hon. JEFFERSON DAVIS,
President of the Confederate States, Richmond:

SIR: Since the commencement of the unhappy difficulties yet pending in the country the people of Kentucky have indicated a steadfast desire and purpose to maintain a position of strict neutrality between the belligerent parties. They have earnestly striven by their policy to avert from themselves the calamity of war and protect their own soil from the presence of contending armies. Up to this period they have enjoyed comparative tranquility and entire domestic peace. Recently a military force has been enlisted and quartered by the U. S. authorities within this State. I have this day addressed a communication and dispatched commissioners to the President of the United States urging the removal of these troops from the soil of Kentucky, thus exerting myself to carry out the will of the people of this State in the maintenance of a neutral position. The people of Kentucky desire to be free from the presence of contending armies, and avert invasion of their soil from either side; and to that object then my efforts are now directed. Although I have no reason to assume that the Government of the Confederate States now contemplate or have ever purposed any violation of the neutral attitude assumed by Kentucky, there seems to be some uneasiness among the people of some portions of the State, occasioned by the collection of bodies of troops along their southern frontier. In order to quiet that apprehension and to secure the people their cherished object of peace, this communication is to represent these facts and to elicit an authoritative assurance that the Government of the Confederate States will continue to respect and observe the neutral position of Kentucky. I am, very respectfully, your obedient servant,

B. MAGOFFIN

*   *   *

Governor Beriah Magoffin Letter to Lincoln, Aug. 19, 1961

Commonwealth of Kentucky
Executive Department

Frankfort Aug 19 1861

Sir,

From the commencement of the unhappy hostilities now pending in the country, the people of Kentucky, have indicated an earnest desire and purpose, as far as lay in their power, while maintaining their original political status, to do nothing by which to involve themselves in the war. Up to this time they have succeeded in securing to themselves and to the state peace and tranquility as the fruits of the policy they dopte adopted — My single object now is to promote the continuance of those blessings to the people of this State.

Until within a brief period, the people of Kentucky were quiet and tranquil, free from domestic strife and undisturbed by internal commotion. They have resisted no law, rebelled against no authority, engaged in no revolution, but constantly proclaimed their firm determination to pursue their peaceful avocations, earnestly hoping that their own soil would be spared the presence of armed troops, and that the scene of conflict would be kept removed from beyond the borders of their state. By thus avoiding all occasions for the introduction of bodies of armed soldiers and offering no provocations for the presence of military force the people of Kentucky have sincerely striven to preserve in this state domestic peace and avert the calamities of sanguinary engagements.

Recently a large body of soldiers have been enlisted in the United States Army and collected in military camps in the central portions of Kentucky. This movement was preceded by the active organization of companies, Regiments &c, consisting of men sworn into the United States service under officers holding commissions from yourself. Ordnance arms, and munitions and supplies of war are being transported into the state and placed in large quantities in these camps In a word an Army is now being organized and quartered within this state supplied with all the appliances of war, without the advice or consent of the Authorities of the State and without consultation of with those most prominently known and recognized as loyal citizens. This movement now imperils that peace and tranquility, which from the beginning of our pending difficulties, have been the paramount desire of this people and which up to this time they have secured to the state.

Within Kentucky there has been and is likely to be no occasion for the presence of military force. The people are quiet and tranquil, feeling no apprehension of any occasion arising to invoke protection from the Federal arm. They have asked that their soil territory be left free from military occupation, and the present tranquility of their communities left uninvaded by soldiers. They do not desire that Kentucky shall be required to supply the battle-fields for the contending Armies or become the theatre of the war.

Now there fore, as Governor of the State of Kentucky and in the name of the people whom I have the honor to represent and with the single and earnest desire to avert from their peaceful homes the horrors of war, I urge the removal from the limits of Kentucky of the military forces now organized and in camp within the state. If such action as is hereby urged, be promptly taken, I firmly believe, the peace of the people of Kentucky will be preserved and the horror of a bloody war will be averted from a people now peaceful and tranquil.

I am very Respectfully your obedient servant,

B. Magoffin

* * *

President Lincoln to Governor Magoffin, August 24, 1861

To His Excellency B. Magoffin
Governor of the State of Kentucky.

Sir:

Your letter of the 19th. Inst. in which you urge the removal from the limits of Kentucky of the military force now organized, and in camp within said State" is received.

I may not possess full and precisely accurate knowledge upon this subject; but I believe it is true that there is a military force in camp within Kentucky, acting by authority of the United States, which force is not very large, and is not now being augmented. I also believe that some arms have been furnished to this force by the United States.

I also believe this force consists exclusively of Kentuckians, having their camp in the immediate vicinity of their own homes, and not assailing, or menacing, any of the good people of Kentucky. In all I have done in the premises, I have acted upon the urgent solicitation of many Kentuckians, and in accordance with what I believed, and still believe, to be the wish of a majority of all the Union-loving people of Kentucky.

While I have conversed on this subject with many eminent men of Kentucky, including a large majority of her Members of Congress, I do not remember that any one of them, or any other person, except your Excellency and the bearers of your Excellency's letter, has urged me to remove the military force from Kentucky, or to disband it. One other very worthy citizen of Kentucky did solicit me to have the augmenting of the force suspended for a time.

Taking all the means within my reach to form a judgment, I do not believe it is the popular wish of Kentucky that this force shall be removed beyond her limits; and, with this impression, I must respectfully decline to so remove it.

I most cordially sympathize with your Excellency, in the wish to preserve the peace of my own native State, Kentucky; but it is with regret I search, and cannot find, in your not very short letter, any declaration, or intimation, that you entertain any desire for the preservation of the Federal Union.

Your Obedient Servant,

A. LINCOLN

Bibliography

Manuscripts

Temple Bodley Papers, Filson Club
Orlando Brown Papers, Filson Club
Breckinridge Family Papers, Library of Congress
Simon Bolivar Buckner Family Papers, Kentucky Historical Society
Thomas Walker Bullitt Collection, Filson Club
Bevie Cain Papers, Western Kentucky University
Caperton Family Papers, Filson Club
Cassius Marcellus Clay Papers, Filson Club
Clay Family Papers, University of Kentucky
Crittenden Papers, Library of Congress
John Curd Miscellaneous Collection, Filson Club
Dicken-Troutman-Balke Papers, University of Kentucky
Duncan Family Papers, University of Kentucky
Fall Family Papers, Kentucky Historical Society
Green Family Papers, Filson Club
Gunn Family Papers, University of Kentucky
Samuel Haycraft Journal, Filson Club
Emily Todd Helm Papers, Kentucky Historical Society
Thomas Henry Hines Papers, University of Kentucky
Hunt-Morgan Family Papers, University of Kentucky
John Janney Papers, Virginia Tech University
John F. Jefferson Papers, Filson Club
Absolom Johnson Diary, Filson Club
George M. Johnson Papers, Kentucky Historical Society
Josiah Stoddard Johnston Papers, Filson Club
Governor Beriah Magoffin Records, Kentucky State Archives

Thomas Robert McBeath Papers, University of Kentucky
Robert Carter Richards Papers, Filson Club
Scrogin/Haviland Papers, Kentucky Historical Society
Uncle Billy Meeting, Filson Club
Underwood Collection, Western Kentucky University
Wallace-Sterling Family Diaries, Kentucky Historical Society
Wickliffe/Preston Papers, University of Kentucky
Yandell Family Papers, Filson Club

Newspapers

Covington Journal [Kentucky]
Kentucky Statesman [Kentucky]
Louisville Courier [Kentucky]
Louisville Daily Journal [Kentucky]
Louisville Commercial [Kentucky]

Government Documents

Acts of the Legislature of the Commonwealth of Kentucky, 1860-1861. Frankfort: Kentucky Yeoman Office, 1866.

Adjutant General's Office. *Report of the Adjunct General of the State of Kentucky*. Frankfort: Harney Press, 1867.

Adjutant General's Office. *Report of the Adjunct General of the State of Kentucky. Confederate Kentucky Volunteers, War 1861-1865*. Utica, Kentucky: Cook and McDowell, 1980.

Constitution of the Commonwealth of Kentucky, 1850.

Journal of the Called Session of the Kentucky General Assembly of the House. Frankfort, Kentucky Yeoman Office, 1861.

Journal of the Called Session of the Kentucky General Assembly of the Senate. Frankfort, Kentucky Yeoman Office, 1861.

Reese, George H. *Proceedings of the Virginia State Convention*. 4 vols. Richmond: Virginia State Library, 1965.

Proceedings of the Convention Held at Russellville, Novr. 18th, 19th, and 20th 1861. Typed transcripts of proceedings at Filson Club.

"Secretary of State of the Kentucky Election Results," 1855-1872. Manuscript volume, Kentucky State Archives.

U. S. War Department, *War of the Rebellion: A Compilation of the Records of the Union and Confederate Armies.* 128 vols. Washington, D. C.: Government Printing Office, 1880-1901.

Books/Published Material

Basler, Roy, ed. *The Collected Works of Abraham Lincoln.* 4 vols. New Brunswick: Rutgers University Press, 1953.

Crittenden, John J. *The Union, the Constitution, and the Laws: Speech of the Hon. John J. Crittenden, at Mozart Hall, on the Evening of August 2nd, 1860.* Lexington: Bradley & Gilbert, 1860.

Holt, Joseph. *The Fallacy of Neutrality: An Address by the Hon. Joseph Holt, to the People of Kentucky, Delivered at Louisville, July 13th, 1861, Also his Letter to J. F. Speed, Esq.* New York: J. G. Gregory, 1961.

Moore, Frank, ed. *Rebellion Record.* 12 vols. New York: G. P. Putman, multiple dates.

Simms, William E. *State of the Union: Speech of Hon. Wm. E. Simms, of Kentucky, Delivered in the House of Representatives, February 9, 1861.* Washington: H. Polkinhorn's Steam Job Press, 1861.

Stevenson, John White. *Speech of Hon. J. W. Stevenson, of Kentucky, on the State of the Union.* Washington: L. Towers, 1861.

Secondary Sources

Unpublished

Bernard, Mary Allen. "Joseph Holt, Judge Advocate General, 1862-1875." Ph.D. Diss., University of Chicago, 1927.

Childers, Robert. "The Secession Crisis and Civil War in Arkansas Through the Eyes of Judge David Walker, Conditional Southern Unionist from Fayetteville." M. A. Thesis, University of Arkansas, 2001.

Finck, James. "Honor and Duty to God and State: John Janney and the Virginia Secession Convention." M. A. Thesis, Virginia Tech, 2002.

Volz, Harry. "Party, State, and Nation: Kentucky and the Coming of the American Civil War." Ph. D. Diss., University of Virginia, 1982.

Williams, Gary Lee. "James and Joshua Speed: Lincoln's Kentucky Friends." Ph.D. Diss., Duke University, 1971.

Articles

Bartman, Roger. "Joseph Holt and Kentucky in the Civil War." *The Filson Club Quarterly*, 40 (April, 1966), 105-122.

Cotterill, Robert. "James Guthrie—Kentuckian, 1792-1869." *Register of Kentucky Historical Society*, 20 (1922), 290-296.

Craig, Berry. "Jackson Purchase Considers Secession." *Register of Kentucky Historical Society*, 99 (Autumn 2001), 339-361.

Harrold, Stanley. "Violence and Nonviolence in Kentucky Abolitionism." *Journal of Southern History*, 57 (Feb. 1991), 15-38.

Lee, R. Alton. "The Corwin Amendment in the Secession Crisis." *Ohio History*, 70 (Jan. 1961), 1-26.

McKinney, William T. "The Defeat of the Secessionists in Kentucky." *Journal of Negro History*, 1 (Oct. 1916), 377-391.

Mering, John V. "The Slave-State Constitutional Unionists and the Politics of Consensus." *Journal of Southern History*, 43 (Aug. 1977), 395-410.

Robertson, James. "Sectionalism in Kentucky from 1855 to 1865." *The Mississippi Valley Historical Review*, 14 (June 1917), 49-63.

Shortridge, Wilson Porter. "Kentucky Neutrality in 1861." *Mississippi Valley Historical Review*, 9 (March 1923), 283-301.

Westwood, Howard C. "The Real Lost Cause: The Peace Convention of 1861." *Military Affairs*, 27 (Autumn 1963), 119-130.

Williams, Kenneth H., and James Russell Harris. "Kentucky in 1860: A Statistical Overview." *The Register of the Kentucky Historical Society*, 103 (Autumn 2005), 743-764.

Yonkers, Charles E. "The Civil War Transformation of George W. Smith: How a Western Kentucky Farmer Evolved From Unionist Whig to Pro-Southern Democrat." *The Register of the Kentucky Historical Society*, 103 (Autumn 2005). 661-690.

Books

Aron, Stephen. *How the West Was Lost: The Transformation of Kentucky from Daniel Boone to Henry Clay.* Baltimore: The Johns Hopkins University Press, 1996.

Carwardine, Richard. *Lincoln: A Life of Purpose and Power.* New York: Knopf, 2006.

Colman, A. M. *Life of J. J. Crittenden.* Philadelphia: J. B. Lippincott and Co., 1871.

Cooling, Benjamin Franklin. *Fort Donelson's Legacy: War and Society in Kentucky and Tennessee, 1862-1863.* Knoxville: University of Tennessee Press, 1997.

Coulter, E. Merton. *The Civil War and Readjustment in Kentucky.* Chapel Hill: University of North Carolina Press, 1926.

Craven, Avery. *The Coming of the Civil War.* Chicago: Phoenix Books, 1957.

Crofts, Daniel. *Reluctant Confederates.* Chapel Hill: The University of North Carolina Press, 1989.

Current, Richard Nelson. *Lincoln's Loyalists: Union Soldiers from the Confederacy.* Boston: Northeast University Press, 1992.

Davis, William C. *Breckinridge: Statesman, Soldier, Symbol.* Baton Rouge: Louisiana State University Press, 1974.

Dew, Charles B. *Apostles of Disunion: Southern Secession Commissioners and the Causes of the Civil War.* Charlottesville: University of Virginia Press, 2001.

Donald, David Herbert. *Lincoln.* New York: Simon & Schuster, 1995.

———. *We Are Lincoln Men: Abraham Lincoln and His Friends.* New York: Simon & Schuster, 2003.

Faust, Drew Gilpin. *A Sacred Circle: The Dilemma of the Intellectual in the Old South, 1840-1860.* Philadelphia: University of Pennsylvania Press, 1986.

Fehrenbach, T. R. *Lone Star: A History of Texas and the Texans.* New York: American Legacy Press, 1983.

Fellman, Michael, Lesley J. Gordon, and Daniel E. Sutherland. *This Terrible War: The Civil War and its Aftermath.* New York: Longman Press, 2003.

Fields, Barbara. *Freedom: A Documentary History of Emancipation 1861-1867.* Ser. I, 9 vols. Cambridge: Cambridge University Press, 1985.

Freehling, William W. *The Road to Disunion: Vol. I, Secessionists at Bay.* Oxford: Oxford University Press, 1990.

———. *The South vs. the South.* Oxford: Oxford University Press, 2001.

Harrison, Lowell H. *The Civil War in Kentucky*. Lexington: The University Press of Kentucky, 1975.

Harrison, Lowell H., and James C. Klotter. *A New History of Kentucky*. Lexington: The University Press of Kentucky, 1997.

Holt, Michael. *The Rise and Fall of the American Whig Party: Jacksonian Politics and the Onset of the Civil War*. New York: Oxford University Press, 1999.

Jordon, Winthrop. *White Over Black: American Attitude Towards the Negro, 1550-1812*. Chapel Hill: University of North Carolina Press, 1968.

Kirwan, Albert D. *John J. Crittenden: The Struggle for the Union*. Lexington: University Press of Kentucky, 1962.

Kleber, John, ed. *The Kentucky Encyclopedia*. Lexington: The University of Kentucky Press, 1992.

Klein, Maury. *History of the Louisville and Nashville Railroad*. Lexington: University Press of Kentucky, 2003.

Mackey, Robert R. *The Uncivil War: Irregular Warfare in the Upper South*. Norman: University of Oklahoma Press, 2004.

McKitrick, Eric L., ed. *Slavery Defended: The View of the Old South*. Englewood Cliffs: Prentice Hall, 1963.

Potter, David M. *The Impending Crisis*. New York: Harper and Row, 1976.

Remini, Robert V. *Henry Clay: Statesman for the Union*. New York: W. W. Norton, 1991.

Scrugham, Mary. *The Peaceable Americans of 1860-1861*. New York: Columbia University Press, 1921.

Shaler, N. S. *Kentucky: A Pioneer Commonwealth*. Boston: Houghton Mifflin Company, 1884.

Shanks, Henry T. *The Secession Movement in Virginia, 1847-1861*. New York: AMS Press, 1971.

Shannon, Jasper, and Ruth McQuown. *Presidential Politics in Kentucky 1824-1948*. Lexington: Bureau of Government Research, College of Arts and Science, University of Kentucky, 1950.

Speed, Thomas. *The Union Cause in Kentucky*. New York: The Knickerbocker Press, 1907.

Tallant, Harold. *Evil Necessity: Slavery and Political Culture in Antebellum Kentucky*. Lexington: University Press of Kentucky, 2003.

Tise, Larry Edward. *Proslavery: A History of the Defense of Slavery in America, 1701-1840*. Athens: University of Georgia Press, 1990.

Woods, James. *Rebellion and Realignment: Arkansas's Road to Secession*. Fayetteville: University of Arkansas Press, 1987.

Index

About the Author

James W. Finck was raised in Virginia, where he developed a deep love of the American Civil War. He received his undergraduate degree in history at the College of William and Mary, a master's degree at Virginia Tech, and his Ph.D. at the University of Arkansas. Dr. Finck taught history at the University of Texas—Pan American. He currently teaches American history at the University of Science and Arts of Oklahoma. He lives in Oklahoma with his wife and three young children. This is his first book.